THE PUSH PIN GRAPHIC

A QUARTER CENTURY OF INNOVATIVE DESIGN AND ILLUSTRATION

BY SEYMOUR CHWAST

EDITED BY STEVEN HELLER AND MARTIN VENEZKY

INTRODUCTION BY MILTON GLASER

CHRONICLE BOOKS

SAN FRANCISCO

THIS BOOK would not be possible if not for the enthusiastic support of our principal editor at Chronicle Books, Alan Rapp, who saw the relevance of the *Push Pin Graphic* for an entirely new generation of designers and artists.

We greatly appreciate the work of dozens of mechanical artists, junior designers, and interns who helped in the production of the eighty-six issues. We are also grateful to Carol Chu, Chwast's design associate, for her critical work in the preparation of this book.

Moreover, much thanks goes to Milton Glaser, without whom there would be no Push Pin Studios, for his invaluable participation in this book. Further thanks goes to Edward Sorel, Reynold Ruffins, Paul Davis, and James McMullan who donated materials to this volume, and, of course, to all the Push Pin associates and representatives who contributed so much to this small slice of design history.—S C , S H , M V

DESIGN BY MARTIN VENEZKY'S APPETITE ENGINEERS AND
SEYMOUR CHWAST, WITH ASSISTANCE BY CAROL CHU,
THE PUSHPIN GROUP.

LIBRARY OF CONGRESS CATALOGING-IN-PUBLICATION DATA AVAILABLE.

ISBN: 0-8118-4103-0

MANUFACTURED IN CHINA.

DISTRIBUTED IN CANADA BY RAINCOAST BOOKS

9050 SHAUGHNESSY STREET

VANCOUVER, BRITISH COLUMBIA V6P 6E5

10 9 8 7 6 5 4 3 2 1

CHRONICLE BOOKS LLC

85 SECOND STREET

SAN FRANCISCO, CALIFORNIA 94105

WWW.CHRONICLEBOOKS.COM

THE CONTENTS

PRE FACE

BY SEYMOUR CHWAST

1 **WAS ONE OF THE LUCKY ONES.** My first job, just weeks after I graduated from Cooper Union in New York in 1951, was as junior designer in the promotion department of the *New York Times*. I acquired valuable experience working for the art director, George Krikorian. Nonetheless, my luck changed when I decided to move on to other opportunities with a couple of magazines, design studios, and an advertising agency. I failed at all of them.

While working at my last full-time job at *House and Garden* magazine, I conspired with my former classmates Edward Sorel and Reynold Ruffins to find a way to attract freelance illustration assignments. Milton Glaser joined us upon his return from his studies in Italy courtesy of a Fulbright scholarship.

The idea of creating a series of mailing pieces was prompted by the work of two designer/illustrators; Jack Wolfgang Beck sent out blotters and John Averill produced brochures, both illustrated, as I recall, with woodcuts. Our mailing pieces took the form of the *Farmers' Almanac* with its horoscope and listing of events for every day of the year. We illustrated short, mostly trivial articles and ads for graphic design suppliers who wanted to reach the same art directors on our mailing list. The slim-jim-sized, sixteen-or-so-paged *Push Pin Almanack* was sent monthly or bimonthly to three thousand art directors. And it worked. The freelance assignments came.

In August of 1954 in a Chinese restaurant a few blocks from our studio loft, we decided to go into business as Push Pin Studios. We realized that the style and message of the *Almanack* (note the cute spelling) was dated and therefore irrelevant. So we invented the *Monthly Graphic* in 1957. It was, at first, the size of a standard newspaper page, printed on one side. It changed to a four-page tabloid and eventually shifted size along with the content. Like the *Almanack*, it demonstrated the kind of work we hoped our clients needed and wanted. Our growing reputation gave us the clout that resulted in commissions. In no small measure, the *Graphic* also served as a vehicle for expression and experimentation.

It was exciting to create ideas of our choosing that were perfect vehicles for our design and illustration. The *Graphic* set a high standard for us since we couldn't blame the limitations of our commercial assignments. Clients responded to a conceptual and witty style that could still apply to most forms of communication and marketing.

Glaser and I were drawn to the then-passé graphics of the Victorian, art nouveau, and art deco periods. Long gone, they offered new possibilities for us and we took advantage in harvesting all that we saw and knew. When the recycled vitality of those movements dissipated, we moved on to producing work closer to our own sensibilities.

The *Monthly Graphic*, after a while, became the *Push Pin Graphic* to identify it with Push Pin Studios and to hide the irregular frequency of publication. Each of the eighty-six issues, spanning the years 1957 to 1980, was financed by other work at the studio, including posters and packaging. We also illustrated for animation, publications, and advertising. The *Graphic* was an extension of our passions not entirely satisfied by our day jobs. Its continuity gave us a kind of legitimacy in the field while the look and feel of its varied sizes and paper stocks and eclectic themes gave us a unique draw. Our promotion piece had a brand name, allowing us to create in any format that suited us without having to explain to the readers what they were getting.

Ours was the first publication of its kind produced by a design firm. Herb Lubalin's *Upper and Lower Case* (promoting the type designs of the International Type Corporation) and *Pentagram Papers* from Pentagram Inc. (occasional brochures covering subjects of visual or literary merit) may have been inspired by the *Push Pin Graphic*.

Paul Davis, Isadore Seltzer, and James McMullan joined Push Pin Studios and collaborated on or produced their own issues of the *Graphic*—with intelligence, wit, and great skill.

In the early seventies, after Glaser left, Push Pin Studios started representing illustrators who worked in their own studios. The *Graphic* became a showcase for talents such as Elwood H. Smith, Haruo Miyauchi, Hedda Johnson, Richard Mantel, John O'Leary, Barbara Sandler, Emanuel Schongut, Stanislaw Zagorski, John Collier, Bernard Bonhomme, George Stavrinos, David Croland, and Michael Hostovich. We presented photographs by Sarah Moon, Benno Friedman, and Arnold Rosenberg as well. They contributed their immense talent to issues on subjects such as "Food and Violence," "Your Body and You," "The Complete History and Knowledge of the World Condensed," "Back to Sleep," and the travel issue, "Exploring New Jersey." This distinctive stage enhanced

their reputations and commissions. In order to properly present their work, I standardized the format of this now-bimonthly magazine to a nine-by-twelve-inch size and thirty-two pages.

With issue number 64, in 1976, I became the art director. Richard Mantel and I were in charge of the layout. I worked with two editors, Paula Scher and Ken Robbins. During this period, they were responsible for collaborating on themes, writing, and finding stories and articles.

Paula, an extraordinary designer who happens to be my wife, wrote many very funny pieces, such as "The History of Chickens," "The Mother Mafia," and "Why Germany Went to War" (because the Germans had no southern outlet for the gas they produced from all the fat food they ate). I am forever grateful to these people for their generosity and imagination.

Pamela Vassil, production coordinator, and Lilly Filipo, editorial manager, became "Trixie and Dixie" for their mock lonely hearts column. We wrote and produced ads that appeared in the *Graphic* in exchange for services we needed for production. These services included printing and typesetting (copy was sent out to type houses in those precomputer days). Some revenue came from other advertisers. More than eight thousand friends and clients were on our mailing list in addition to three thousand paid subscribers. After five years in the latest iteration, I realized that the remaining costs were too high. I produced the last issue in 1980.

Seymour Chwast, 1978.

Looking back at these issues produced over a quarter century, I can finally be objective about the work. My aspiring German expressionism of the fifties turned into my own kind of flat proto–art deco in the sixties and surrealism in the seventies. The elegant drawings of Milton Glaser and James McMullan were less subject to mainstream evolution while Paul Davis's paintings were slave to no trend and inspired others, notably with his folk art style, which he initiated for illustration. Much of what we did entered the mental filing system of art director and art buyer readers. Awards were bestowed. Museum shows were held and "Push Pin" became a subject taught in design courses. The *Graphic* was a catalyst for reaching millions through the media.

I was driven by a need to please my peers and my mother, who still hangs up every printed piece of mine that she comes across.

Four decades after publishing the first *Push Pin Monthly Graphic*, I am still excited. In fact, this "amateur effort" continues today with a modest occasional journal called the *Nose*. At this writing, I just finished number 8 and can't wait to start the next one. ❧

INTRO
DUCTION

BY MILTON GLASER

1T STARTED AT COOPER UNION when we were a sweetly naive group of students looking for a place to work and socialize after school hours. We rented the back end of a loft on Thirteenth Street not far from Cooper that we shared with Calvin Holt, a dancer who later cofounded Serendipity 3, an updated version of a New York soda shop and retail store. One of our early jobs was the design of his logo, still in use, although Calvin passed away some years ago. The loft was often used as a rehearsal studio by such notables as Merce Cunningham and John Cage, although at the time we scarcely knew who they were. Before we graduated, we had formed a business called Design Plus, whose only activity turned out to be printing cork place mats with a primitive silk screen set up in the corner of the loft. What a miserable summer that was. The heat of a New York summer in an un-air-conditioned loft, coupled with the noxious assault of the silk-screen paint thinner, made for horrible working conditions. After one sale to the old Wanamaker's department store, we abandoned the business but kept renting the loft.

After graduating from Cooper Union in 1951, we all went out and found jobs. Seymour Chwast in the *New York Times* promotion department, Ed Sorel at the William D. MacAdams Advertising Agency, Reynold Ruffins at the Tony Martin Studio, and me in the promotion department of *Vogue* magazine until I received a Fulbright grant and went to study etching in Bologna with Giorgio Morandi. When I returned from my sojourn in Italy in 1952, I discovered that Seymour, Reynold, and Ed had started to promote their illustration work with a small intermittent brochure called the *Push Pin Almanack,* an idiosyncratic and charming mailing piece that was effective in calling attention to their work, if not generating a lot of financial rewards. They generously invited me to join them and at the same time we hired Koodin Lapow, a packaging design firm I had occasionally worked for, to represent the group. We all had day jobs and gathered at the loft after work to do our freelance assignments. Ben Koodin and Harry Lapow were busy keeping their own business afloat but managed to find us enough work to occupy most of our evenings.

At a certain moment in 1954 Seymour, Ed, and I had a collective epiphany—we could start a full-time studio of our own. Reynold joined us later in 1955. It was very much, in retrospect, like that moment in many early Mickey Rooney and Judy Garland films when someone says, "Let's do a show!" Of course we knew nothing about running a business let alone an art studio, but passion and energy were enough, as it turned out. In those days you could rent a loft space for $100 a month, a pay phone for $7, and you were in business. Not to mention the fact that expensive computer equipment didn't exist as a professional expense. But most important, we had a way of reaching our potential customers that even we didn't fully appreciate until years later.

We named the studio Push Pin after the *Almanack* because it had developed a modest reputation in the field for a fresh way of thinking about design and illustration, and we were getting an increasing amount of work from agencies, publishers, and magazines. A design historian might call us premature postmodernists. This was the early fifties, a time when Swiss modernism and the Westport School of Illustration, most frequently characterized by the work appearing in the *Saturday Evening Post,* were dominant in our visual culture even though that ideological combination is almost incomprehensible. Another characteristic that defined our work was our integration of design, typography, and illustration into a single practice. We believed strongly that the separation of these disciplines into specialized activities was arbitrary and unproductive. We knew, like all emerging generations, that we wanted to discover something of our own. We were children of modernism but turned to the past for inspiration just as the artists of the arts-and-crafts movement had. We were excited by the very idea that we could use anything in the visual history of humankind as influence. Art nouveau, Chinese wash drawing, German woodcuts, American primitive paintings, the Viennese secession, and cartoons of the thirties were an endless source of inspiration. All the things that the doctrine of orthodox modernism seemed to have contempt for—ornamentation, narrative illustration, visual ambiguity—attracted us. Not that all of this was very well thought out; we were blundering along but felt we were onto something. At one point the *Almanack* seemed to be too confining in size and references. Its implicit relationship to early American themes, graphic art such as illustrated chapbooks, no longer served the studio's perception of itself, even though the brochure had been our basic way of reaching people.

My personal interest in stylistic diversity (as far as I can analyze it) came from two major sources: Picasso and my first stay in Italy. I have often cited the first time (I was in high school) I saw his etching, illustrating a story by Balzac, that shows a bull in a variety of styles going from naturalism to a kind of reductive symbolism. That one work convinced me that there was no truth in style and that it was simply a device to reflect an expressive intention. My stay in Italy exposed me to art history in an overwhelming way. Inevitably, like most artists, I fell in love with the Renaissance, Piero della Francesca, Titian, Tiepolo, baroque architecture, and all the other things the ideology of modernism was suspicious of.

We decided to launch a new publication that would be more expansive and reflect our point of view more clearly, called the *Monthly Graphic*. We had hired Myrna Mushkin, a bright and attractive young woman, as a "do-anything person" in part because we loved to hear her say, "I'm Mushkin from Push Pin." One of her many jobs was finding editorial material for the *Graphic*. One day she called our attention to the fact that since she and we had other things to do, the promise of a "Monthly" *Graphic* was almost never realized. Rather than meet what we considered to be an oppressive deadline, we changed the name to the *Push Pin Graphic*.

The editorial process was disorderly. Anyone could come up with an idea. It would be discussed, researched, and executed collectively or individually. By 1956 Ed Sorel had left the studio to pursue a brilliant career as a social commentator and caricaturist; as a result none of his work ever appeared in the *Graphic*. Reynold Ruffins left the studio in 1960 but is well represented in issue numbers 2, 5, 6, 12, 14, 15, 17, 18, 19, 20, 21, 22, 23, and 24. Seymour and I continued to run the studio and managed to attract a number of brilliant colleagues. John Alcorn, a boyish-looking design prodigy, came to work and added to our visual vocabulary (issue numbers 4, 5, 8, 10, and 16). Later he and his family moved to Italy, where John single-handedly transformed the Italian book jacket scene. He died suddenly in 1992 at the age of fifty-six.

Paul Davis arrived at the studio almost immediately after graduating from the School of Visual Arts (SVA) in New York. He was wide-eyed and refreshingly innocent of big-city ways. Although he was interested in what might be called primitive expressionism, his technical and painterly skills were impressive. At the studio he began to fuse two unrelated ideas, American primitive painting and surrealism, into an unexpectedly personal idiom (issue number 39). Paul later married Myrna and went on to become a famous illustrator and designer particularly celebrated for his theatrical

posters and editorial work. Myrna is currently the director of the Art Directors Club (ADC) of New York.

James McMullan had already started his career as an illustrator when he joined us. He drew like an angel, in a more fluid naturalistic style than any of the rest of us were able to master. He worked on issue numbers 46, 50, and 52 and added to the studio's range and reputation. Later he became known for his outstanding theatrical posters for Lincoln Center and many children's books. He is considered to be an exceptional drawing teacher at the School of Visual Arts, and his book *High-Focus Drawing* is must-reading for those possessed by the desire to draw.

Isadore Seltzer had been educated and worked on the West Coast, and although his sensibility reflected this geographical influence, he fit right into the Push Pin genre in issue numbers 30, 34, and 43. His versatility was an asset to the studio, as well as to his own illustration career after he left the studio. In recent years he has turned to painting as his major activity,

Other contributors included Hedda Johnson, Barry Zaid, Christian Piper, Haruo Miyauchi, David Croland, Arnold Rosenberg, Joyce MacDonald, and many more. Those early years were golden. The studio had prospered and become an influence on the history of American graphic design due in no small part to our modest publication. At a certain point, the Push Pin point of view was defined in design circles as an alternative to modernism, so much so it became almost generic.

In the sixties I started *New York* magazine with Clay Felker and began designing restaurants with Joe Baum and supermarkets for Sir James Goldsmith. I wanted to go on to do other things, and in 1975 Seymour and I parted after twenty exciting years. The last issue I worked on was number 64. We accomplished more than we had ever dreamed of, and although Seymour and a new cast of contributors continued generating one delightful issue after another, what we produced together in those early years still fills me with pride and appreciation for an extraordinary time. ✪

Milton Glaser, 1972.

9

THE PUSH PIN EFFECT

BY STEVEN HELLER

PUSH PIN STUDIOS had phenomenal sway over visual culture during the fifties, sixties, and seventies. If it's not too presumptuous to make a parallel, in its own way the studio was like the Beatles of illustration and design. Push Pin pressed the limits of tradition while establishing its own. It developed generational codes and styles. It transformed mainstream culture. It was more than the sum of its parts. And it spawned many offspring who went forth and multiplied.

Nonetheless, it is difficult to convey the excitement that graphic artists felt when Push Pin Studios came to the fore initially through its quaint, though arresting, *Push Pin Almanack* and later through the more experimental *Push Pin Monthly Graphic.* Their creative groundswell altered the course of graphic style and design practice for subsequent generations.

Push Pin's inventive methods awoke a somnambulant postwar field with cage-rattling effect comparable to

when during the 1920s the New Typography, practiced by the Bauhaus, de Stijl, and the constructivists, revolutionized advertising and book design and ushered in radical change throughout fine and applied arts. Although Push Pin was not fanatically avant-garde, through its reinvention of discarded mannerisms it did spark profound shifts in commercial art away from the cold rationalism of the corporate modern movement on the one hand and the staid conventions of common commercial practice on the other, and into new realms of pictorial expression. Like the Beatles, Push Pin did not merely "cover" or copy old standards. While exhuming Victorian, art nouveau, and art deco mannerisms (two decades before postmodernism encouraged similar reappraisals of the past and the passé), Push Pin remained contemporary in a formal sense and fresh in its conceptual outlook. Push Pin was not nostalgic or faddish, but it created a foundation on which graphic design could be practiced beyond Push Pin's own sphere of influence.

Illustration from poster announcing a fifteenth anniversary exhibition at the Mead Library of Ideas, 1972, designed by Chwast and Glaser.

Push Pin's principal cofounders, Seymour Chwast (b. 1931) and Milton Glaser (b. 1929), two native New Yorkers who met while attending Manhattan's Cooper Union, brought distinct tastes and preferences—as well as chemistry—to their unique partnership. Chwast savored American comic strips and pop culture while Glaser studied etching in Italy and was passionate for Italian Renaissance painters. The former injected a cartoonist's abandon into his artwork, the latter introduced a sublime elegance. Despite their formal differences, both shared the conviction that postwar design and illustration should not be limited to prevailing practices—either sentimental realism or reductive simplicity. They rejected rote methods and rigid styles while concocting incomparable ways of transforming old into new, just like the alchemists who, legend has it, transformed base metals into gold. "We had come to the end of the evolution of the modernist style," recalls Chwast. "We began to look around for new sources of inspiration. It was a timely process of discovery."

Discover was the operative verb, but *eclectic* was the adjective that underscored Push Pin's spirit. It was also fitting insofar as the studio's palette, typography, and imagery were bright, spirited, and stylish compared to the strict asceticism of the Swiss School and International Style, which in the fifties were methods of choice for most institutional design programs. But Push Pin's carnivalesque aesthetic was not undisciplined—various forms were consciously rejected while others were selected based on the tastes of all members. For example, during an era when photography was becoming increasingly more popular among art directors than hand-rendered illustration, Push Pin stubbornly used paint, brush, and collage in expressionistic ways. Moreover, Push Pin revived the once seamless intersection of art and typography—illustration and design—deemed passé by modernists who revered machine age tools and aesthetics. Illustrated posters with original lettering (à la the early-twentieth-century *affichistes*) formed a significant part of Push Pin's repertoire. Yet contrary to appearances Push Pin was not solely about revivalism. *Modern* has always been an ambiguous term, and Push Pin possessed a keen ability for achieving newness while avoiding the more dogmatic aspects of modernism. Glaser's famous 1967 "Dylan Poster," a harmonious marriage of a Persian miniature ornament and a Marcel Duchamp self-portrait, is a characteristic example of transmuting two conflicting historical references into a single work. Along the way, the poster became an icon of the sixties.

Studio members voraciously experimented with many means borrowed or scavenged from high and low art to build unique visual personas. Which, incidentally, was not without precedent. Long before Push Pin, modern designers since World War I jerry-rigged new visual languages from bits of vintage and vernacular type and image that they found in old commercial print shops and sample books. The Swiss and German Dada movements incorporated nineteenth-century typefaces and printers' clichés to distinguish their antiestablishment periodicals and posters from the trite, commercial mainstream. Later, in the 1930s and 1940s, this influenced more mannered work by Alexey Brodovitch, Lester Beall, and Alvin Lustig, among others, who fused old with new. Yet compared to Push Pin, these designers timidly dabbled with pastiche while Chwast and Glaser avidly unearthed cultural relics—and their quotations of such graphic idioms as German Jugendstil and French art moderne were applied with missionary zeal.

But their mission was not solely an attack on modernism. In fact, like the modernists, Push Pin believed design could make a significant difference in the well-being of society, not only by making messages more accessible through clear systems, but also by brightening daily life through expressive form. The means of achieving this goal was, however, through visibility in the marketplace. So building Push Pin's commercial identity and obtaining prestigious clients in the process was paramount to its mission. Besides taking on the role of experimental hothouse for illustration and design, the studio was in business to do business.

Push Pin Studios was officially founded, as Milton Glaser notes in his introduction, during the muggy New York summer of 1954. Chwast, Glaser, and their Cooper Union classmates Edward Sorel (b. 1929) and later Reynold Ruffins (b. 1930) rented a small flat in a brownstone on East Seventeenth Street. The back room, where Sorel slept at night and Glaser reviewed unsolicited portfolios (in his bathing suit) during the day, was so damp they called it the "fungus room." This may have been an inauspicious venue to launch an influential studio, but it was not

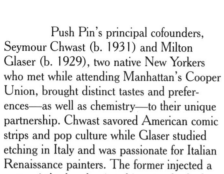

Classmates Glaser (far left), Reynold Ruffins, Chwast (third and fourth from left), George Leavitt (far right), and unnamed friends, 1950.

12

LEFT
Outside Pushpin's Woodstock studio, 1962. From left: Chwast (front), Glaser (rear), Isadore Seltzer, and Paul Davis.

RIGHT & BELOW
The Push Pin Almanack,
1954, 1955.

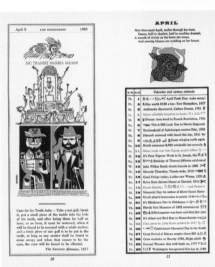

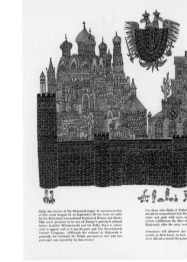

their first attempt to crack into the design business.

Three years earlier, while sophomores at Cooper, they collectively rented a loft on East Thirteenth Street and called themselves Design Plus. Their business card, which Glaser designed as a type class project, with a "d+" logo that looked a bit like a sideways Egyptian ankh against a tic-tac-toe background, signaled the group's eccentricity. At the time they earned a few small professional commissions, including producing a gross of silk-screen place mats and a flier for a droll monologist named Brother Theodore, who performed in a small theater downtown. But these jobs were not enough to support a full-fledged studio, and inevitably after graduation each member except Glaser, who went off to study in Italy, took a staff position elsewhere. Their mini-diaspora was less professionally productive than they had hoped, so in the evenings Chwast, Sorel, and Ruffins conceived, and in 1953 produced, the *Push Pin Almanack,* the first of fifteen occasional self-promotion mailers designed to showcase their individual talents and free themselves from workaday servitude. Glaser joined the group upon his return from Italy.

In the tradition of the old *Farmers' Almanac* and Will H. Bradley's esoteric chapbooks (published during the 1890s), the *Push Pin Almanack* was a miscellany filled with arcane facts and curious quotes that were elegantly typeset and illustrated with comical line drawings and chiaroscuro woodcuts. At the time, Chwast notes, illustrated blotters were the most common medium for self-promotion, but the popularity of the ballpoint pen made them obsolete. So the almanac idea was seized upon as a novel way to attract the attention of potential clients.

The genteel subtitle on the cover announced "The choicest morsels of essential information gathered for those persons in the graphic arts," which indicates that the *Almanack* was not intentionally designed to disrupt mainstream commercial art with convention-busting avant-gardisms. The cover design, with its smiling-face-push-pin logo sandwiched between an old-fashioned script typeface that spelled the words *Push Pin* and its nineteenth-century

13

RIGHT
From left, Chwast, John
Alcorn, Ruffins, 1958.

OPPOSITE LEFT
Chwast and Glaser, 1968.

OPPOSITE RIGHT
Display of Push Pin's work.

typeface that read *Almanack*, was as decorous as the name *Push Pin* was quaint. "Quaintness was popular in those days," Chwast recalls.

While the logo and the type treatment were constant, distinctive color combinations—including orange and pink, navy and green—were changed on each cover to signal the new issue. Given its eclectic spirit, the *Almanack* stayed within the bounds of commercial taste and was also consistent with emerging design trends in historical pastiche, including some editorial layouts by *McCall's* magazine art director Otto Storch, who at the time used blocky Victorian wood type. This penchant for things old-fashioned returned partly as a reaction to the somber neutrality of modernism and partly because it was just fun to play with ironic and romantic graphic forms.

Six issues of the *Almanack* were published before Push Pin Studios officially began, and nine after. The typesetting and the printing of three thousand copies were basically done at cost in exchange for the free design of the paper, type, and printing suppliers' advertisements that ran in each edition. Other operating expenses were paid through the sale of small-space ads. Within weeks of the first issue's mailing, designers and art directors began to take notice and the *Almanack* brought in enough paying work from New York–based book, advertising, and film-strip clients for Chwast, Glaser, and Sorel to be able to leave their jobs and start their consortium (Ruffins joined later). Push Pin became the de facto studio name owing to the success of the *Almanack*. Chwast recalls, "We included the 's' in studio because we liked the pretentious sound."

In the year that Push Pin Studios hung its shingle, romantic realism continued to dominate illustration with only a few expressionist blips appearing here and there. Illustration was patently literal and overly narrative (often images were taken verbatim from text passages decided upon by editors or art directors and then captioned to avoid any ambiguity). Push Pin's more conceptual and metaphorical image-making pried an opening in the conservative precincts of illustration, especially changing aesthetic attitudes toward book jackets and record covers, and spruced up advertisements, too. At the same time, however, postwar corporate modernism had arguably become a predictable assortment of limited typefaces and templates used for business reports and sign systems. As a style it was at the height of usability (and was ubiquitous), but as a utopian design ethic born of social turmoil in the twenties it had run out of steam, because in the hands of some of its more slavish followers it evoked the air of numbing sameness.

Minimalist design wasn't all it was cracked up to

be anyway, and when it was applied to products that demanded variety, the public became indifferent. Helvetica, the quintessential modern typeface (designed in 1957 by Max Miedinger for the Haas foundry in Switzerland), was eventually so widely and generically used for everything from signs and packages to annual reports and advertisements that while readable, it was overlookable. The modernist argument that ornament was superfluous and bourgeois—and so jettisoned in favor of asymmetrical, unfettered layout—had also become a stylistic conceit as superficial as what it originally rebelled against. After rejecting arabesques and curlicues, modernism substituted black and red rectangular bars, which were simply another kind of ornament. The original argument against decoration made some theoretical sense, but in extremis reductionism sacrificed the serendipitous quirks that gave graphic design its surprise factor. So in response to the status quo Push Pin exploited as many quirks as it could.

If the Viennese architect Adolph Loos was correct when in 1908 he charged that ornament was a crime, then Push Pin was guilty—yet with extenuating circumstances. Its felonious activity was partly a generational protest against the rising tide of conformity brought on by stodgy design *isms*. But more important its members truly found beauty born of eccentricity in wedding classical and novelty typefaces, mixing vibrant colors, and clashing intricate patterns. The accidents created by unforeseen juxtapositions, and the dynamic tension caused by mixing harmonious and cacophonous textures together on a page, challenged the stereotypically drab fifties and inspired, among other things, the psychedelic sixties. Victor Moscoso, the maestro of psychedelic concert posters, credits Push Pin as one of his key influences.

The Push Pin doctrine (although studio members would be loath to write it into fast-drying cement) decreed there was more to graphic design than dutifully following geometric grids. Instead Push Pin members sought their own ideal of beauty by giving the appearance that they worked from the inside out rather than starting from rigid blueprints, and even when they used identifiable design tropes the result was often unanticipated. The more massive the armory of graphic options at the member's disposal, the more visually and intellectually explosive the result.

Among other things, Push Pin's reprise of vintage graphic style caused a renaissance of graphic arts history, and the studio's own reference library was quite an impressive stockpile of vintage books, posters, and magazines that grew larger commensurate with the members' creative needs and Chwast and Glaser's increased income. The range of source materials rivaled most commercial picture (or scrap) collections and brimmed over with curious booty that was

Members on the roof of Push
Pin Studio, 1970. From left,
Chwast, George Leavitt,
Tim Lewis, James McMullan,
Vincent Ceci, and Glaser.

incorporated into Push Pin's stylistic vocabulary. The wealth
of exotic inspirations included Persian and Indian miniatures
that Glaser had collected and Victorian children's books and
toys that Chwast had acquired at flea markets and second-
hand bookshops. If any single factor should be credited for
the uniqueness of the Push Pin style (aside from its princi-
pals' vision, of course), reference material is key. The slab
serif Victorian, curvilinear art nouveau, rectilinear art deco,
spiky German Fraktur, and other esoteric typefaces, as well as
the bevy of cartouches, swashes, flourishes, and other vintage
printers' rules, borders, and fleurons borrowed from old type
catalogs were customized for the studio's use. Push Pin routinely created distinct motifs that both defined its own look
and influenced others. Chwast, for instance, was attracted to
twenties decorative art, which he transformed into what he
called "Roxy Style" before he knew it was art deco, which
along with Glaser's variation on the same theme influenced
the sixties art deco revival and morphed into psychedelic chic.
The editor and critic Harold Hayes wrote in the *New York
Times Magazine* (March 6, 1977) that Push Pin prompted
revivals "not only in graphic design but as manifest now in
interior decorating, fashion and furnishings as well."

The astounding degree to which Push Pin influenced contemporary aesthetics was not, however, only
through its commercial commissions but more directly
through the *Push Pin Monthly Graphic.* Influences flowed
into the design and illustration fields through this experimental periodical, which in 1957 replaced the *Almanack.* Glaser
notes that it took a year after ceasing the *Almanack* in 1956
to launch the *Graphic* because "since we weren't in the publishing business, when the *Almanack* gave out, we did not
have an instant alternative—it had to evolve." And evolve it
did over eighty-six issues from an assortment of broadsheet
posters to a newsprint miscellany of thematic design and
illustration into a magazine with a wellspring of curios and
commentary.

The *Graphic* was for Push Pin Studios what in
1967 *Sgt. Pepper's Lonely Hearts Club Band,* the first
"high-concept" rock/pop album of the sixties, was for the
Beatles. Sure there were differences—*Sgt. Pepper* was a one-
shot encapsulation of the Beatles' innovation to that date
(and perhaps the group's greatest innovation), while the
Graphic was ongoing and cumulative—but both were creative investigations that found acceptance outside the laboratory in the public arena. By allowing studio members to
experiment and play with different methods, to explore style,
content, and structure, the *Graphic* served as a kind of incu-
bator that few professional studios had the ability to offer.
Rather than limit itself to one marketable studio style, Push

Pin showed clients that it was always expanding its range—
but Push Pin did not arbitrarily impose its new ideas on
paying customers. The *Graphic* served as a catalog of
options from which clients could choose.

Perpetually in flux, the *Graphic* was not locked into
a single format (until much later). The only truly consistent
anchor was its masthead, a Black Letter cartouche with a
vivaciously swirling linear swash designed by Glaser, but
everything else was mutable, including the size and shape of
the publication. It began as a broadsheet newspaper printed
in black and white; later it transformed into a two-color,
four-page tabloid, veered from that with a handful of anom-
alous sizes and shapes, and eventually ended its long run as
a standard-sized full-color magazine. Yet it was never totally
confined by these dimensions when a good idea demanded
novel form (which was often the case).

"Expect the unexpected," a well-known sixties-era
advertising slogan, fit the *Push Pin Monthly Graphic* to a T.
Its conceptual and visual unpredictability, even in its standard formats, fostered such anticipation among a growing
audience of designers and illustrators that when on frequent
occasions it was late for its so-called monthly release date,
there was palpable consternation. Unlike the leading professional journals—*Graphis, Print,* and *Communication Arts*—
the *Graphic* did not simply report on (or reproduce examples
of) current design trends but rather developed its own trends
in real time and space. It was blue sky in a proscribed uni-
verse. Readers were engaged by the *Graphic* because it was
not merely a sample of successful jobs, but a model of design
"authorship" created under real-world conditions (i.e., printing limitations) yet free from clients' restrictive criteria. In
fact, so influential was the idea of the *Graphic* that other
design and illustration studios eventually followed suit. So
inspiring was the content of the *Graphic* that in the months
following a specific issue a particular trait or motif (whether
major or minor) often appeared in other designers' work.
Chwast recalls an instance when Glaser introduced simple
round-corner boxes that framed line illustrations, only to
notice a few months later that round corners were springing
up elsewhere. In commercial art's continual quest to find the
next big (or small) wave, the *Graphic* was a veritable ocean.

The *Almanack* revealed Push Pin's adolescent
potential while the *Graphic* embodied its maturity. But this
did not happen overnight.

Thanks to attention garnered by the *Almanack,*
Push Pin was on a trajectory toward prominence. It experienced a major growth spurt in 1956 and so moved from

Seventeenth Street to a small apartment on East Fifty-seventh Street (in the same building that housed the Bettmann Archive, which made its fortune from selling historical prints clipped from old magazines to art directors and designers). Sorel left the partnership that year to be an illustrator and political caricaturist (one of America's most acerbic), and a couple of years later Ruffins also resigned, to start his own freelance illustration career as a children's book artist. Chwast and Glaser inherited sole proprietorship of Push Pin Studios, and by 1958 the work was so plentiful they moved into a duplex flat in a well-kept brownstone with its own backyard garden on East Thirty-first Street. Their success was beyond their expectations, and they were forced to expand. In addition to pasteup assistants, Chwast and Glaser hired a few more artists who conformed to "the Push Pin Spirit," including the young illustrators John Alcorn, Paul Davis, Norman Green, and designers Samuel Antupit and Herb Leavitt. The work was sometimes decorative, other times conceptual, but all times contemporary. In 1965 during the height of Push Pin's creative popularity (and as its international reputation soared owing to articles appearing in *Graphis* and other journals), Chwast and Glaser purchased a townhouse on East Thirty-second Street (which Glaser still occupies). Among other additions to the staff was James McMullan, an illustrator with an established reputation and elegant style of representational drawing. Eventually more exponents of the Push Pin method, including Isadore Seltzer, Barry Zaid, Tim Lewis, Vincent Ceci, Haruo Miyauchi, and Hedda Johnson joined the critical mass and contributed to the ongoing *Graphic*.

Informally Chwast and Glaser shared editor, art director, and publisher roles, but, as Glaser notes, "all members were given the opportunity to conceive issues based on their personal interests"—and everyone collaborated on an issue when a particular theme demanded it. Paul Davis, who later became an iconic poster designer, introduced his distinctive hybrid folk art style—paintings on wood—in a special solo *Graphic* devoted to primitive targets (number 32, page 83), which earned him considerable recognition among illustrators and art directors. The range of other subjects included "English Royalty: How They Died" (number 27, page 72), "Limericks and Other Nonsense" (number 20, page 58), "The Meaning of Dreams" (number 49, page 120), "The Dark Side of Good People" (number 56, page 138), "The Mouth" (number 62, page 168), and "Teens and Bikers on Cars" (number 48, page 118). Esoteric issues were also devoted to railroads, westerns, and Tolstoy's *War and Peace*—each topic was fuel for conceptual illustration. Personal obsessions and discoveries were routinely

expressed as well. For example, Chwast produced an issue inspired by his first trip to Italy. Some of these issues were printed in conventional ways, but many involved intricate die cuts, foldouts, gatefolds, and other special printing and manufacturing effects. Nothing was impossible as long as the results merited the effort.

Many of the *Graphic*'s themes were admittedly ephemeral while others were, as Glaser recalls, "more overtly political at a time when civil rights and the Vietnam War were foremost on our minds." Given the socially and politically polarized times, it was no small decision for a studio's ostensible "promotional organ" to be critical of hot-button issues and events (even in a liberal town like New York). Such things could easily have backfired and alienated clients, but apparently this did not deter Chwast or Glaser when they believed it was necessary to speak out. Chwast's "The South" issue (number 54, see facsimile insert) was a heartfelt statement that took a stand on what was one of the most critical crossroads in the Nation's history. And yet not all recipients of the *Push Pin Graphic* could be expected to greet the publication with open arms. Nonetheless conscience came before commerce, and The South issue was one of the most trenchant graphic commentaries during a period known for its social and political activism. Another key issue was Glaser's critique of rampant violence in America (number 55, page 135), which was a trompe l'oeil arrangement of images on successive pages, each page with a die cut that revealed images on the successive page that posed a perceptual quandary.

The *Graphic* was not "edited" in the strictest sense, but rather its themes were conceived either through deliberation and consensus or on a whim. Usually quotes or excerpts were collected from existing arcane sources and used as text. Chwast and Glaser oversaw the art direction, and from 1960 to 1965 Myrna Mushkin shepherded issues into publishable form and found editorial content as well. In the early 1970s, after the *Graphic* became a more standardized magazine (and Glaser was no longer intimately involved), initially Paula Scher and later Ken Robbins took writing and editorial roles. In retrospect, the fact that the *Graphic* had a regular publishing schedule was an act of will (incidentally the word *Monthly* was dropped from the title with issue number 35 to avoid embarrassing expectations). Momentum was maintained for eighty-six issues because even in its later incarnation it filled a need for those involved to have an outlet for discovery, and for the readers to be stimulated by what Push Pin, in turn, discovered.

So the *Graphic* cannot be measured by commercial success alone—or perhaps at all for that matter. It was a

18 Present and former members posed for this photograph for *The Push Pin Style*, published in 1970.

financial failure. However, it certainly boosted Push Pin's reputation and reaped commissions. The *Graphic*'s readership included avid followers as well as art directors and creative directors who purchased the studio's design and illustration, but rarely were boardroom moguls of major corporations on the subscription list. Despite its increasing notoriety, Push Pin Studios never appealed to corporate clients, for whom the *Graphic* was too whimsical. Push Pin Studios was more likely to be hired by pop entrepreneurs and mass-culture businesses, including periodical, book, and record publishers, entertainment and arts producers, and advertising agencies. Hard-core multinational industry was, however, just too uptight.

Throughout the sixties and seventies various exhibitions, including the prestigious 1970 retrospective at the Louvre's Musée des Arts Décoratifs in Paris, showcased Push Pin's work. And two books in particular chronicled its extensive output—*The Push Pin Style* (Communication Arts, 1970) and *The Push Pin Style Design and Illustration* (Idea Publishing, 1972). Yet paging through these books today, we see how much of the work is dated—in a good way (e.g., icons like Glaser's Dylan poster or Chwast's "End Bad Breath" anti–Vietnam War poster) but also in a locked-in-its-own-time way, owing to those many works that were inextricably bound to current fashions. Juxtaposing the wide range of Push Pin's illustration and type styles in these book/catalog formats does not, however, do equal justice to the studio's legacy as represented in the collected *Push Pin Graphic*. Since the *Graphic* was so meticulously art directed and thematically fine-tuned, even the more dated issues have

an integral creative essence that neutralizes the onus of stylistic decrepitude. Each *Graphic* represents an evolutionary stage for artist and studio; so even viewed together as an entire run, the issues convey a strong sense of uniformity born of the synchronic passions that define the Push Pin vision.

Nonetheless, by the mid-1970s even the *Push Pin Graphic* had lost some luster if only because Push Pin Studios had settled comfortably into a mainstream groove that made the studio's style more predictable. There was also a limit to the kinds of clients Push Pin attracted—Push Pin had a grip on popular culture and the clients that purveyed it—and within those parameters the work sometimes evoked déjà vu. Chwast and Glaser have long maintained an extraordinary capacity for reinvention, but their experimental intensity (when compared with the early days of Push Pin) had become more evolutionary than revolutionary. To further diversify into different design areas, Glaser (who in 1968 cofounded the remarkably successful *New York* magazine and was its design director) left Push Pin Studios to found his own design firm, Milton Glaser Inc. He took on a broader range of editorial and identity projects, including restaurant and product design, and further expanded his own graphic idioms (in fact, he did his most internationally recognized icon, "I ♥ NY," after leaving Push Pin). Chwast, who was almost pathologically diverse in his methods and styles (his book *Happy Birthday, Bach* features almost three hundred different stylistic approaches), retained the Push Pin Studios franchise and continues to operate the studio in numerous incarnations. He also delved further into the art

1 Jerry Smokler
2 Vincent Ceci
3 Edward Sorel
4 Cosmos Sarchiapone
5 Tim Lewis
6 Milton Glaser
7 George Leavitt
8 Sam Antupit
9 Norman Green
10 Jerry Joyner
11 Paul Davis
12 Jason McWhorter
13 Herb Levitt
14 James McMullan
15 Reynold Ruffins
16 Barry Zaid
17 Loring Eutemy
18 Isadore Seltzer
19 Seymour Chwast
20 John Alcorn

and authorship of children's books and produced a prodigious number of significant posters. In yet another nod to the Beatles, even though Chwast and Glaser expanded their practices and furthered their individual reputations, after their monumental (though amicable) split, they will always be remembered for their Push Pin collaboration.

In 1976, after briefly suspending publication, Chwast revamped the *Graphic* into a standard nine-by-twelve-inch magazine format printed in full color. His goal was to be more commercially viable through the sale of advertising and paid subscriptions (ultimately resulting in three thousand subscribers) at the rate of $15 yearly. Eleven thousand copies of each issue were printed. This run continued for four years and twenty-two fairly regular issues. Since Push Pin had also started to aggressively represent outside illustrators, the *Graphic* was used to showcase the studio's potential. Still, it was not used like a conventional catalog that featured previously printed assignments but rather work produced exclusively to illustrate the *Graphic*'s quirky themes.

The new series, which began with issue number 64, was not more ambitious than the earlier *Graphics*, but it followed magazine conventions and the production values—the slick, coated paper and standard size exuded a decidedly different tactile and conceptual sensation. By this time other studio "authorial" publications (most notably the *Pentagram Papers*—an eclectic collection of visual and textual curiosa) had been in circulation for a while, so the exclusivity, and thus the novelty, of the earlier *Graphics* had faded somewhat. Semitrade, self-published journals like *Upper and Lower Case*, conceived and designed by Herb Lubalin, also siphoned some electricity from the revamped *Graphic*. But Chwast was determined to produce a publication that not only built upon the *Graphic*'s past glories but also contributed a new point of view.

After a transitional uncoated paper issue devoted to the aesthetics of chickens (number 63, page 170), which hatched the *Graphic*'s new "chicken logo" (the Eustace Tilly of Push Pin), Chwast premiered the first magazine version devoted to "Mothers" (number 64, page 174). The content was something akin to a variety show of diverse acts playing harmoniously within a thematic construct. The most notable editorial element was an illustrated series of famous artists' mothers (humorously rendered in the artistic style of their

progeny), peppered throughout eccentric texts on motherhood. Other issues had ironic themes like "Indigestion" (number 70, page 189), "The Garden (!) State" (number 72, page 194), "Animal Follies" (number 76, page 207), "The Best of Us" (number 80, page 216), and "Good Luck Bad Luck" (number 85, page 232). Each issue was more whimsical than scabrous, but overall a sense of mild satire reigned. In addition, Chwast included real information when possible. The cover of the "Total Disaster" issue (number 78, page 212), for example, was a hand-colored photograph of a hotel destroyed during the San Francisco earthquake of 1906, while the inside was a Baedeker of real and imagined disasters.

Despite the abundance of advertisements from graphic arts suppliers (most of these ads were actually designed by Chwast and provided for free in return for the suppliers' services), financial pressures ultimately took a toll. The "Crime" issue (number 86, page 234) was the very last *Push Pin Graphic*, and perhaps not coincidentally it was the least stimulating of all the issues. Maybe a fizzle is not the best way to end, but there were so few of those in the course of a quarter century that it can be overlooked. Although the steam ran out, the sheer number—eighty-six issues covering the gamut from ephemeral to profound—was nothing short of a historic accomplishment. From its early incarnation the *Push Pin Monthly Graphic* had an incalculable influence by introducing conceptual illustration and eclectic graphic design to America (indeed the world). Now, studied as a totality, these issues document the evolution of a generation-shaping graphic method and manner that had as much impact on popular style as on design culture. ❡

19

THE PUSH PIN GRAPHIC

MANY of the *Push Pin Graphics* reproduced on the following pages are among only a few extant copies. Since the earlier issues were printed on inexpensive newsprint they are predictably showing the effect of age. Most are yellowing, some are crumbling, and all are quite fragile. The editors, however, decided not to enhance them in any way but to retain their look because they are artifacts. Of course, those printed on better quality paper have held up fairly well over time, and often the design and typography appear timeless. Nonetheless, all of these editions are rare documents of design and illustration history.

Published by The Push Pin Studios, 211 East 57 Street, New York 22, PLaza 3-8646. Designers & Illustrators to Advertising & Industry. Miss Rosalie Janpol, representative.

Devil's Apple.
(Solanum mammosum L.)

FLORA AND **FAUNA** IN **WOOD**

NUMBER

1

MARCH 1957

The premiere issue of the *Graphic* proudly declared that members of Push Pin Studios were "Designers and Illustrators to the Advertising Industry." With that said, the cover of this issue, a woodcut by Seymour Chwast, used a bold technique that challenged the style of contemporary commercial art.

21

Reynold Ruffins illustrated these excerpts and axioms about the nature of good and evil with brush and pen ink drawings. The design of this *Graphic* was curiously cluttered in the manner of a Dada or futurist journal, yet it befitted Push Pin's eclectic nature and penchant for stylistic variety.

THE PUSH PIN — Monthly Graphic. — MARCH 1957

NUMBER TWO

SUPPLEMENT

Published by The Push Pin Studios, 211 East 57 Street, New York 22, PLaza 3-8616 — Designers & Illustrators to Advertising & Industry — Miss Rosalie Janpol, representative.

NUMBER THREE

THE PUSH PIN **Monthly Graphic.** APRIL 1957

Published by The Push Pin Studios, 211 East 57 Street, New York 22, PLaza 3-8616 | *Designers & Illustrators to Advertising & Industry* | *Miss Rosalie Janpol, representative.*

EXPRESSION**ISM**

NUMBER

3

APRIL 1957

The *Graphic* was a design laboratory and in this issue Milton Glaser showed his newfound interest in calligraphic drawing, using a Japanese reed pen as his basic tool. He also took a small image and enlarged it to enhance its graphic impact.

23

ABOUT FISHING

NUMBER

4

APRIL 1957

The fishing theme of this issue with its text, "Hints for Anglers," gave John Alcorn a chance to experiment with a cutout style that wed decorative and expressionist sensibilities. The antimodern, eclectic typographic treatment typified the Push Pin aesthetic.

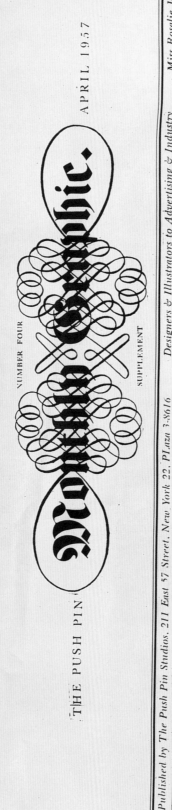

Monthly Graphic. APRIL 1957

NUMBER FOUR SUPPLEMENT

THE PUSH PIN

Published by The Push Pin Studios, 211 East 57 Street, New York 22, PLaza 3-8616 Designers & Illustrators to Advertising & Industry Miss Rosalie Jampol, representative.

HINTS FOR ANGLERS

Wet Garments: Never sit down to rest or remain quiet with feet
or legs wet. Keep the f... and le... wet and in action, thus ward-
ing off a possible chil... Wading ...: Those made of canvas are
the best. Leather sh... ...arden ... the feet. Hob-nails: The
bottoms of wading-s... ...ould b... ...th malleable iron hob-
nails. Don't use ... ...ls, ...ly become smooth as
glass. Take it ... ...t ma... ... fishing. Rest a
couple of hours ... ...spec... ... Behave well: The
angler is always ... ...an- ...r forget when strangers are met at ... ...so... ... O... ...
you are in the w... ...an... ...t i... ...
and not as a servan... ...w ... ...care... ...ct
th... ... your hooks in all kinds of fishing, and ... ...at they
a... ... and perfect. If the point is dull, exchange o... ... or
e... ...e to ... ...rfect poin... for which ...rpose a fine fil...
always be c... Tackle ...tal: All ... ...used upon tac...
be eith... ... silver... ...rass, nic... ...ated. Brig...
Spoons: ... ...oons l... ...ir brill... ...ey can ... ...tened
by th... ...tle n... ...mercur... ...on w... ... of
cham... ...Nets... ...arry s... ...ne...
fish... ... cum... ...it wi... ...so... ...t
com... ...uy... ...y yo... ...ack... ...g-
ul... ... ...t a... ...not... ...rd-
wa... ...l ... ...th... ...A Ga... ...sh:
A ... ...d ... ...e ... ...good ... ...eat.
Cle... ...us... ... ...ers. ...ght
Fish... ...ts... ...r ... ... Bott...
Spri... ...vo... ...ng. Fish
alway... ... Fi... ...days are
always ... ...ng. ... ...cape to pre-
vent a "s... ...ish Al... ... is to carry
a net about ... ...g, with a ... ...open at one
end. The fish ar... ...ed in the bag, w... ... immersed in the
water. These nets can be had at ... tackle store. Big Trout: If
fishing with a fly ... ...y a few inches under
water. It wil... ... ...big trout rarely
come to the ... ...wary trout can
sometimes ... ...le-leaf, and
with a sm... ...t h... ... the ... ...n; suspend
the hook ... ...press ... ...ather, ... it down-stream,
and the ... ...pretty su... ...e it. Sm... ...ater: Perfectly
smooth we... ...arely affords... ...ful fly fish... Sunrise and sun-

John Alcorn

WORK, CRAFT, AND PLEASURE

NUMBER 5

JUNE 1957

The front page of this tabloid, with its clean columns of type, is an elegant homage to a nineteenth-century newspaper. Inside, however, the issue contained a very contemporary double-page illustration of a lion tamer drawn by Chwast with a Speedball pen and wash, which on newsprint allowed the ink to bleed in a serendipitous way.

The full page of custom-made advertisements promoted Push Pin and its vendors.

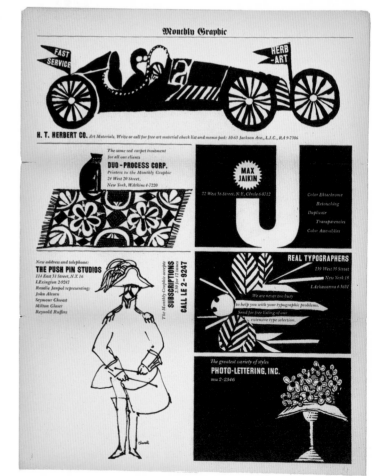

NUMBER SIX

THE PUSH PIN **Monthly Graphic.** JULY 1957

Published by The Push Pin Studios, 114 East 31 Street, New York 16, LExington 2-9247 *Subscriptions: $2.50 for one year*

Oscar Wilde

Delivered to the Art Students of the Royal Academy at their Club in Golden Square, Westminister, on June 30, 1883.

What Makes an Artist? and What Does the Artist Make?

In the lecture which it is my privilege to deliver before you tonight I do not desire to give you any abstract definition of beauty at all. For, we who are working in art cannot accept any theory of beauty in exchange for beauty itself, and, so far from desiring to isolate it in a formula appealing to the intellect, we, on the contrary, seek to materialise it in a form that gives joy to the soul through the senses. We want to create it, not to define it. The definition should follow the work: the work should not adapt itself to the definition.

Nothing, indeed, is more dangerous to the young artist than any conception of ideal beauty: he is constantly led by it either into weak prettiness or lifeless abstraction: whereas to touch the ideal at all you must not strip it of vitality. You must find it in life and re-create it in art.

While, then, on the one hand I do not desire to give you any philosophy of beauty – for, what I want tonight is to investigate how we can create art, not how we can talk of it.

To begin with, such an expression as English art is a meaningless expression. One might just as well talk of English mathematics. Art is the science of beauty, and Mathematics the science of truth: there is *no* national school of either. Indeed, a national school is a provincial school, merely. Nor is there any such thing as a school of art even. There are merely artists, that is all.

And as regards histories of art, they are quite valueless to you unless you are seeking the ostentatious oblivion of an art professorship. It is of no use to you to know the date of Perugino or the birthplace of Salvator Rosa: all that you should learn about art is to know a good picture when you see it, and a bad picture when you see it. As regards the date of the artist, all good work looks perfectly modern: a piece of Greek sculpture, a portrait of Velasquez – they are always modern, always of our time. And as regards the nationality of the artist, art is not national but universal. As regards archaeology, then, avoid it altogether: archaeology is merely the science of making excuses for bad art; it is the rock on which many a young artist founders and shipwrecks. How worthless archaeology is in art you can estimate by the fact of its being so popular. Popularity is the crown of laurel which the world puts on bad art. Whatever is popular is wrong.

As I am not going to talk to you, then, about the philosophy of the beautiful, or the history of art, you will ask me what I am going to talk about. The subject of my lecture tonight is what makes an artist and what does the artist make; what are the relations of the artist to his surroundings, what is the education the artist should get, and what is the quality of a good work of art.

Now, as regards the relations of the artist to his surroundings, by which I mean the age and country in which he is born. All good art, as I said before, has nothing to do with any particular century; but this universality is the quality of the work of art; the conditions that produce that quality are different. And what, I think, you should do is to realise completely your age in order completely to abstract yourself from it; remembering that if you are an artist at all, you will be not the mouthpiece of a century, but the master of eternity; that all art rests on a principle, and that mere temporal considerations are no principle at all; and that those who advise you to make your art representative of the nineteenth century are advising you to produce an art which your children, when you have them, will think old-fashioned. But you will tell me this is an inartistic age, and we are an inartistic people, and the artist suffers in this nineteenth century of ours.

Of course he does. I, of all men, am not going to deny that. But remember that there never has been an artistic age, or an artistic people, since the beginning of the world. The artist has always been, and will always be, an exquisite exception. There is no golden age of art; only artists who have produced what is more golden than gold.

What, you will say to me, the Greeks? were not they an artistic people?

Well, the Greeks certainly not, but, perhaps, you mean the Athenians, the citizens of one out of a thousand cities. Not a bit of it. What is an artistic people but a people who love their artists and understand their art? The Athenians could do neither.

How did they treat Phidias? To Phidias we owe the great era, not merely in Greek, but in all art – I mean of the introduction of the use of the living model.

And what would you say if all the English bishops, backed by the English people, came down from Exeter Hall to the Royal Academy one day and took off Sir Frederick Leighton in a prison van to Newgate on the charge of having allowed you to make use of the living model in your designs for sacred pictures?

Would you not cry out against the barbarism and the Puritanism of such an idea?

Would you not rush off and burn down Newgate, if necessary, and say that such a thing was without parallel in history?

Without parallel? Well, that is exactly what the Athenians did.

And do you think that this was an exceptional case? The sign of a Philistine age is the cry of immorality against art, and this cry was raised by the Athenian people against every great poet and thinker of their day – Aeschylus, Euripides, Socrates. It was the same with Florence in the thirteenth century. Good handicrafts are due to guilds not to the people. The moment the guilds lost their power and the people rushed in, beauty and honesty of work died.

And so, never talk of an artistic people; there never has been such a thing.

But, perhaps, you will tell me that the external beauty of the world has almost entirely passed away from us, that the artist dwells no longer in the midst of the lovely surroundings which, in ages past, were the natural inheritance of every one, and that art is very difficult in this unlovely town of ours, where, as you go to your work in the morning, or return from it at eventide, you have to pass through street after street of the most foolish and stupid architecture that the world has ever seen; architecture, where every lovely Greek form is desecrated and defiled, and every lovely Gothic form defiled and desecrated, reducing three-fourths of the London houses to being, merely, like square boxes of the vilest proportions, as gaunt as they are grimy, and as poor as they are pretentious – the hall door always of the wrong colour, and the windows of the wrong size, and where, even when wearied of the houses you turn to contemplate the street itself, you have nothing to look at but chimney-pot hats, men with sandwich boards, vermilion letterboxes, and do that even at the risk of being run over by an emerald-green omnibus.

Is not art difficult, you will say to me, in such surroundings as these? Of course it is difficult; but then art was never easy; you yourselves would not wish it to be easy; and; besides, nothing is worth doing except what the world says is impossible. Still, you do not care to be answered merely by a paradox. What are the relations of the artist to the external world, and what is the result of the loss of beautiful surroundings to you, is one of the most important questions of modern art; and there is no point on which Mr. Ruskin so insists as that the decadence of art has come from the decadence of beautiful things: and that when the artist can not feed his eye on beauty, beauty goes from his work.

I remember in one of his lectures, after describing the sordid aspect of a great English city, he draws for us a picture of what were the artistic surroundings long ago.

Think, he says, in words of perfect and picturesque imagery, whose beauty I can but feebly echo, think of what was the scene which presented itself, in his afternoon walk, to a designer of the Gothic school of Pisa – Nino Pisano or any of his men.

And then look at the depressing, monotonous appearance of any modern city, the sombre dress of men and women, the meaningless and barren architecture, the colourless and dreadful surroundings. Without a beautiful national life, all the arts will die . . .

But, as regards the general idea of that bit of prose . . . Is it true that beautiful surroundings are necessary for the artist? I think not; I am sure not. Indeed, to me the most inartistic thing in this age of ours is not the indifference of the public to the beautiful things, but the indifference of the artist to the things that are called ugly. For, to the real artist, nothing is beautiful or ugly in itself at all. With the facts of the object he has nothing to do, but with its appearance only, and appearance is a matter of light and shade, of masses, of position, and of value.

Appearance is, in fact, a matter of effect merely, and it is with the effects of nature that you have to deal, not with the real condition of the object. What you, as painters, have to paint is not things as they are but things as they seem to be, not things as they are but things as they are not.

No object is so ugly that, under certain conditions of light and shade, or proximity to other things, it will not look beautiful; no object is so beautiful that, under certain conditions, it will not look ugly. I believe that in every twenty-four hours what is beautiful looks ugly, and what is ugly looks beautiful, once. And, the commonplace character of so much of our painting seems to me due to the fact that so many of our young artists look merely at what we may call 'ready-made beauty', whereas you exist as artists not to copy beauty but to create it in your art, to wait and watch for it in nature.

What would you say of a dramatist who would take nobody but virtuous people as characters in his play? Would you not say that he was missing half of life? Well, of the young artist who paints nothing but beautiful things, I say he misses one half of the world.

Do not wait for life to be picturesque, but try and see life under picturesque conditions. These conditions you can create for yourself in your studio, for they are merely conditions of light. In nature, you must wait for them, watch for them, choose them; and, if you wait and watch, come they will. In Gower Street at night you may see a letterbox that is picturesque; on the Thames Embankment you may see picturesque policemen.

Even Venice is not always beautiful, nor France.

To paint what you see is a good rule in art, but to see what is worth painting is better. See life under pictorial conditions. It is better to live in a city of changeable weather than in a city of lovely surroundings.

Now, having seen what makes the artist, and what the artist makes, who is the artist? There is a man living amongst us who unites in himself all the qualities of the noblest art, whose work is a joy for all time, who is, himself, a master of all time. That man is Mr. Whistler.

But, you will say, modern dress, that is bad. If you cannot paint black cloth you could not have painted silken doublet. Ugly dress is better for art – facts of vision, not of the object.

What is a picture? Primarily, a picture is a beautifully coloured surface, merely, with no more spiritual message or meaning for you than an exquisite fragment of Venetian glass or a blue tile from the wall of Damascus. It is, primarily, a purely decorative thing, a delight to look at.

All archaeological pictures that make you say 'How curious!' all sentimental pictures that make you say 'How sad!' all historical pictures that make you say 'How interesting!' all pictures that do not immediately give you such artistic joy as to make you say 'How beautiful!' are bad pictures.

We never know what an artist is going to do. Of course not. The artist is not a specialist. All such divisions as animal painters, landscape painters, painters of Scotch cattle in an English mist, painters of English cattle in a Scotch mist, racehorse painters, bull-terrier painters, all are shallow. If a man is an artist he can paint everything.

The object of art is to stir the most divine and remote of the chords which make music in our soul; and colour is, indeed, of itself a mystical presence on things, and tone a kind of sentinel.

Am I pleading, then, for mere technique? No. As long as there are any signs of technique at all, the picture is unfinished. What is finish? A picture is finished when all traces of work, and of the means employed to bring about the result, have disappeared.

In the case of handicraftsmen – the weaver, the potter, the smith – on their work are the traces of their hand. But it is not so with the painter; it is not so with the artist.

Art should have no sentiment about it but its beauty, no technique except what you cannot observe. One should be able to say of a picture not that it is 'well painted,' but that it is 'not painted.'

What is the difference between absolutely decorative art and a painting? Decorative art emphasises its material: imaginative art annihilates it. Tapestry shows its threads as part of its beauty: a picture annihilates its canvas; it shows nothing of it. Porcelain emphasises its glaze: water-colours reject the paper.

A picture has no meaning but its beauty, no message but its joy. That is the first truth about art that you must never lose sight of. A picture is a purely decorative thing.

And I shall have some peace there, For peace comes dropping slow,/Dropping from the ve

ART
AND
SEEING

NUMBER
6

JULY 1957

The typography on this front page is consistent with the nineteenth-century theme and a lecture given by Oscar Wilde to members of the Royal Academy. Ruffins illustrated the entire issue.

29

norning To where the cricket sings;/There midnights all aglimmer, and noon a purple glow,/And evening full of the linnet's wings,

Mussolini (tenth from right, top row) marches on Rome/Oct. 28, 1922

NUMBER SEVEN

THE PUSH PIN **Monthly Graphic.** AUGUST 1957

Published by The Push Pin Studios, 114 East 31 Street, New York 16, LExington 2-9247 Subscriptions: $2.50 for one year

BLACK AND WHITE

NUMBER

7

AUGUST 1957

This was not a thematic issue. So the cover essay about Franz Kline and double page drawing inside have little in common except that Glaser's interest in calligraphic gesture, similar in some ways to Kline's, was the basis for this drawing of Mussolini marching on Rome. Although Glaser did not feel that this drawing was particularly accomplished, the distribution of black and white was interesting to him. At the same time, he was developing a crosshatch drawing that derived from his experience etching in Italy.

FRANZ KLINE INTERVIEWED

The following is an excerpt from Selden Rodman's recent book, "Conversations with Artists," published by Devin-Adair

The abstract expressionists have a meeting place where they get together for discussions. It is called, simply, The Club. But recently, one of the members told me, "some of us tried to organize it, give it a regular home, weekly nights, dues, etc. The result is that nobody goes any more." The unofficial and still popular rendezvous of the artists is the Cedar Bar. It is a nondescript tavern with tables in back and nothing to distinguish it from hundreds of others like it except that, facing the bar, between two conventional prints, hangs a small, unframed, unobtrusive canvas containing several slashes of green and gray paint. The artist, a young painter named Charles Brady, has not signed the picture, but under it in pencil some irreverent patron has scrawled on the wall with a pencil: "Horace Horsecollar watching the Mating Penguins."

I met Franz Kline at the Cedar Bar for lunch about a month after the party we had attended. I asked him whether he had been approached by the management to contribute a mural.

"...you really are cheating the mural's nice," he said, "but the idea was fantastic. People would come up to you while you were eating a hamburger and say, 'You do that? What does it mean? We come here to get away from all that. As long as it's the kind of nondescript place it is, we'll keep coming."

Kline is forty-six, of medium height and stocky. He has a trim black moustache and black hair, crew cut. He is friendly, relaxed, sure of himself without being insistent in his view of other ways of painting.

"People have the crazy idea that an abstract painter doesn't like realism," he said. "I like Hyman Bloom's work and, going back further, Ryder's, and even Eakins's. But the thing is that painters like Daumier and Ryder don't ever really paint things the way they look. Nobody can ever look at a boat by Ryder—like a hunk of black tar—and say to me that a boat ever looked like that! Or one of Daumier's faces, composed of slabs of paint, deliberately crude! The final test of painting, theirs, mine, any other, is: does the painter's emotion come across?" He scoffed at Aline Saarinen's theory, expressed in her appreciation of Steichen's "Family of Man" photograph show, that photography might have replaced painting as the great visual art form of our age, and that perhaps painters "should now be reinforced in their conviction that they have no responsibility toward depicting the outward appearance of the world or even finding 'the hidden significance in a given text.'"

"Dali once told me my work was related to John of the Cross, whom he called 'the poet of the night.' Not having read him, I wouldn't know."

We took a crosstown to Kline's studio apartment, which is at the top of a three-story house facing a big playground on Avenue B. It is a typical abstract expressionist's apartment, except for a roof porch in front of the street-front room which gives the studio an exceptional amount of light. A few cheap tables and work benches; a chaotic bedroom; paint spattered on the floor; old magazines and paperbacks in a pile; not a picture of any description on the walls. (I finally found an old Kline behind a desk and hung it behind him for a photograph.) The flat is stripped for action—which doubtless is as it should be, since "action painting" is the objective. A single large white canvas standing against the wall had a couple of sketches of black paint on it, against both of which sheets of yellowing newspaper had been made—to make the paint dry quickly," Kline explained.

I asked him to describe, if he could, what distinguished the procedures of his kind of painting from that of artists in the past.

"Procedure is the key word," he said. "The difference is that we don't begin with a definite sense of procedure. It's free association from the start to the finished state. The old idea was to make me of your talent. This, we feel, is often to take the line of least resistance. Even a painter like Larry Rivers uses his creative gift in the old way—which is O.K. I'm not criticizing him or saying that for him it may not be the right way—but painters like Rothko, Pollock, Still, perhaps in reaction to the tendency to analyze which has dominated painting from Seurat to Albers, associate, with very little analysis. A new form of expressionism inevitably followed. With de Kooning, the procedure is continual change, and the immediacy of the change. With Pollock, the confidence you feel from the concentration of his energy in a given picture."

"And you?"

He held up his hand. "Let me make one further point. If Picasso had spent his whole life making drawings and portraits capable of standing up beside Ingres's—which he amply demonstrated that he could do—he'd have ended up another Augustus John, a man who did no more than follow the bent of his talent, and not Picasso."

"So, to come back," I said, "it's the luck of procedure—"

"And the surprise element which that entails. But, as I said earlier, the emotion must be there. If I feel a painting I'm working on doesn't have imagery or emotion, I paint it out and work over it until it does." "Then you organize, at least to that extent," I said, referring to Mathieu's remark to Tobey which I had already related to him.

"Of course. And so does Mathieu. To think of ways of disorganizing can be a form of organization, you know. The thing is that a person who wants to explore painting naturally reflects: 'How can I be my work be most expressive?' Then the forms develop."

Kline's work caught on with the art world in 1950, following his first show of abstractions. It hasn't changed greatly since, and the few pictures in which he has tried to vary the black-white pattern with color have not been successful. "Most of my life I've had no money and managed to get along," he says. "Right now I sell a few pictures. Nothing changes. I don't count on it lasting." When Noguchi took photographs of his work to Japan in 1951, their kinship with Oriental calligraphic art was instantly recognized. Sabro Hasegawa sought him out on a visit to this country several years later, and this led to some talk of Kline being influenced by Eastern brushes, but without foundation. "Everybody likes calligraphy," he says. "You don't have to be an artist to like it, or go to Japan. Mine came out of drawing, and light. When I look out the window—I've always lived in the city—I don't see trees in bloom or mountain laurel. What I do see—or rather, not what I see but the feelings aroused in me by that looking—is what I paint."

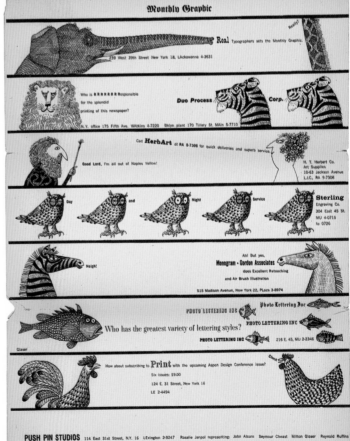

THE ART OF OBJECTS

NUMBER 8

SEPTEMBER 1957

The text on the front page by art historian Arnold Hauser is a subtle tease for the extravagant visuals that Alcorn made from cut and pasted textured papers in a marriage of abstract and representational forms. Alcorn also designed the advertisements with a children's book sensibility.

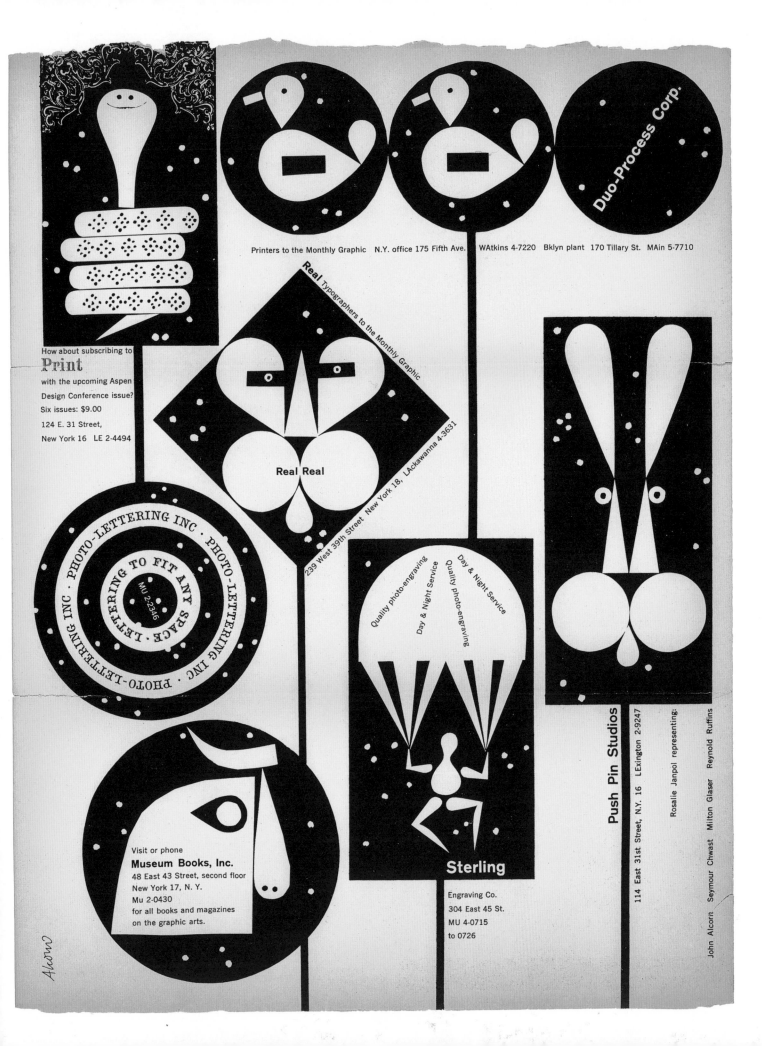

How about subscribing to

Print

with the upcoming Aspen Design Conference issue?
Six issues: $9.00
124 E. 31 Street,
New York 16   LE 2-4494

Printers to the Monthly Graphic   N.Y. office 175 Fifth Ave.   WAtkins 4-7220   Bklyn plant 170 Tillary St.   MAin 5-7710

Duo-Process Corp.

Real Typographers to the Monthly Graphic

Real Real

239 West 39th Street New York 18, LAckawanna 4-3631

PHOTO-LETTERING INC · PHOTO-LETTERING INC · PHOTO-LETTERING INC · PHOTO-LETTERING INC · LETTERING TO FIT ANY SPACE ·

MU 2-2346

Quality photo-engraving
Day & Night Service

Day & Night Service
Quality photo-engraving

Visit or phone
Museum Books, Inc.
48 East 43 Street, second floor
New York 17, N. Y.
Mu 2-0430
for all books and magazines
on the graphic arts.

Sterling

Engraving Co.
304 East 45 St.
MU 4-0715
to 0726

Push Pin Studios

114 East 31st Street, N.Y. 16   LExington 2-9247

Rosalie Janpol representing:

John Alcorn   Seymour Chwast   Milton Glaser   Reynold Ruffins

Alcorn

33

THE PUSH PIN · **Monthly Graphic.** · NUMBER NINE

October, 1957   Published by The Push Pin Studios, 114 East 31 Street, New York 16, LExington 2-9247   Subscriptions: $2.50 yearly

THE LIBIDO FOR THE UGLY
H. L. MENCKEN

On a Winter day some years ago, coming out of Pittsburgh on one of the expresses of the Pennsylvania Railroad, I rolled eastward for an hour through the coal and steel towns of Westmoreland county. It was familiar ground; boy and man, I had been through it often before. But somehow I had never quite sensed its appalling desolation. Here was the very heart of industrial America, the center of its most lucrative and characteristic activity, the boast and pride of the richest and grandest nation ever seen on earth—and here was a scene so dreadfully hideous, so intolerably bleak and forlorn that it reduced the whole aspiration of man to a macabre and depressing joke. Here was wealth beyond computation, almost beyond imagination—and here were human habitations so abominable that they would have disgraced a race of alley cats.

I am not speaking of mere filth. One expects steel towns to be dirty. What I allude to is the unbroken and agonizing ugliness, the sheer revolting monstrousness, of every house in sight. From East Liberty to Greensburg, a distance of twenty-five miles, there was not one in sight from the train that did not insult and lacerate the eye. Some were so bad, and they were among the most pretentious—churches, stores, warehouses, and the like—that they were downright startling; one blinked before them as one blinks before a man with his face shot away.

Reprinted with the permission of Alfred A. Knopf, Inc.

From Prejudices: Sixth Series, 1927

URBAN DISASTERS

NUMBER
9
OCTOBER 1957

H. L. Mencken wrote ironically about America's visual blight in the cities and countryside as "the love of ugliness for its own sake, the lust to make the world tolerable." In his center spread illustration Chwast saw the ubiquitous newsstand— the museum in which so much popular art is hung—as representing good and bad blight.

THE FIRST HOLIDAY ISSUE

NUMBER

10

NOVEMBER 1957

Glaser experimented with the use of limited color and overprinting in this issue and says he learned a lot in the process. "It would have been child's play with the computer, but of course, the hand was the primary 'digital' tool back then." Ruffins did other illustrations in this issue.

SEASON'S GREETINGS

THE PUSH PIN Monthly Graphic. NUMBER TEN

November, 1957 *Published by The Push Pin Studios, 114 East 31 Street, New York 16, LExington 2-9247* *Subscriptions: $2.50 yearly*

CHARLES DICKENS:

THE STORY OF THE GOBLINS WHO STOLE A SEXTON

In an old abbey town, down in this part of the country, a long, long while ago—so long, that the story must be a true one, because our great grandfathers, implicitly believed it—there officiated as sexton and gravedigger in the churchyard, one Gabriel Grub. It by no means follows that because a man is a sexton, and constantly surrounded by the emblems of mortality, therefore he should be a morose and melancholy man; your undertakers are the merriest fellows in the world; and I once had the honour of being on intimate terms with a mute, who in private life, and off duty, was as comical and jocose a little fellow as ever chirped out a devil-may-care song, without a hitch in his memory, or drained off the contents of a good stiff glass without stopping for breath. But, notwithstanding these precedents to the contrary, Gabriel Grub was an ill-conditioned, cross-grained, surly fellow—a morose and lonely man, who consorted with nobody but himself, and an old wicker bottle which fitted into his large, deep waistcoat-pocket—and who eyed each merry face, as it passed him by, with such a deep scowl of malice and ill-humour, as it was difficult to meet, without feeling something the worse for.

"A little before twilight, one Christmas Eve, Gabriel shouldered his spade, lighted his lantern, and betook himself towards the old churchyard; for he had got a grave to finish by next morning, and, feeling very low, he thought it might raise his spirits, perhaps, if he went on with his work at once. As he went his way, up the ancient street, he saw the cheerful light of the blazing fires gleam through the old casements, and heard the loud laugh and the cheerful shouts of those who were assembled around them he marked the bustling preparations for next day's cheer, and smelt the numerous savoury odours consequent thereupon, as they steamed up from the kitchen windows in clouds. All this was gall and wormwood to the heart of Gabriel Grub; and when groups of children bounded out of the houses, tripped across the road, and were met, before they could knock at the opposite door, by half a dozen curly-headed little rascals who crowded round them as they flocked upstairs to spend the evening in their Christmas games, Gabriel smiled grimly, and clutched the handle of his spade with a firmer grasp, as he thought of measles, scarlet fever, thrush, hooping-cough, and a good many other sources of consolation.

"In this happy frame of mind, Gabriel strode along; returning a short, sullen growl to the good-humoured greetings of such of his neighbours as now and then passed him; until he turned into the dark lane which led to the churchyard. Now, Gabriel had been looking forward to reaching the dark lane, because it was, generally speaking, a nice, gloomy, mournful place, into which the townspeople did not much care to go, except in broad daylight, and when the sun was shining; consequently, he was not a little indignant to hear a young urchin roaring out some jolly song about a merry Christmas, in this very sanctuary, which had been called Coffin Lane ever since the days of the old abbey, and the time of the shaven-headed monks. As Gabriel walked on, and the voice drew nearer, he found it proceeded from a small boy, who was hurrying along, to join one of the little parties in the old street, and who, partly to keep himself company, and partly to prepare himself for the occasion, was shouting out the song at the highest pitch of his lungs. So Gabriel waited until the boy came up, and then dodged into a corner, and rapped him over the head with his lantern five or six times, to teach him to modulate his voice. And as the boy hurried away with his hand to his head, singing quite a different sort of tune, Gabriel Grub chuckled very heartily to himself, and entered the churchyard: locking the gate behind him.

"He took off his coat, put down his lantern, and getting into the unfinished grave, worked at it for an hour or so, with right good will. But the earth was hardened with the frost, and it was no very easy matter to break it up, and shovel it out; and although there was a moon, it was a very young one, and shed little light upon the grave, which was in the shadow of the church. At any other time, these obstacles would have made Gabriel Grub very moody and miserable, but he was so well pleased with having stopped the small boy's singing, that he took little heed of the scanty progress he had made, and looked down into the grave, when he had finished work for the night, with grim satisfaction: murmuring as he gathered up his things:

" 'Brave lodgings for one, brave lodgings for one,
A few feet of cold earth, when life is done;
A stone at the head, a stone at the feet,
A rich, juicy meal for the worms to eat;
Rank grass over head, and damp clay around,
Brave lodgings for one, these, in holy ground.'

" 'Ho! ho!' laughed Gabriel Grub, as he sat himself down on a flat tombstone which was a favourite resting-place of his; and drew forth his wicker bottle. 'A coffin at Christmas! A Christmas Box. Ho! ho! ho!'

" 'Ho! ho! ho!' repeated a voice which sounded close behind him. "Gabriel paused, in some alarm, in the act of raising the wicker bottle to his lips; and looked around. The bottom of the oldest grave about him, was not more still and quiet, than the churchyard in the pale moonlight. The cold hoar-frost glistened on the tombstones, and sparkled like rows of gems, among the stone carvings of the old church. The snow lay hard and crisp upon the ground; and spread over the thickly strewn mounds of earth so white and smooth a cover that it seemed as if corpses lay there, hidden only by their winding-sheets. Not the faintest rustle broke the profound tranquility of the solemn scene. Sound itself appeared to be frozen up, and all was so cold.

" 'It was the echoes' said Gabriel Grub, raising the bottle to his lips again.

" 'It was not,' said a deep voice.

"Gabriel started up, and stood rooted to the spot with astonishment and terror; for his eyes rested on a form that made his blood run cold.

"Seated on an upright tombstone, close to him, was a strange unearthly figure, whom Gabriel felt at once, was no being of this world. His long fantastic legs which might have reached the ground, were cocked up, and crossed after a quaint, fantastic fashion; his sinewy arms were bare; and his hands rested on his knees. On his short round body he wore a close covering, ornamented with small slashes; a short cloak dangled at his back; the collar was cut into curious peaks, which served the goblin in lieu of ruff or neckerchief; and his shoes curled up at his toes into long points. On his head, he wore a broad-brimmed sugarloaf hat, garnished with a single feather. The hat was covered with the white frost; and the goblin looked as if he had sat on the same tombstone very comfortably, for two or three hundred years. He was sitting perfectly still; his tongue was put out, as if in derision; and he was grinning at Gabriel Grub with such a grin as only a goblin could call up. 'It was not the echoes,' said the goblin. Gabriel Grub was paralysed, and could make no reply. 'What do you do here on Christmas Eve?' said the goblin sternly. 'I came to dig a grave, sir,' stammered Gabriel Grub. 'What man wanders among graves and churchyards on such a night as this?' cried the goblin.

" 'Gabriel Grub! Gabriel Grub!' screamed a wild chorus of voices that seemed to fill the churchyard. Gabriel looked fearfully round—nothing was to be seen.

" 'What have you got in that bottle?' said the goblin.

" 'Hollands, sir,' replied the sexton, trembling more than ever; for he had bought it of the smugglers, and he thought that perhaps his questioner might be in the excise department of the goblins.

" 'Who drinks Hollands alone, and in a churchyard, on such a night as this?' said the goblin.

" 'Gabriel Grub! Gabriel Grub!' exclaimed the wild voices again. 'The goblin leered maliciously at the terrified sexton, and then raising his voice, exclaimed:

" 'And who, then, is our fair and lawful prize?'

"To this inquiry the invisible chorus replied, in a strain that sounded like the voices of many choristers singing to the mighty swell of the old church organ—a strain that seemed borne to the sexton's ears upon a wild wind, and to die away as it passed onward; but the burden of the reply was still the same, 'Gabriel Grub! Gabriel Grub!'

"The goblin grinned a broader grin than before, as he said, 'Well, Gabriel, what do you say to this?'

"The sexton, gasped for breath.

" 'What do you think of this, Gabriel?' said the goblin, kicking up his feet in the air on either side of the tombstone, and looking at the turned-up points with as much complacency as if he had been contemplating the most fashionable pair of Wellingtons in all Bond Street.'

" 'It's—it's—very curious, sir,' replied the sexton, half dead with fright; 'very curious, and very pretty, but I think I'll go back and finish my work, sir, if you please.'

" 'Work!' said the Goblin, 'what work?'

" 'The grave, sir; making the grave,' stammered the sexton. 'Oh, the grave, eh?' said the goblin; 'who makes graves at a time when all other men are merry, and takes pleasure in it?'

"Again the mysterious voices replied, 'Gabriel Grub!

" 'I'm afraid my friends want you, Gabriel,' said the goblin, thrusting his tongue further into his cheek than ever—and a most astonishing tongue it was—'I'm afraid my friends want you, Gabriel,' said the goblin.

" 'Under favour, sir' replied the horror-stricken sexton, 'I don't think they can, sir; they don't know me, sir; I don't think they have ever seen me, sir.'

" 'Oh, yes they have, replied the goblin; 'we know the man with the sulky face and grim scowl, that came down the street to-night, throwing his evil looks at the children, and grasping his burying spade the tighter. We know the man who struck the boy in the envious malice of his heart, because the boy could be merry, and he could not. We know him, we know him.'

"Here the goblin gave a loud shrill laugh, which the echoes returned twentyfold; and throwing his legs up in the air, stood upon his head, or rather upon the very point of his sugar-loaf hat, on the narrow edge of the tombstone: whence he threw a somerset with extraordinary agility, right to the sexton's feet, at which he planted himself in the attitude in which tailors generally sit upon the shopboard.

" 'I—I—am afraid I must leave you, sir,' said the sexton, making an effort to move.

" 'Leave us,' said the goblin, 'Gabriel Grub going to leave us. Ho! ho! ho!'

"As the goblin laughed, the sexton observed, for one instant, a brilliant illumination within the windows of the church, as if the whole building were lighted up; it disappeared, the organ pealed forth a lively air, and whole troops of goblins, the very counterpart of the first one, poured into the churchyard, and began playing at leapfrog with the tombstones; never stopping for an instant to take breath, but 'overing' the highest among them, one after the other, with the most marvellous dexterity. The first goblin was a most astonishing leaper, and none of the others could come near him; even in the extremity of his terror the sexton could not help observing, that while his friends were content to leap over the common-sized gravestone, the first one took the family vaults, iron railings and all, with as much ease as if they had been so many street posts.

"At last the game reached to a most exciting pitch; the organ played quicker and quicker; and the goblins leaped faster and faster; coiling themselves up, rolling head over heels upon the ground, and bounding over the tombstones like footballs. The sexton's brain whirled round with the rapidity of the motion he beheld, and his legs reeled beneath him, as the spirits flew before his eyes: when the goblin-king, suddenly darting towards him, laid his hand upon his collar, and sank with him through the earth.

"When Gabriel Grub had had time to fetch his breath, which the rapidity of his descent had for the moment taken away, he found himself in what appeared to be a large cavern, surrounded on all sides by crowds of goblins, ugly and grim; in the centre of the room, on an elevated seat, was stationed his friend of the churchyard; and close beside him stood Gabriel Grub himself, without power of motion.

" 'Cold to-night,' said the king of the goblins, 'very cold. A glass of something warm, here!'

"At this command, half a dozen officious goblins, with a perpetual smile upon their faces, whom Gabriel Grub imagined to be courtiers, on that account, hastily disappeared, and presently returned with a goblet of liquid fire, which they presented to the king.

" 'Ah!' cried the goblin, whose cheeks and throat were transparent, as he tossed down the flame, 'this warms one, indeed! Bring a bumper for Mr. Grub.'

"It was in vain for the unfortunate sexton to protest that he was not in the habit of taking anything warm at night; one of the goblins held him while another poured the blazing liquid down his throat; the whole assembly screeched with laughter as he coughed and choked, and wiped away the tears which gushed plentifully from his eyes, after swallowing the draught.

" 'And now,' said the king, fantastically poking the taper corner of his sugar-loaf hat into the sexton's eye, and thereby occasioning him the most exquisite pain: 'And now, show the man of misery and gloom, a few of the pictures from our own great storehouse!'

"As the goblin said this, a thick cloud which obscured the remoter end of the cavern, rolled gradually away, and disclosed, apparently at a great distance, a small and scantily furnished, but neat and clean apartment. A crowd of little children were gathered round a bright fire, clinging to their mother's gown, and gambolling around her chair. The mother occasionally rose, and drew aside the window-curtain, as if to look for some expected object: a frugal meal was ready spread upon the table; and an elbow-chair was placed near the fire. A knock was heard at the door: the mother opened it, and the children crowded round her, and clapped their hands for joy, as their father entered. He was wet and weary, and shook the snow from his garments, as the children crowded round him, and seizing his cloak, hat, stick, and gloves, with busy zeal, ran with them from the room. Then, as he sat down to his meal before the fire, the children climbed about his knee, and the mother sat by his side, and all seemed happiness.

"But a change came upon the view, almost imperceptibly. The scene was altered to a small bedroom, where the fairest and youngest child lay dying; the roses had fled from his cheek, and the light from his eye; and even as the sexton looked upon him with an interest he had never felt or known before, he died. His young brothers and sisters crowded round his little bed, and seized his tiny hand, so cold and heavy; but

John Alcorn

Milton Glaser

they shrunk back from its touch, and looked with awe on his infant face; for calm and tranquil as it was, and sleeping in rest and peace as the beautiful child seemed to be, they saw that he was dead, and they knew that he was an Angel looking down upon, and blessing the, from a bright and happy Heaven.

"Again the light cloud passed across the picture, and again the subject changed. The father and mother were old and helpless now, and the number of those about them was diminished more than half; but content and cheerfulness sat on every face, and beamed in every eye, as they crowded round the fireside, and told and listened to old stories of earlier and bygone days. Slowly and peacefully, the father sank into the grave, and, soon after, the sharer of all his cares and troubles followed him to a place of rest. The few, who yet survived him, knelt by their tomb, and watered the green turf which covered it, with their tears; then rose, and turned away: sadly and mournfully, but not with bitter cries, or despairing lamentations, for they knew that they should one day meet again; and once more they mixed with the busy world, and their content and cheerfulness were restored. The cloud settled upon the picture, and concealed it from the sexton's view.

"What do you think of that?" said the goblin, turning his large face towards Gabriel Grub.

"Gabriel murmured out something about its being very pretty, and looked somewhat ashamed, as the goblin bent his fiery eyes upon him.

"You a miserable man!" said the goblin, in a tone of excessive contempt. "You!" He appeared disposed to add more, but indignation choked his utterance, so he lifted up one of his very pliable legs, and flourishing it above his head a little, to insure his aim, administered a good sound kick to Gabriel Grub; immediately after which, all the goblins in waiting, crowded round the wretched sexton, and kicked him without mercy; according to the established and invariable custom of courtiers upon earth, who kick whom royalty kicks, and hug whom royalty hugs.

"Show him some more!" said the king of the goblins.

"At these words, the cloud was dispelled, and a rich and beautiful landscape was disclosed to view—there is just such another, to this day, within half a mile of the old abbey town. The sun shone from out the clear blue sky, the water sparkled beneath his rays, and the trees looked greener, and the flowers more gay, beneath his cheering influence. The water rippled on, with a pleasant sound; the trees rustled in the light wind that murmured among their leaves; the birds sang upon the boughs; and the lark carolled on high her welcome to the morning; Yes, it was morning; the bright, balmy morning of summer; the minutest leaf, the smallest blade of grass, was instinct with life. The ant crept forth to her daily toil, the butterfly fluttered and basked in the warm rays of the sun; myriads of insects spread their transparent wings, and revelled in their brief but happy existence. Man walked forth, elated with the scene; and all was brightness.

"You a miserable man!" said the king of goblins, in a more contemptuous tone than before. And again the king of the goblins gave his leg a flourish; again it descended on the shoulders of the sexton; and again the attendant goblins imitated their chief.

"Many a time the cloud went and came, and many a lesson it taught to Gabriel Grub, who, although his shoulders smarted with pain from the frequent applications of the goblins' feet, looked on with an interest that nothing could diminish. He saw that men who worked hard and earned their scanty bread with lives of labour, were cheerful and happy; and that to the most ignorant, the sweet face of nature was a never-failing source of cheerfulness and joy. He saw those who had been delicately nurtured, and tenderly brought up, cheerful under privations, and superior to suffering that would have crushed many of a rougher grain, because they bore within their own bosoms the materials of happiness, contentment, and peace. He saw that women, the tenderest and most fragile of all God's creatures, were the oftenest superior to sorrow, adversity, and distress; and he saw that it was because they bore, in their own hearts, an inexhaustible well-spring of affection and devotion. Above all, he saw that men like himself, who snarled at the mirth and cheerfulness of others, were the foulest weeds on the fair surface of the earth; and setting all the good of the world against the evil, he came to the conclusion that it was a very decent and respectable sort of world after all. No sooner had he formed it, than the cloud which closed over the last picture, seemed to settle on his senses, and lull him to repose. One by one, the goblins faded from his sight; and as the last one disappeared, he sunk to sleep.

"The day had broken when Gabriel Grub awoke, and found himself lying, at full length on the flat gravestone in the churchyard, with the wicker bottle lying empty by his side, and his coat, spade, and lantern, all well whitened by the last night's frost, scattered on the ground. The stone on which he had first seen the goblin seated, stood bolt upright before him, and the grave at which he had worked, the night before, was not far off. At first, he began to doubt the

---

that if a man turn sulky and drink by himself at Christmas-time, he may make up his mind to be not a bit the better for it: let the spirits be never so good, or let them be even as many degrees beyond proof, as those which Gabriel Grub saw in the Goblin's cavern."

37

Seymour Chwast

Reynold Ruffins

reality of his adventures, but the acute pain in his shoulders when he attempted to rise, assured him that the kicking of the goblins was certainly not ideal. He was staggered again, by observing no traces of footsteps in the snow on which the goblins had played at leap-frog with the gravestones, but he speedily accounted for this circumstance when he remembered that, being spirits, they would leave no visible impression behind them. So Gabriel Grub got on his feet as well as he could, for the pain in his back; and brushing the frost off his coat, put it on, and turned his face towards the town.

"But he was an altered man, and he could not bear the thought of returning to a place, where his repentance would be scoffed at, and his reformation disbelieved. He hesitated for a few moments; and then turned away to wander and seek his bread elsewhere.

"The lantern, the spade, and the wicker bottle, were found, that day, in the churchyard. There were a great many speculations about the sexton's fate, at first, but it was speedily determined that he had been carried away by the goblins; and there were not wanting some very credible witnesses who had distinctly seen him whisked through the air on the back of a chestnut horse blind of one eye, with the hind-quarters of a lion, and the tail of a bear. At length all this was devoutly believed; and the new sexton used to exhibit to the curious, for a trifling emolument, a good-sized piece of the church weathercock which had been accidentally kicked off by the aforesaid horse in his aerial flight, and picked up by himself in the churchyard, a year or two afterwards.

"Unfortunately, these stories were somewhat disturbed by the unlooked-for reappearance of Gabriel Grub himself, some ten years afterwards, a ragged, contented, rheumatic old man. He told his story to the clergyman, and also to the mayor; and in course of time it began to be received, as a matter of history, in which form it has continued down to this very day. The believers in the weathercock tale, having misplaced their confidence once, were not easily prevailed upon to part with it again, so they looked as wise as they could, shrugged their shoulders, touched their foreheads, and murmured something about Gabriel Grub having drunk all the Hollands, and then fallen asleep on the flat tombstone; and they affected to explain what he supposed he had witnessed in the goblin's cavern, by saying that he had seen the world, and grown wiser. But this opinion, which was by no means a popular one at any time, gradually died off; and be the how it may, as Gabriel Grub was afflicted with rheumatism to the end of his days, this story has at least one moral, if it teach no better one—and that is,

CUBISM
AND
SURREALISM

NUMBER
11

DECEMBER 1957

Glaser had long been interested in both surrealism and Dada; Apollinaire's typographical experiments were also very important. A friend of Glaser's, filmmaker Stanley Vanderbeek, had in his home a collection of surreal furniture objects he had made. Glaser used them as the basis for this *Graphic*.

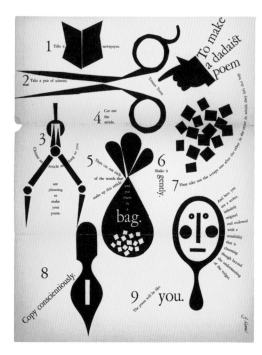

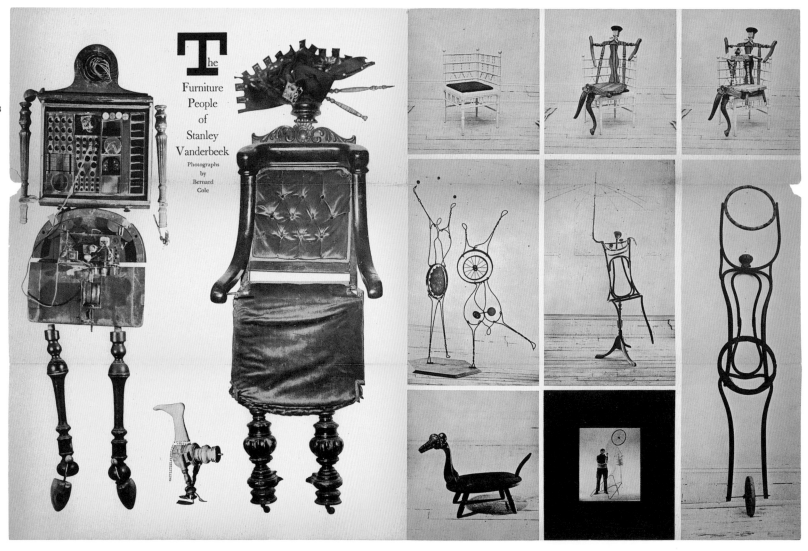

The
Furniture
People
of
Stanley
Vanderbeek
Photographs by
Bernard Cole

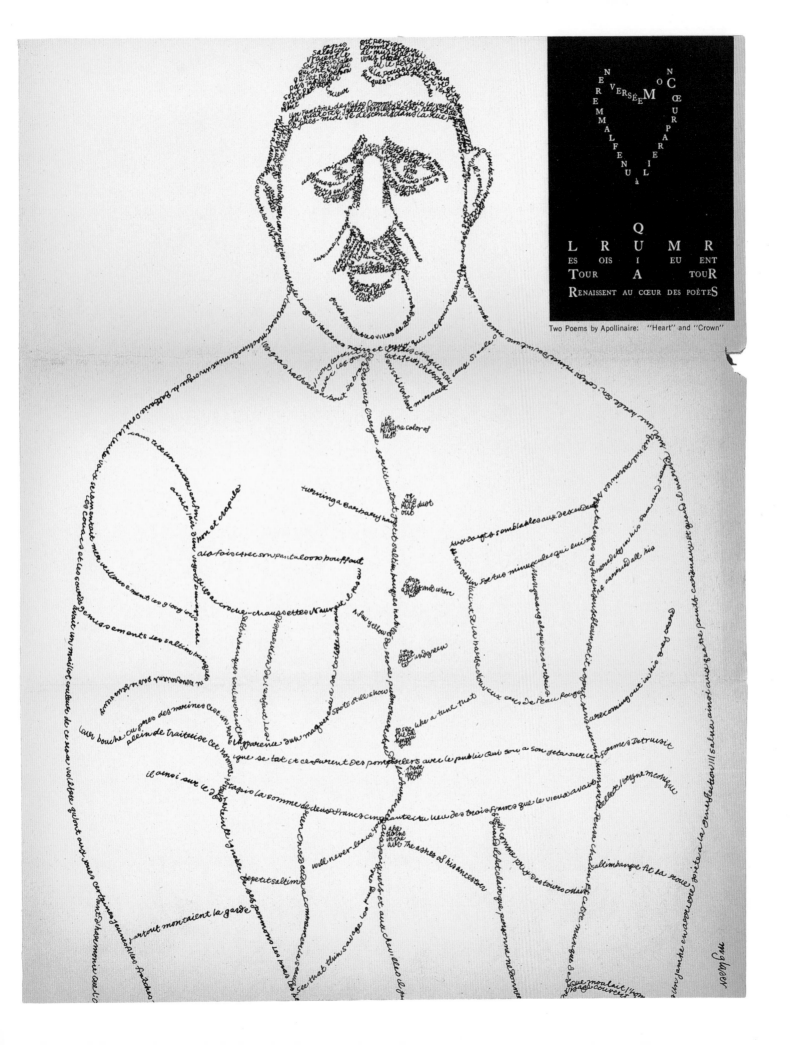

Two Poems by Apollinaire: "Heart" and "Crown"

39

THE QUATTROCENTO

NUMBER

12

JANUARY 1958

Chwast was fascinated by a collection of
eighteenth-century puppets he had
found during his maiden trip to Venice.
He created a linocut comic strip that
illustrated a tale by Giovanni Boccaccio.
The main text was by Hauser from his
book *The Social History of Art.*

THE PUSH PIN **Monthly Graphic.** NUMBER TWELVE

January, 1958   Published by The Push Pin Studios, 114 East 31 Street, New York 16, LExington 2-0247   Subscriptions: $2.50 yearly

The Concept
of the
Renaissance

Continued on page 6

40

Dianora's Story

Adapted from a story by Giovanni Baccaccio as related in "The Decameron"

In the country of Friuli, which, though cold, is enlivened with noble mountains there lived a lovely lady called Dianora. She was married to a lord of great wealth and charm called Gilberto, but such was the lady's beauty that it obtained her the love of Ansaldo, a mighty baron.

Dianora, weary of the baron's solicitations (she denied him everything) thought her task an impossible one. The baron was resoved to determine if it could be done, and sent messengers to various countries to find out whether there were anyone to help him. At last a wizard presented himself. He offered to create the garden for a fabulous sum.

Again and again I have pressed my suit, but to no avail, Dianora. If there is any way to prove that I love you tell me how.

Make my garden as beautiful in January as it is in May. Let me be be rid of you until you do.

Come next January your lady's garden will be filled with verdant lawns and the most beautiful fruits, flowers and leafy shrubs.

Please don't be angry, but consider the purity of my intention and banish your wrath with better judgment.

I'll try.

Finally the first of January came and bitter and cold it was, with ice and snow covering the face of the earth. Nevertheless, when Dianora walked into her garden, she saw that it was as green as in May. All day long she brooded upon it until she could no longer conceal her dispair. She was compelled to speak and told Gilberto everything as it happened.

Gilberto granted Dianora what perhaps no other man would, prompted by fear of the wizard who might work them some dreadful mischief

Dianora, it is not proper for a discreet and modest woman to make any bargain involving her chastity. I want you to go to Ansaldo. If you can manage to make him release you from your pledge. If not—this once only, yield your body to him, but not your soul.

It is not any love I bear you but the command of my husband, who, considerate of the labors of your ungoverned passion, obliged me to come. I am ready to do your will for this once only.

My lady, since things are what you say, far be it for me to wreck the honor of one who is considerate of my love; you may go home in peace, render my thanks to your husband for such supreme courtesy, and assure him that henceforth he has in me a brother and faithful servant.

Touched by Gilberto's liberality his passion gave way to tenderness.

Dianora was beside herself with this assurance. She said that nothing could have made her believe her come to Ansaldo could have any other outcome than this and she will always be grateful to him for it. Bidding him goodby, she returned to her husband.

After seeing Gilberto so generous with his honor and with your love, I should also be generous with my reward. Keep your money then.

That's too much.

Ansaldo was embarrassed by such liberality but his coaxing was of no avail. On the third day the magician removed the garden and returned to his land. From that time onward Dianora, Gilberto and Ansaldo were bound in a close tie of friendship.

Seymour Chwast

GEORGE BERNARD SHAW

NUMBER
13

JANUARY 1958

Glaser says that most
portrait of George Bernard
Shaw do not really look like him,
this by way of admitting that
he had never been very good at
likeness. But the ones in this issue
worked well and also demonstrated
Push Pin's collective interest in
work with various graphic
techniques, line, tone, and mixed.

42

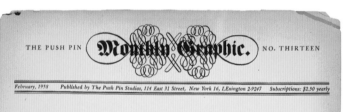

THE PUSH PIN Monthly Graphic. NO. THIRTEEN

February, 1958   Published by The Push Pin Studios, 114 East 31 Street, New York 16, LExington 2-9247   Subscriptions: $2.50 yearly

G.B.S. sat down without a word. His face was white and drawn. We guessed that he needed quiet and therefore brought out books on art, which he examined with the greatest of care. He knew few of the modern names, showed an antipathy to abstract work, and confused Picasso with Pissarro.

"Old Camille Pissarro was an excellent artist but (turning to Picasso's work) what a son!"

He was obviously thinking of Pablo and not Lucien and blamed the latter for indulging in abstract pattern to deceive an ignorant public. He visualized Lucien Pissarro as a young, irresponsible, irrepressible fellow with a great big indulgent father. I showed him a photograph of Lucien with long grey beard. G.B.S. smiled and said:

"That's where men have the advantage. They can always grow a beard to cover a chin. I myself am not too good without a beard, I have a nasty jowl which needs softening with natural hair." Again he denounced Lucien as one who ought to know better. I explained that he was a personal friend, a hard, conscientious worker, the nearest person we have to William Morris in this country. I told G.B.S. of the wonderful friendship that existed between father and son and quoted a letter from Camille to Lucien:

"Remember that I have a rustic, melancholy temperament, that I am coarse and wild in appearance, it is only after a long time that I can appeal to anyone if the person who looks at me has a little indulgence. But the passer-by passes too cursory a glance and goes on...."

G.B.S. said: "When I was an art critic I recognized the moment I saw the work of the impressionists that a new vision and a new vitality had entered art. When an artist's work produces violent controversy people are apt to regard it with that sort of seriousness which is very appropriately called deadly. The same sort of thing happened in literature and the theater: they were almost done to death by the earnest disciples. Be earnest, certainly, but if you believe in a thing you can laugh at it. Atheists, whose religion is that there is no God, laugh at God and end up as theosophists. Do you remember St. John Ervine's story, when he and Galsworthy were watching a performance of my play? They were suddenly harangued by a funeral usher, an earnest student of the drama. He must have entered the theater after depositing a body in a cellar. He pointed to the dozen persons in the theater and exclaimed: 'And even then don't take it seriously! Three blows of the mallet were heard, the artistic substitute for the orchestra, and the play was resumed."

I thought that the best bit of pungent criticism I had ever read was of Courbet by Alexandre Dumas, fils; I read it to G.B.S.:

"From what fabulous crossing of a slug with a peacock, from what genital antithesis, from what sebaceous oozing can have been generated, for instance, this thing called Mr. Gustave Courbet? Under what gardener's bell, with the help of what manure, as a result of what mixture of wine, beer, corrosive mucus and

G B S on A R T

flatulent oedema can have grown this sonorous and hairy pumpkin, this aesthetic belly, this imbecilic and impotent incarnation of the Self? Wouldn't one say he was the force of God, if God, whom this something has wanted to destroy, were capable of playing pranks, and could have mixed Himself up with this?"

G.B.S. laughed and thought it good stuff. "It was no doubt the making of Courbet," he said. "Philosophically Dumas was all wrong. God is capable of playing pranks, and He's always mixing Himself up with artists. It's the only company He cares to keep. All the same, I'm all out for a healthy Philistinism which will laugh, though not ungently, at the mystic pretensions of our workers in paint, in stone, or in print."

"You prefer to think of yourself as a 'healthy' Philistine?"

He dropped his head and made up his mind quickly. "How else," he answered, "is one to be free from the diseased languor of aestheticism?"

In that phrase I saw the *Yellow Book*, and the artists and writers Max pilloried so tenderly.

"You know," he continued, "Dumas could have said all that of Rodin's sculpture, or of my work, or compositely, or Rodin's sculpture of me. Rodin was an extraordinary man really. He liked to work in his garden, and, whenever he wanted anything moved he would call the nearest person, even the postman, to help him lift the sculpture, and the amazing thing was that he did it! We got on very well together. He could not speak English and I could not speak French, so conversation was smooth, as I did all the talking. He was really uneducated and like Anatole France had never heard of me before my wife asked him to do a bust of me. I don't think he had even heard of William Morris. He lived in grand style in a mansion with a large garden and a factotum who ran all his affairs very efficiently for him."

"You mean Rilke, the poet?"

"Was he a poet?" He was obviously taken aback. I waited to hear something about Rilke but he had nothing to say about him.

"Rodin was a very good draftsman," he continued, "and Charlotte, who managed to get round everybody, impressed him enough for him to give her one of his drawings, a nude, but he was delicate enough to drape this drawing before he presented it, in deference to my wife's modesty. Which reminds me of a sweet story about Ruskin.

"He had heard that a lady whom he had loved in his youth was dying, and he expressed a desire to see her. The reply came that he could only see her if he said that he loved God more than her. He did not go."

"It was well," I said, "that Ruskin didn't see her."

"I had a similar experience with Janet Achurch. My last meeting with her was at the Court Theatre. I had not seen her for ages, and I made an odd mistake. I went into the wrong room and found three women dressing; I went straight to the one made up as an old woman and kissed her hand. She was obviously surprised and quietly directed me to the next landing."

"Did Janet make you promise to put God before her?" I asked.

"No, it was I who was always preaching religion. Look how religion transformed Annie Besant. Mrs. Besant, the secularist, became coarser and stouter every year, while as a theosophist she became a teetotalist and vegetarian and looked quite attractive in her white robes. Annie had no taste. She bought an umbrella for me: it was so ugly that I wouldn't be seen at a funeral with it. I returned it to her, and she threw it over a fence in Regent's Park. To tease her, I did a drawing of the field with lots of little umbrellas coming through."

"You are inclined to ride roughshod over people's feelings," I remarked.

"Well I had to show the cloven hoof even if it was—" G.B.S. had been living with one foot in the grave, on and off, for more than years than I can remember, on the foot that was in the grave.

Reprinted by permission of the publishers, The Vanguard Press, from "Days with ... *by Stephen Winsten. Copyright, 1949, by Vanguard Press, Inc.*

43

Milton Glaser

GAUGUIN
AND THE
SOUTH SEAS

NUMBER

14

MARCH 1958

Working its way through writings of great artists, the *Graphic* in this issue published text from Paul Gauguin's South Seas journal and illustrations by Ruffins. The typography of the advertisements shows a growing penchant for Victorian and art nouveau lettering.

THE PUSH PIN **Monthly Graphic.** NO. FOURTEEN

March, 1958   Published by The Push Pin Studios, 114 East 31 Street, New York 16, LExington 2-9247   Subscriptions: $2.50 yearly

Silence! I am learning to know the silence of a Tahitian night.

In this silence I hear nothing except the beating of my heart.

But the rays of the moon play through the bamboo reeds, standing equidistant from each other before my hut, and reach even to my bed. And these regular intervals of light suggest a musical instrument to me—the reed-pipe of the ancients, which was familiar to the Maori, and is called *vivo* by them. The moon and the bamboo reeds made it assume an exaggerated form—an instrument that remained silent throughout the day, but that at night by grace of the moon calls forth in the memory of the dreamer well-loved melodies. Under this music I fell asleep.

Between me and the sky there was nothing except the high frail roof of pandanus leaves, where the lizards have their nests.

In my sleep I could see the space above me, the vault of heaven, not the prison walls which I had made for myself. I was far, far away from the prisons that European houses are.

A Maori hut does not separate man from life, from space, from the infinite . . .

In the meantime I felt myself very lonely here.

The inhabitants of the district and I mutually watched each other, and the distance between us remained the same.

By the second day I had exhausted my provisions. What to do? I had imagined that with money I would be able to find all that was necessary for life. I was deceived. Once beyond the threshold of the city, we must turn to Nature in order to live. She is rich, she is generous, she refuses to no one who will ask his share of her treasures of which she has inexhaustible reserves in the trees, in the mountains, in the sea. But one must know how to climb the tall trees, how to go into the mountains, in order to return weighed down with heavy booty. One must know how to catch fish, and how to dive to tear loose the shellfish so firmly attached to stones at the bottom of the sea.—One must know how, one must be able to do these things.

Here was I, a civilized man, distinctly inferior in these things to the savages. I envied them. I looked at their happy, peaceful life round about me, making no further effort than was essential for their daily needs, without the least care about money. To whom were they to sell, when the gifts of Nature were within the reach of every one?

There I was sitting with empty stomach on the threshold of my hut, sadly considering my state, and thinking of the unforeseen, perhaps insurmountable, obstacles which Nature has created for her protection and placed between herself and him who comes from a civilized world, when I saw a native gesticulating and calling out something to me. The expressive gesture interpreted the words, and I understood that my neighbor was inviting me to dinner. With a shake of the head I declined. Then I re-entered my hut, ashamed, I believe equally because charity had been offered me, and because I had refused it.

A few minutes later a little girl without saying anything left some cooked vegetables in front of my door, and also fruit wrapped neatly in green freshly picked leaves. I was hungry, and likewise without a word I accepted the gift.

A little later, the man passed in front of my hut, and, smiling, but without stopping, said in a questioning tone, "Paia?"

I divined, "Are you contented?"

This was the beginning of a reciprocal understanding between the savages and myself.

"Savages!" This word came involuntarily to my lips when I looked at these black beings with their cannibal-like teeth. However, I already had a glimpse of their genuine, their strange grace . . . I remembered the little brown head made it assume an exaggerated form, which from under the clusters of large gigantic leaves watched me one morning without my knowing it, and I fled when my glance met hers . . .

NOA NOA

An excerpt from a journal of the south seas by
PAUL GAUGUIN,
translated by O. E. Theis, reprinted with the permission of
The Noonday Press.

⚫—⚫—⚫

As they were to me, so was I to them, an object for observation; a cause of astonishment—one to whom everything...

close to a blue. Golden figures in the brooks and on the seashore enchanted me. Why did I hesitate to put all this glory of the sun on my canvas?

Oh! the old European traditions! The timidities of expression of degenerate races!

In order to familiarize myself with the distinctive characteristics of the Tahitian face, I had wished for a long time to make a portrait of one of my neighbors, a young woman of pure Tahitian extraction.

One day she finally became emboldened enough to enter my hut, and to look at photographs of paintings which I had hung on one of the walls of my room. She regarded the *Olympia* for a long time and with special interest.

"What do you think of her?" I asked. I had learned a few Tahitian words during the two months since I had last spoken French.

My neighbor replied, "She is very beautiful!"

I smiled at this remark, and was touched by it. Had she then a sense of the beautiful? But what reply would the professors of the Academy of Fine Arts have made to this remark?

Then suddenly after a perceptible silence such as precedes the thinking out of a conclusion, she added, "Is it your wife?"

"Yes."

I did not hesitate at this lie. I—the *tané* of the beautiful *Olympia!*

While she was curiously examining certain religious compositions of the Italian primitives, I hastened, without her noticing it, to sketch her portrait.

She saw it, and with a pout cried out abruptly, "*Aïta* (no)!" and fled.

An hour later she returned, dressed in a beautiful robe with *tiaré* behind the ear. Was it coquetry? Was it the pleasure of consenting of her own free will after having refused? Or was it simply the universal attraction of the forbidden fruit which one denies one's self? Or more probably still, was it merely a caprice without any other motive, a pure caprice of the kind to which the Maoris are so given?

Without delay I began work, without hesitation and all of a fever. I was aware that on my skill as painter would depend the physical and moral possession of the model, that it would be like an implied, urgent, irresistible invitation.

She was not at all handsome according to our aesthetic rules.

She was beautiful.

All her traits combined in a Raphaelesque harmony by the meeting of curves. Her mouth had been modeled by a sculptor who knew how to put into a single mobile line a mingling of all joy and all suffering.

I worked in haste and passionately, for I knew that the consent had not yet been definitely gained. I trembled to read certain things in these large eyes—fear and the desire for the unknown, the melancholy of bitter experience which lies at the root of all pleasure, the involuntary and sovereign feeling of being mistress of herself. Such women submit to us when we ourselves are conquered. All the force which has in it something di-

THE PUSH PIN Monthly Graphic. NO. FIFTEEN

April, 1958   Published by The Push Pin Studios, 114 East 31 Street, New York 16, LExington 2-9247   Subscriptions: $2.50 yearly

SIMILARITY AND DIFFERENCE BETWEEN PAINTING AND POETRY

The imagination is to reality as the shadow to the body that casts it and as poetry is to painting, because poetry puts down her subjects in imaginary written characters, while painting puts down the identical reflections that the eye receives, as if they were real, and poetry does not give the actual likeness of things, and does not, like painting, impress the consciousness through the organ of sight.

The imagination cannot visualize such beauty as is seen by the eye, because the eye receives the actual semblances or images of objects and transmits them through the scene organ to the understanding where they are judged. But the imagination never gets outside the understanding (sensus communis); it reaches the memory and stops and dies there if the imagined object is not of great beauty; thus poetry is born in the mind or rather in the imagination of the poet who, because he describes the same things as the painter, claims to be the painter's equal! But in truth he is far removed, as has been shown above. Therefore, in regard to imitation, it is true to say that the science of painting stands to poetry in the same relation as a body to its cast shadow; but the difference is even greater, because a shadow penetrates through the eye to the understanding while the object of the imagination does not come from without but is born in the darkness of the mind's eye. What a difference between forming a mental image of such light in the darkness of the mind's eye and actually perceiving it outside the darkness!

If you, poet, had to represent a murderous battle you would have to describe the air obscured and darkened by fumes from frightful and deadly engines mixed with thick clouds of dust polluting the atmosphere, and the panicky flight of wretches fearful of horrible death. In that case, the painter will be your superior, because your pen will be worn out before you can fully describe what the painter can demonstrate forthwith by the aid of his science, and your tongue will be parched with thirst and your body overcome by sleep and hunger before you can describe with words what a painter is able to show you in an instant. In his picture only the soul is wanting; each figure is represented so as to show completely that part which has the given direction. What long and tedious work it would be for poetry to describe all the movements of the fighters in such a battle and the actions of their limbs and their ornaments. This is accomplished with great directness and truth in painting and placed before you, and in such a picture only the sound of the engines, the terrifying shouts of the victors, and the cries and wailing of the terrified victims are wanting, and neither can the poet convey these to the sense of hearing.

The only true office of the poet is to invent the words of people who are conversing together—only then can he transmit to the sense of hearing an equivalent of nature, for the words created by the human voice are natural phenomena in themselves.

Painting serves a nobler sense than poetry and represents the works of nature with more truth than a poet. The works of nature are much nobler than speech which was invented by man; but the works of man are to the works of nature as man is to God. Therefore, it is a nobler profession to imitate the things of nature which are the true and actual likenesses than to imitate in words the actions and speeches of men. And if you, poet, wish to confine yourself exclusively to your own profession in describing the works of nature, representing diverse places and forms of various objects, you will be out-distanced by the painter's infinitely greater power. But if you clothe yourself in other sciences that are outside the realm of poetry and are not yours, such as astronomy, rhetoric, theology, philosophy, geometry, arithmetic, and so forth, then you are no longer a poet. You have changed into something else and no longer enter into the present consideration. Do you not see that in describing nature you do so with the aid of sciences made by others, while the painter proceeds unaided and without drawing on scientific or other aids works of nature.

Thereby lovers are made to turn to the portraits of their beloved, to speak to the painting which represents them. Thereby the peoples are stirred with fervent vows to seek out the images of the gods (but this does not apply to the works of poets who describe the same gods with words); thereby are animals deceived. I once saw a dog, deceived by a portrait of his master, giving him a joyful welcome; and I have observed dogs barking and trying to bite dogs represented in a painting; and I saw a monkey indulging in endless pranks with another monkey represented in a painting. I have seen swallows fly to perch on iron bars painted in imitation of lattices that protrude from the windows of buildings.

MUSIC MAY JUSTLY BE CALLED THE YOUNGER SISTER OF PAINTING

Music cannot be called otherwise than the sister of painting, for she is dependent upon hearing, a sense second to sight, and her harmony is composed of the union of its proportional parts sounded simultaneously, rising and falling in one or more harmonic rhythms. These rhythms may be said to surround the proportionality of the members composing the harmony, just as the contour bounds the members from which human beauty is born.

But painting excels and ranks higher than music, because it does not fade away as soon as it is born, as is the fate of unhappy music. On the contrary, it endures and has all the appearance of being alive, though in fact it is confined to one surface. Oh wonderful science, which can preserve the transient beauty of mortals and endow it with a permanence greater than the works of nature; for these are subject to the continual changes of time which leads them towards inevitable old age! And such a science is in the same relation to divine nature as its works are to the works of nature, and for this it is to be adored.

LEONARDO

NUMBER

15

APRIL 1958

From Gauguin to Leonardo da Vinci, this issue surveyed the latter's notebooks and included drawings of animals by Ruffins and Renaissance equestrians by Glaser.

Proud of our work, sure of our skill. The Weaver Organization produces fine offset printing and color lithography. Printers to the Monthly Graphic.

WEAVER ORGANIZATION, ST 4-9400, 46-13 11 ST., L. I. C.

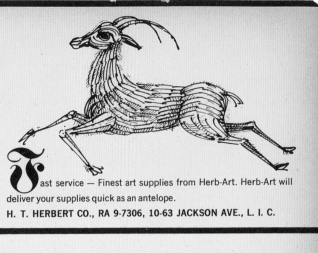

Fast service — Finest art supplies from Herb-Art. Herb-Art will deliver your supplies quick as an antelope.

H. T. HERBERT CO., RA 9-7306, 10-63 JACKSON AVE., L. I. C.

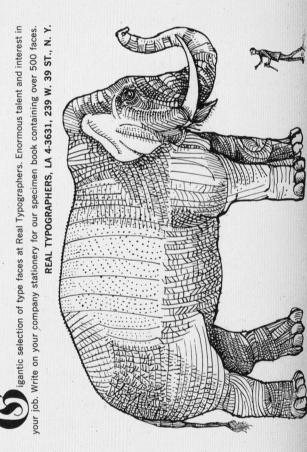

Gigantic selection of type faces at Real Typographers. Enormous talent and interest in your job. Write on your company stationery for our specimen book containing over 500 faces.
REAL TYPOGRAPHERS, LA 4-3631, 239 W. 39 ST., N. Y.

Dependable — You can always depend on the Push Pin Studios to give you creative design and illustration. Rosalie Janpol representing John Alcorn, Seymour Chwast, Milton Glaser, Reynold Ruffins.
THE PUSH PIN STUDIOS., LE 2-9247 — 114 E. 31 ST., N. Y.

Unique Photo-Lettering, Mu. 2-2346

May, 1958   *Published by The Push Pin Studios, 114 East 31 Street, New York 16, LExington 2-9247*   *Subscription: $2.50 yearly*

Ambrose Bierce:

Peace

O, what's the loud uproar assailing
  Mine ears without cease?
'Tis the voice of the hopeful, all-hailing
  The horrors of peace.

Ah, Peace Universal; they woo it—
  Would marry it, too.
If only they knew how to do it
  'Twere easy to do.

They're working by night and by day
  On their problem, like moles.
Have mercy, O Heaven, I pray,
  On their meddlesome souls!

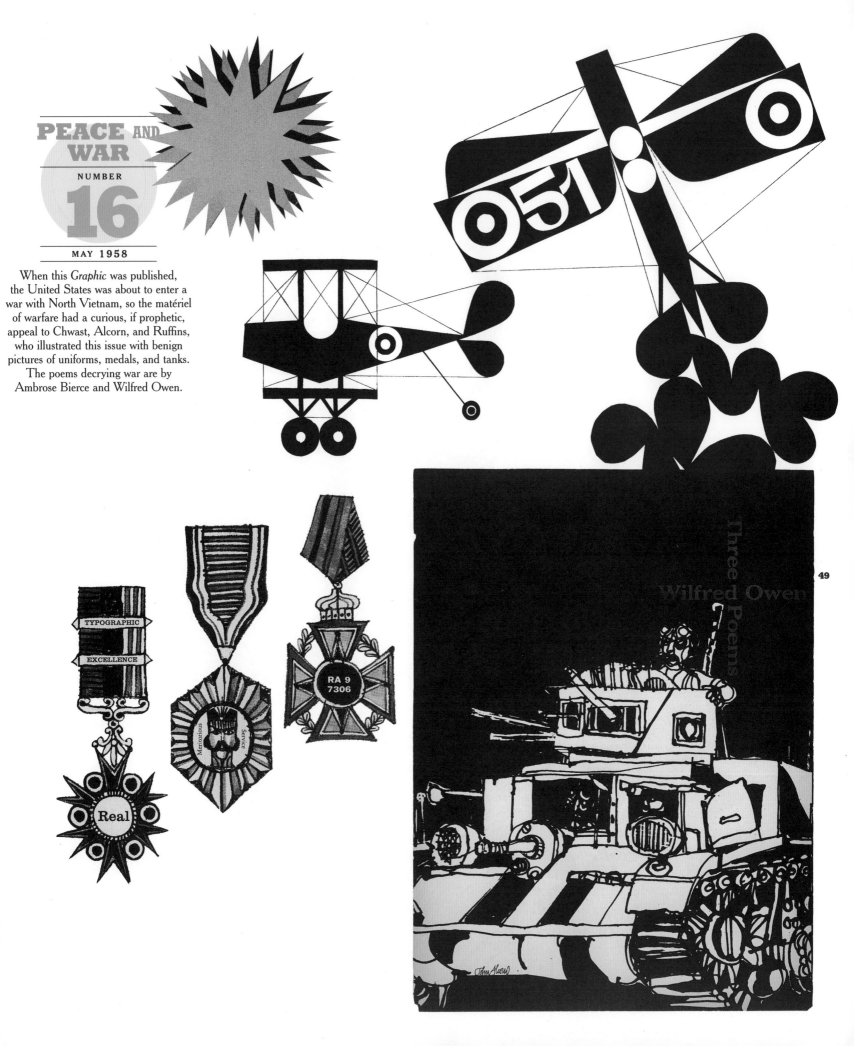

PEACE AND WAR

NUMBER

16

MAY 1958

When this *Graphic* was published, the United States was about to enter a war with North Vietnam, so the matériel of warfare had a curious, if prophetic, appeal to Chwast, Alcorn, and Ruffins, who illustrated this issue with benign pictures of uniforms, medals, and tanks.

The poems decrying war are by Ambrose Bierce and Wilfred Owen.

TYPOGRAPHIC

EXCELLENCE

Real

Meritorious Service

RA 9 7306

Three Poems

Wilfred Owen

49

1ST DRAGOONS

Hurrah for the English "Royals," boys!
*   Still over the trembling ground*
The clanging hoofs of our charger's ring
*   With victory in the sound.*

Our standards stricken with ball and blast
*   May droop over surging heads,*
But only to float aloft at last
*   In laurelled and glorious shreds.*

Ay, the cavaliers, and Ironsides
*   Never came from a stock of loons,*
And their loyalty and faithfulness,
*   Are bent in the first dragoons.*

Hurrah for the English "Royal," boys!
*   In the days of Wellington*
We had plenty of spirit in Portugal
*   And plenty of fight and fun.*
We had plenty to do in Moorish Spain
*   Till we marched it through and through.*
And swept like a wave in the "heavy's" charge
*   Or the field of Waterloo.*

Ay, the Cavaliers, etc.

Hurrah for the English "Royals," boys!
*   And mates of former days,*
Ould Erin "Enniskilliners,"
*   And bonnie Scotland's sheeny "Greys"*
We have shared in many a bivouac,
*   And many a refrain trolled,*
As the sun's gone down on the battlefield,
*   In it's glory of purple and gold.*

Ay, the Cavaliers, etc.

13TH HUSSARS

With a glow of the war-light on each face,
*   As a tough athlete of Mars,*
What Corps is that of the white and blue
*   The old 13th Hussars*
And the stalwart band of the lion-hearts
*   Of the Island Queen are they,*
Who oft at the muster-roll of fame
*   Have dashingly won their way!*

Ay we have beat the foe in Belgium,
*   And we charged him out of Spain,*
And the front of Sevastopol
*   We thrashed o'er again*
The jolly old corps
*   Forever more will conquer again and again.*

With a glistening heat of Hindoostan,
*   With the guerilla's track,*
With the hunger and cold of the Crimea,
*   We have shared the bivouac,*
And the victory clarions oft have sent
*   Their call o'er the battle plain,*
As we've swept the enemy like the swath,
*   Of the mower through the grain.*

Ay we beat the foe, etc.

And oh, when Peace her rainbow lights
*   In the heavens and land and wave,*
When love warms womans dewy lips
*   For the faithful and the brave,*
Then rife and ready with lithesome tread
*   As in happy days of yore,*
To the welcome home of true sweethearts
*   We merrily march once more.*

Ay we beat the foe, etc.

© 1958 by The Push Pin Studios, 114 East 31 Street, New York 16, LExington 2-9247

Subscription: $2.50

A DARING RAILWAY ROBBERY

DES MOINES, Iowa, July 22.—The express train on the Chicago, Rock Island and Pacific Railroad bound east, due here at 10:15 last evening, was thrown from the track about 7 o'clock, attacked and robbed, and the engineer killed. It occurred about four miles west of Adair Summit, between the Mississippi and Missouri Rivers, and some sixty miles west of here. The spot selected was favorable for the deed, there being no habitation within several miles, and none in sight, and withal it was at a sharp curve.

The robbers, who were all but one masked, had removed the plates connecting one rail with those next to it, and putting a rope through the holes in one end, awaited the coming of the train. When the train was within two rods of the place, the rope was pulled, and the rail was thrown across the track. Simultaneously several shots were fired in quick succession. The engineer saw the displaced rail and reversed his engine and applied the air-brakes, which was his last act. Engine, tender, and two baggage-cars were

thrown into and across the ditch, and the forward trucks of the first passenger coach were thrown from the track. At once two of the scoundrels, one unmasked, attacked the express-car, compelled the messenger to give up the keys by holding revolvers at their heads, and took from the safe nearly $1,700 and one sealed bag of Wells, Fargo & Co.'s, amount not known. Pistols were also held at the head of the registry clerk and Mr. Rice, Assistant Superintendent of the road, who was also in the car, and had hardly recovered from the shock of the concussion when the robbers entered.

The engineer, John Rafferty, was found with his neck broken, caused by falling at the time of the crash. He was also wounded by a pistol shot in the thigh. At first it was supposed he was shot dead, but this proves not to have been true. Dennis Faby, the fireman, when the concussion was over, found himself lying on the floor of the cab unhurt, with the dead body of the engineer on top of him. Dragging the body on the track, he started to

alarm the others on the train, but was compelled to turn back by the robbers. Putting out the furnace fire, he let the water out of the boiler, thus avoiding an explosion. No others on the train were injured, but several were fired at. The conductor, Mr. William Smith, had two bullets through his clothing.

While the robbery was going on the passenger-coaches were guarded by the remaining robbers, so that no aid could be afforded from that source. At the first shock the passengers were thrown forward, and after the recoil many started forward to the scene of the wreck, but were driven back by threats, mingled with oaths and occasional shots. The passengers, however, were not otherwise maltreated, the robbers confining themselves entirely to the mail and express car. Fortunately the through registered letter package from San Francisco to New-York was unnoticed by the thieves, while three and a half tons of bullion express matter were undisturbed. As soon as they were satisfied the thieves jumped from the car, mounted and rode away south-

ward, less than ten minutes from the time of the attack.

As soon as word could be got to Chicago the company offered a reward of $5,000 for the discovery of the robbers. To this the Government will add the highest amount allowed by law. The whole southwestern part of the State is aroused, and the line of the Burlington and Missouri River Road is heavily guarded. Special trains with armed men left Council Bluffs last evening in parallel lines to intercept the robbers, and a large scouting party left Atlantic, some fifteen miles south of the disaster. Five miles south of the spot, the trail of five horsemen has been struck, and followed to Nodaway River, some thirty-eight miles southward. A full description of the horses, it is believed, has been obtained, and it is thought the robbers can hardly escape. The general opinion is, that they are a set of Missouri guerrillas, similar to those who robbed a bank at Corydon, in this State, some two or three years ago.

From The New York Times, July 23, 1873.

WESTERN BANDITS AT WORK

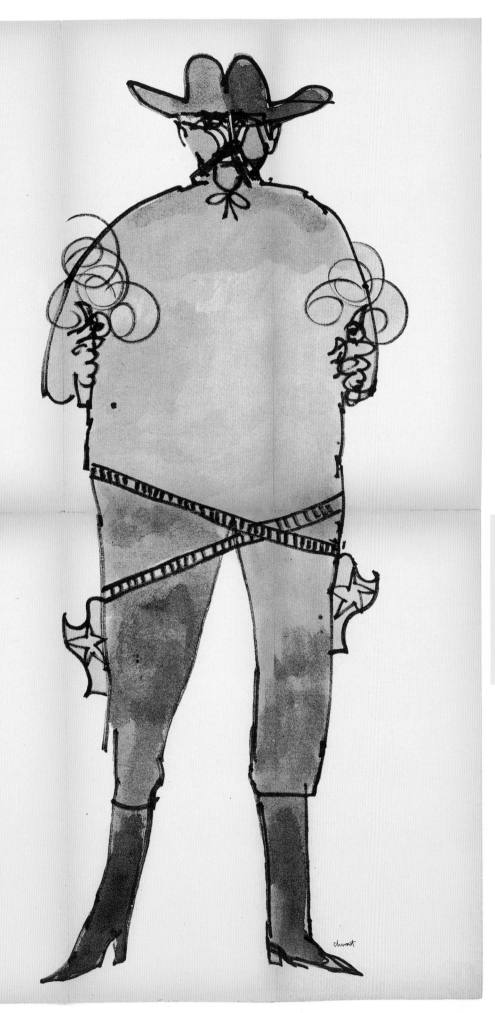

Des Moines, Iowa, July 22.—A thousand conjectures are current here in regard to the persons who robbed the train. The most probable one is that the robbery was committed by persons living near where the robbery took place. A valise, in which they carried off money taken from the Express Company's safe, was found five miles south of the wrecked train to-day. Vigilant parties are scouring South-western Iowa, and it is confidently believed the robbers will be caught if they remain within the State. A telegram received here late to-night says they crossed the Burlington and Missouri Railroad last night at midnight. William A. Smith, conductor of the ill-fated train, testified to-day at the Coroner's inquest, on the body of John Rafferty, the engineer, who was killed, that the train was wrecked two and a half or three miles west of Adair Station, and 600 or 700 feet east of Turkey Creek Bridge. I was in the smoking-car near the front end. From the noise I thought the engine was in a ditch, with one or two cars piled upon it. I was thrown under the seat in front of me; don't remember which side of the car. I got on out on the bulk. I went forward to see who was hurt. The first person I met was one of the masked men near the baggage-car door, who pointed a revolver in each hand toward me and told me to get back, firing at one and the same time. I backed down as far as the sleeping-coach before I felt I was out of his way. There I met Dennis Foley, the fireman. He says, "Billy, Jack is dead." The passengers were in a hubbub, and the women and children were crying. I told the passengers I thought the masked men were trying to rob the baggage-car, and tried to borrow a revolver, but failed. I could still see the man from where I was. Saw another passing up and down on the opposite side of the train. Think he was firing at me also. Some of the passengers asked me to get into the train, as these men were firing at me, and I would be the cause of some of them being killed. I then went into the sleeping-car at the rear, still trying to get a revolver, and urging the passengers to keep quiet, as these men were robbing the baggage-car. I went out of the ladies'-car up to the bank, and thence to the engine. Two balls passed through my clothing while I was on the bank. These shots came from the south side of the train. Did not see a man on the north side then. Did not see or hear anything more of the masked men; after the passengers had got quiet I went forward to investigate the cause of the wreck. At the hind truck of the smoking-car I found the fishplate had been removed from the rail on the north side, disconnecting a rail at both ends. A rope and straps were tied in the bolt-holes of the disconnected rail at the west end, and a rope passed under the south rail across the ditch and upon the bank. A piece of rope was also found on the bank which seemed to have been broken from the other. It was a new rope, the common size. The west end was loose of the rail when I saw it. It was only a few inches from the south rail. The hind trucks of the smoking-car were still on the track. We had been running eighteen or twenty miles an hour.

THE SCENE WAS TERRIBLE

The passengers on the train report that the scene was terrible, and baffles description. When the crash came all were thrown forward, some entirely out of their seats. Then came a recoil, and immediately after this they heard firing, but supposed that it came from the wreck. Many of the men jumped from the cars and started to get forward, and were ordered back by the robbers, who continued their firing, and enforced their commands by terrible oaths and threats. Back they went, and in the cars found women and children, half crazed with fright, shrieking, crying, and fainting, imploring men to protect them, and exclaiming, "My God! we shall be killed! we shall be killed!" The stoutest hearts quailed, and felt they were at the mercy of desperadoes. Altogether it was a scene unprecedented in the history of railroading in this country, as never before has so reckless and daring a scheme been carried to completion. All Western Iowa is in a fever of excitement. Farmers for miles around are leaving the harvest fields with their families and visiting the scene of the robbery.

The engine and baggage-cars remain as they were last night. The former is badly wrecked. Superintendent Royce estimates the loss sustained by the company at about $3,000. Gov. Carpenter issued a proclamation to-day offering a reward of $500 for the arrest of each person engaged in the robbery.

The management of the Chicago, Rock Island and Pacific Railroad have offered a reward of $5,000 for the detection of the parties who attacked and robbed the train on that road near Adair, Iowa, last night.

From The New York Times, July 23, 1873.

EXTRA! EXTRA!

NUMBER 17

1958

Two ripped-from-the-headlines news stories taken from the *New York Times* of July 23, 1873, about crime sprees in the old west, inspired Chwast's double-page gun-toting outlaw. Ruffins and Herbert Leavitt, a junior designer at Push Pin, drew the period-looking trains on the cover and as a separate insert.

The Push Pin Studios now represented by Miss Jane Lander Editorial and Advertising art

The Push Pin Studios
114 E. 31 St. N. Y. 16, N.Y.
Le 2-9247

SPICES

NUMBER

18

1959

This special holiday issue featured recipes from old cookbooks and a spice chart with artwork keyed to descriptions of the various fare. The drawings were by Ruffins and Glaser, and Chwast's woodcut illustrated verse about spice.

When you are leyd in bed so softe
A cage of gold that hange slofte
Wythe longe peper ſtyre burning
And cloues that be ſwete ſmelling,
That when ye ſlepe, the taſte may come,
And yf ye no reſt can take
Till ſyght myraſtreſs for you ſhall wake.

The Squire of Low Degree

Seymour Chwast

The Push Pin Monthly Graphic Spice Chart

HENRY JAMES
AND
ITALY

NUMBER
19

1959

Glaser had done some drawings of the Porta Portense while living in Rome and thought one of them would be suitable in a travel section of the *Graphic*. He had also done a sort of gestural drawing derived from a combination of Japanese wash drawings and Picasso, which is demonstrated in the *Bathers and Umbrellas* illustration.

ROME

I pocketed my scepticism and spent a long afternoon on the Corso. Almost every one was a masker, but you had no need to conform; the pelting rain of confetti effectually disguised you. I can't say I found it all very exhilarating; but here and there I noticed a brighter episode — a capering clown inflamed with contagious jollity, some finer humourist forming a circle every thirty yards to crow at his indefatigable sallies. One clever performer so especially pleased me that I should have been glad to catch a glimpse of the natural man. You imagined for him that he was taking a prodigious intellectual holiday and that his gaiety was in inverse ratio to his daily mood. Dressed as a needy scholar, in an ancient evening-coat and with a rusty black hat and gloves fantastically patched, he carried a little volume carefully under his arm. His humours were in excellent taste, his whole manner the perfection of genteel comedy. The crowd seemed to relish him vastly, and he at once commanded a gleefully attentive audience. Many of his sallies I lost; those I caught were excellent. His trick was often to begin by taking some one urbanely and caressingly by the chin and complimenting him on the *intelligenza della sua fisionomia*. I kept near him as long as I could; for he struck me as a real ironic artist, cherishing a disinterested, and yet at the same time a motived and a moral, passion for the grotesque. I should have liked, however — if indeed I shouldn't have feared — to see him the next morning, or when he unmasked that night over his hard-earned supper in a smoky *trattoria*. As the evening went on the crowd thickened and became a motley press of shouting, pushing, scrambling, everything but squabbling, revellers. The rain of missiles ceased at dusk, but the universal deposit of chalk and flour was trampled into a cloud made lurid by flaring pyramids of the gas-lamps that replaced for the occasion the stingy Roman luminaries. Early in the evening came off the classic exhibition of the *moccoletti*, which I but half saw, like a languid reporter resigned beforehand to be cashiered for want of enterprise. From the mouth of a side-street, over a thousand heads, I caught a huge slow-moving illuminated car, from which blue-lights and rockets and Roman candles were in course of discharge, meeting all in a dim fuliginous glare far above the house-tops. It was like a glimpse of some public orgy in ancient Babylon. In the small hours of the morning, walking homeward from a private entertainment, I found Ash Wednesday still kept at bay. The Corso, flaring with light, smelt like a circus. Every one was taking friendly liberties with every one else and using up the dregs of his festive energy in convulsive hootings and gymnastics. Here and there certain indefatigable spirits, clad all in red after the manner of devils and leaping furiously about with torches, were supposed to affright you. But they shared the universal geniality and bequeathed me no midnight fears as a pretext for keeping Lent, the *carnevale dei preti*, as I read in that profanely radical sheet the *Capitale*. Of this too I have been having glimpses. Going lately into Santa Francesca Romana, the picturesque church near the Temple of Peace, I found a feast for the eyes — a dim crimson-toned light through curtained windows, a great festoon of tapers round the altar, a girdle of lamps before the sunken shrine beneath, and a dozen white-robed Dominicans scattered in the happiest composition on the pavement. It was better than the *moccoletti*.

CAPRI

Beautiful, horrible, haunted: that is the essence of what, about itself, Capri says to you — dip again into your Tacitus and see why.

57

Everyone involved in Push Pin was fascinated with odd letterforms and spent a lot of time digging through old type specimen manuals. This is one example of their discoveries. The illustrations by Ruffins, Glaser, and Chwast fit into boxes with rounded corners. Chwast notes that this "started a trend for such corners among designers at the time."

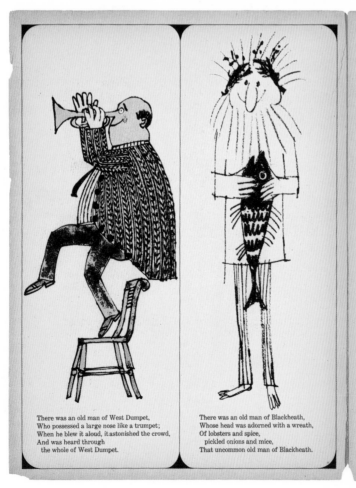

There was an old man of West Dumpet,
Who possessed a large nose like a trumpet;
When he blew it aloud, it astonished the crowd,
And was heard through
the whole of West Dumpet.

There was an old man of Blackheath,
Whose head was adorned with a wreath,
Of lobsters and spice,
pickled onions and mice,
That uncommon old man of Blackheath.

There was an Old Person of Cheadle,
Was put in the stocks by the beadle;
For stealing some pigs,
some coats and some wigs,
That horrible person of Cheadle.

There was an Old Lady whose folly,
Induce her to sit in a holly;
Whereon by a thorn,
her dress being torn,
She quickly became melancholy.

There was an Old Man with a beard,
Who said, 'It is just as I feared!'—
Two Owls and a Hen,
four Larks and a Wren,
Have all built their nests in my beard!'

There was an old man of Boulak,
Who sate on a Crocodile's back;
But they said, 'Tow'rds the night,
he may probably bite,
Which might vex you, old man of Boulak!'

There was an Old Man of the Hague,
Whose ideas were excessively vague;
He built a balloon,
to examine the moon,
That deluded Old Man of the Hague.

There was a young person of Janina,
Whose uncle was always a fanning her;
When he fanned off her head,
she smiled sweetly, and said,
'You propitious old person of Janina!'

There was an old person of Ware,
Who rode on the back of a bear:
When they ask'd,—'Does it trot?'
he said 'Certainly not!
He's a Moppsikon Floppsikon bear!'

There was a Young Lady whose bonnet,
Came untied when the birds sate upon it;
But she said, 'I don't care!
all the birds in the air
Are welcome to sit on my bonnet!'

There was an old man in a garden,
Who always begged every-one's pardon;
When they asked him, 'What for?'
He replied 'You're a bore!
And I trust you'll go out of my garden.'

There was an old person of Wilts,
Who constantly walked upon stilts;
He wreathed them with lilies,
and daffy-down-dillies,
That elegant person of Wilts.

THE PUSH PIN **Monthly Graphic.** NO. TWENTY ONE

60

This issue is an example of Push Pin's political interests, with quotes from *Consumer Reports*, Linus Pauling, Albert Schweitzer, and the *London Times* about the dangers of nuclear catastrophe. Glaser's stark drawing of a pregnant woman derives from the same formal influences that inspired his illustration in issue number 19. Chwast's strolling children were done in pen and ink to gain more control in the details than with woodcut. Ruffins drew this eerily reclining child.

61

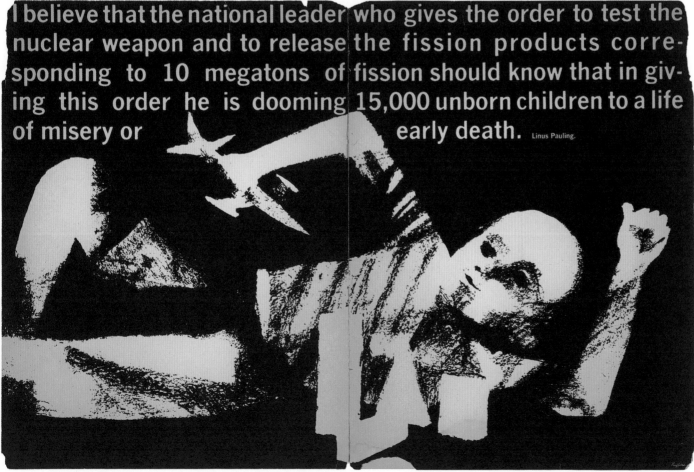

I believe that the national leader who gives the order to test the nuclear weapon and to release the fission products corresponding to 10 megatons of fission should know that in giving this order he is dooming 15,000 unborn children to a life of misery or early death. Linus Pauling.

Glaser moved through stylistic and technical experiments with hurricane speed. Below he drew in ink on thin newsprint and then used the mirror image on the opposite side of the paper for reproduction, while Chwast's bird (right) was rendered in highly diluted oil paint, which gave it a blotchy texture.

In any approach towards the creation of a World Authority, certain disruptive forces raise difficulties which at times seem almost insuperable. The opposition between Communism and Capitalism is the most notable obstacle to world unity at the present day; but there is another, namely nationalism, which would remain if Communism and Capitalism had learnt to tolerate each other. Nationalism in each nation consists partly of beliefs as to one's own nation's excellence, and partly of ethical maxims supposed to follow from these beliefs.

I shall be speaking mainly of the bad aspects of nationalism, but I wish to say emphatically that it has also its good aspects. It would not be a good thing if people all over the world were alike. Culturally, the differences between different nations give a desirable variety and are a stimulus in literature and art. It is only when nationalism leads to armed strife that it becomes a danger. It is wholly a good thing when a nation has indepedence in everything except violent hostility to other nations. If an International Authority is ever created, it will have to limit its interferences with national States to matters likely to disturb international peace. If it does more than this, it becomes tyranny.

But, having said this, we must now turn our attention to the dangerous aspects of nationalism. Unlike Capitalism and Communism, nationalism is not a single, world-wide system, but is a different system in each nation. It consists essentially in collective self-glorification and in a conviction that it is right to pursue the intrests of one's own nation however they may conflict with those of others. In the eighteenth century, the British proclaimed the slogan, 'Britons never shall be slaves, and proceeded to make slaves of as many non-Britons as they could. The French, shortly afterwards, proclaimed, 'Let impure blood water our furrows' —the impure blood being that of Austrians. I recently received a letter from a German explaining that 'Deutschland uber alles' does not mean that Germany shall rule the world, but that a German should think only of German interests. One could multiply examples indefinitely, but the phenomenon is too familiar to need further illustration.

It is rather odd that emphasis upon the merits of one's own nation should be considered a virtue. What should we think of an individual who proclaimed: 'I am morally and intellectually superior to all other individuals, and, because of this superiority, I have the right to ignore all interests except my own'? There are, no doubt, plenty of people who feel this way, but if they proclaim their feeling too openly, and act upon it too blatantly, they are thought ill of. When, however, a number of such individuals, constituting the population of some area, collectively make such a declaration about themselves, they are thought noble and splendid and spirited. They put up statues to each other and teach schoolchildren to admire the most blatant advocates of the national conceit.

Loose Dentures
Logy
Hot Flashes
Unsightly Fat
Brittle Splitting Nails
Internal Bad Breath
Gas
Heartburn
Nagging Backache
Tired Blood

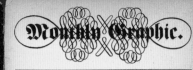

Monthly Graphic.

Number 23   Subscription: $2.50 for 12 issues, Canada and Foreign; $3.50

*The
Push Pin Guide
for the
discerning*

Hypochondriac

*comprising
Smelter's Shakes
The Frenzy
Spontaneous Combustion
Bed Case
Ainhum
Cachexy
Tarantism
Raynaud's Disease
Mania
Risus Sardonicus
Obesity
Falling of the Hair
Scrivener's Palsy
Ephimera
Measles
Tara
Hypochondriasis*

*©1959
The Push Pin Studios
114 East 31 Street, N.Y.
LE 2-9247*

64

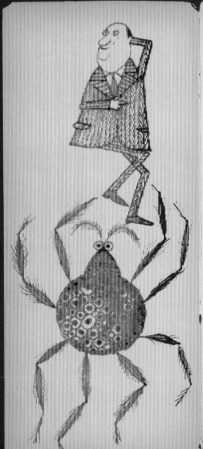

Tarantism

A variety of dancing mania, popularly believed to be caused by the bite of a tarantula and to be cured by dancing.

Raynaud's Disease

Description: A vascular change, seen chiefly in the extremities, in which a persistent ischaemia or a passive hyperaemia leads to disturbance of function or to loss of vitality with necrosis. Women are more frequently attacked than men. Neurotic and hysterical patients are more prone to the disease. Several members of a family may be affected, ranging in age from six months to 77 years. Damp and cold weather appears to favor its occurrence.

Symptoms: In mild cases, the hands alone may be affected. With this condition, known as "beefsteak hand," one finger may be white and the adjacent ones red and blue. Severe cases attack fingers and toes at once, and with them sometimes the tip of the nose and the ears. The skin is a deep purple and the toes black. However, severe attacks of this sort last only 3 months, and the patient may recover with merely a snip off the ears, and a scar on the tip of the nose.

Mania

Causes: A great quantity of incorrupt blood flowing to the brain.

Symptoms: Similar to the frenzy, except that the frenzy comes with a fever, and this without.

Bed Case

Description: A not uncommon form of hysteria.

Symptoms: Subjects of it live in bed; they are tranquil, cheerful, have good digestions and like the kind attentions of sympathizing friends. Often impressed with the belief that there is serious disease in spine or innards: there are certain movements which they think cannot be made without "horrible" pain.

Ainhum

Description: A disease of the fifth toe, found mainly in warm climates. It may occur in families, and is more common in males. There is endarteritis, with proliferation of the epidermis.

Symptoms: It is a local disease, without warning symptoms. A groove forms and the toe drops off. This process usually takes about two years. There is rarely any pain.

Cachexy

Description: Signifies a bad habit or constitution of body, proceeding from unsound viscera or distempered juices occasioned usually by the eating of gross, glutinous or viscous food.

Symptoms: Persons grow weary without having exercised; hate to stir about; have a coldness of their limbs; an inclination to sleep; they become stupid,

MEDICAL ADVICE

NUMBER

23

1959

This satiric guide, designed and illustrated by Glaser, Ruffins, and Chwast in a narrow format resembling the earlier *Push Pin Almanack*, is the epitome of Push Pin's typographic commingling of Black Letter (Fraktur) and Roman typefaces.

Smelters' Shakes

Description: An affliction resulting from exposure to brass dust or fumes.

Symptoms: Hair stained somewhat green; slight greenish deposit in the teeth and gums; green tint to perspiration. Acute chills, sweating, feeling of nausea followed by: vomiting; great thirst; a rapid, feeble pulse; a rise of temperature. Many patients are most liable to it on Mondays.

The Frenzy

Causes: Comes from a great abundance of blood or choler filling up the brain.

Symptoms: They who have the frenzy are troubled with a continual fever and madness with great wakefulness and little sleep, and when they wake, they roar and cry and cannot tell what they say or do. If it comes from blood, they laugh; if from choler, they fight and brawl and cannot be controlled without cords or chains.

Spontaneous Combustion

An affection in which persons, more especially individuals in the habit of indulging in the use of spiritous liquors, who take fire and are consumed.

Occurs mainly in aged persons upwards of sixty years old; more frequently in women than in men; and chiefly when of indolent habits, a debilitated frame and intemperate in their mode of living.

(One case described is that of a woman found two feet from her chimney. There was no appearance of fire in the room, but all that remained was skull, bones of the lower extremities and some vertebrae.)

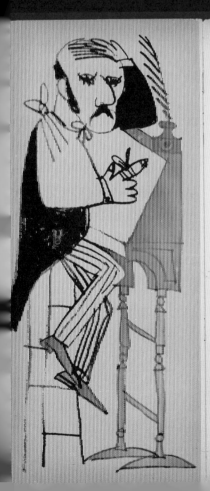

Scrivener's Palsy

Description: A condition, more frequent in men, found most usually in writers and piano or violin players, but also among such persons as milkmaids, weavers and cigarette-rollers. Persons of nervous temperament are more liable to the disease. The most common form of the disease, known as "writer's cramp," is most reasonably explained as resulting from a deranged action of the nerve centres presiding over the muscular movements involved in the act of writing, a condition which has been termed irritable weakness.

Symptoms: These may described as a cramp or spasm — a combined movement of flexion and adduction of the thumb so that the pen may be twisted from the grasp and thrown some distance, or a lock-spasm in which the fingers become so firmly contracted upon the pen that it cannot be removed

Ephimera

Description: An ague which endures but one day. The vital spirits are in a terrible unnatural heat, without putrefaction, as a result of much sadness, anger, hunger or drunkenness.

Symptoms: Great heat in the body and a fever ending in a sweat or vapor.

Measles

Causes: Nature purging all the corruption from the inward parts of the body.

Symptoms: The signs be evident to the sight.

Tara

A kind of jumping disease, prevailing in Siberia.

Hypochondriasis

Description: An affection originating in the melancholy imagination. Does not arise in youth, but about or after the thirty-fifth year and generally increases with age.

Symptoms: Languor, sadness, a great fear of death, peevishness, all kinds of groundless apprehensions from trifling causes.

§§§§§

Sources

"American Illustrated Medical Dictionary, The"; 19th ed.; Philadelphia; W. B. Saunders Company; 1941. Reprinted with the kind permission of the publisher. (*Tarantism, Tara*)

"Principles and Practice of Medicine, The"; Sir William Osler, M.D.; and Thomas McRae, M.D.; 9th ed.; New York; D. Appleton & Company; 1922. Reprinted with the kind permission of Appleton-Century-Crofts, Inc. (*Smelters' Shakes, Ainhum, Raynaud's Disease, Scrivener's Palsy*)

"Compendium on the Practice of Physic"; E. G. Clarke, M.D.; Philadelphia; 1818. (*Hypochondriasis*)

"Curiosities of Medical Experience"; J. G. Miller, M.D.; Philadelphia; Haswell, Barrington and Haswell; 1858. (*Spontaneous Combustion*)

"Family Magazine, The"; Part II; London; 1741 (*Cachexy*)

"Index of Diseases and Their Treatment, An"; Thomas Hayes Tanner, M.D.; 2nd ed. revised by W. H. Broadbent, M.D.; London; Henry Renshaw; 1876. (*Bed Case, Obesity*)

"Modern Practice of Physic, The"; Robert Thomas, M.D.; London; Longman, Hurst, Rees, Orme & Brown; 1816. (*Risus Sardonicus*)

"Treasury of Healthe, The"; Pope John XXI; 13th c. (*The Frenzy, Mania, Falling of the Hair, Ephimera, Measles*)

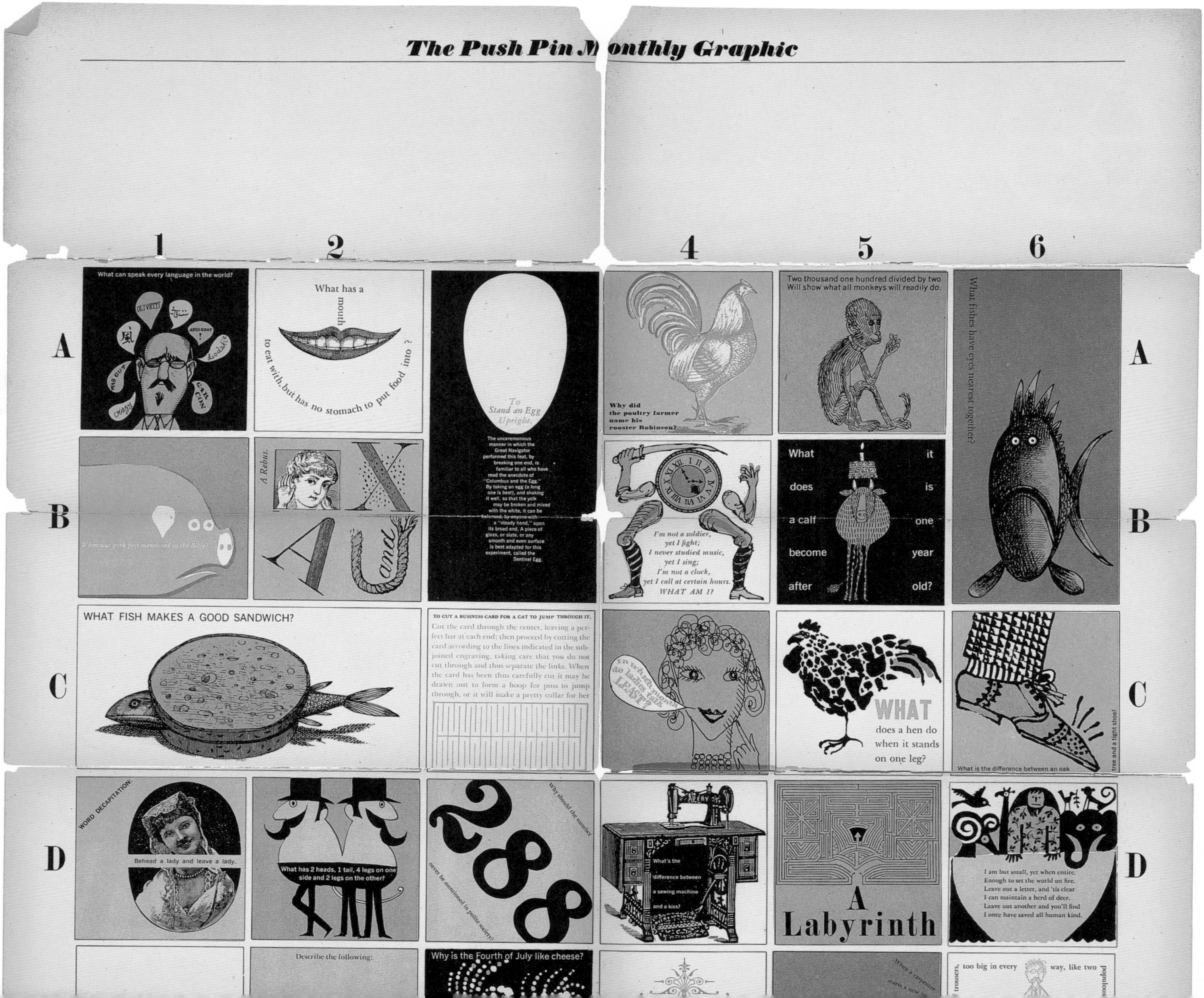

The Push Pin Monthly Graphic

A6. What fishes have eyes nearest together?

C6. tree and a tight shoe!

What is the difference between an oak

D6. I am but small, yet when entire,
Enough to set the world on fire.
Leave out a letter, and 'tis clear
I can maintain a herd of deer.
Leave out another and you'll find
I once have saved all human kind.

populous

way, like two

trousers,

too big in every

A5. Two thousand one hundred divided by two
Will show what all monkeys will readily do.

B5. What does a calf become after it is one year old?

C5. WHAT does a hen do when it stands on one leg?

D5. A Labyrinth

When a carpenter

saves a nail

A4. Why did the poultry farmer name his rooster Robinson?

B4. I'm not a soldier, yet I fight;
I never studied music, yet I sing;
I'm not a clock, yet I call at certain hours.
WHAT AM I?

C4. In which sense do ladies count LEAST?

What's the difference between a sewing machine and a kiss?

D4.

A2. To Stand an Egg Upright.

The uncommon manner in which the Great Navigator performed this feat, is familiar to all who have read the anecdote of Columbus and the Egg. By taking an egg by the large end, and shaking it so that you break the yolk, it may be broken and mixed with the white, it can be "stood on end," upon its broad end. A piece of grain, or table, or any smooth surface is best adapted for this experiment, called the Sentinel Egg.

B2. TO CUT A BUSINESS CARD FOR A CAT TO JUMP THROUGH IT.

Cut the card through the center, leaving a perfect bar at each end; then proceed by cutting the card according to the lines indicated in the subjoined engraving, taking care that you do not cut through and thus separate the links. When the card has been thus carefully cut it may be drawn out to form a hoop for puss to jump through, or it will make a pretty collar for her

C2. Why should the number 288 never be mentioned in polite society?

D2. Why is the Fourth of July like cheese?

Describe the following:

A1. What can speak every language in the world?

GAR CON

If the cap with fits, wear it put on it in the Bible.

B1. A Rebus.

C1. WHAT FISH MAKES A GOOD SANDWICH?

D1. What has 2 heads, 1 tail, 4 legs on one side and 2 legs on the other?

WORD DECAPITATION.

Behead a lady and leave a lady

A2 (center). What has a mouth to eat with, but has no stomach to put food into?

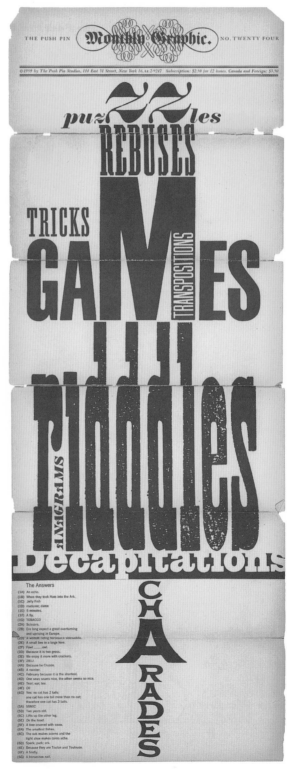

This cover represents the way Push Pin used passé typography early on. Glaser notes that although they were not the only people doing this, they were among the earliest practitioners. Morgan Press, a type house specializing in Victorian wood type, was an invaluable resource. Chwast notes that with this issue Push Pin received many jobs to create work using old engravings in a boxed grid.

Chwast had been making papier-mâché sculpture in his spare time, but he decided to use one in this issue in addition to his woodcut technique for seriously comic portraits of famous people. The quotations included Queen Elizabeth on her epitaph, Ernest Hemingway on morality, Herbert Hoover on politics, and Napoleon's saying "The best constitution is short and obscure."

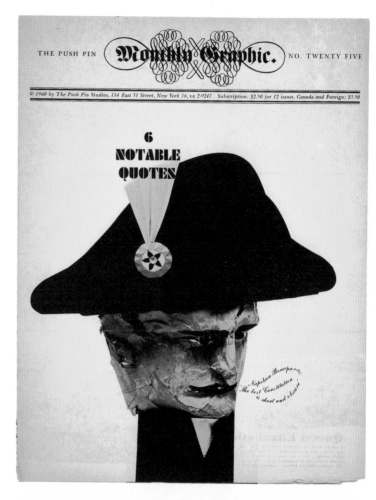

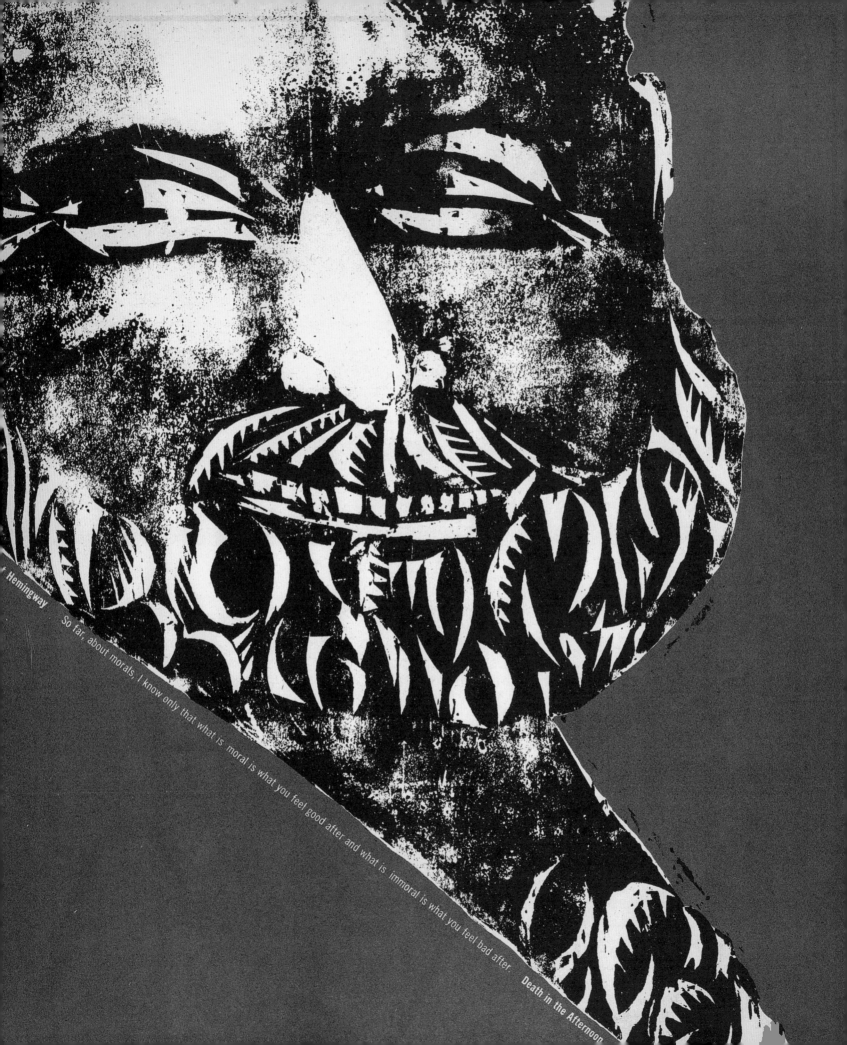

Hemingway   So far, about morals, I know only that what is moral is what you feel good after and what is immoral is what you feel bad after   Death in the Afternoon

Another hot news story from the *New York Times* suggested the use of space-age artwork by children. The advertisement page employed a mechanical-style "art of space aliens" to give an enhanced futuristic aura.

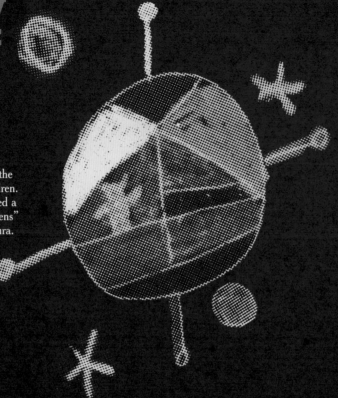

THE PUSH PIN  Monthly Graphic. NO. TWENTY SIX

© 1960 by The Push Pin Studios, 114 East 31 Street, New York 16, ca 2-9747   Subscription: $2.50 for 12 issues. Canada and Foreign: $3.50

RUSSIANS SUGGEST 1908 BLAST IN SIBERIA MAY HAVE BEEN NUCLEAR

HIGH RADIOACTIVITY CITED IN STUDY OF MYSTERIOUS EXPLOSION IN SIBERIA

By Walter Sullivan

Soviet scientists, whose achievements have often won the respect of their Western colleagues, have recently come up with some ideas that have set their fellow scientists agog.

Among these Soviet suggestions are the following:

¶A gigantic nuclear explosion of extraterrestrial origin may have taken place over Siberia on June 30, 1908.

¶The two small moons of Mars may be artificial satellites, placed in orbit by a civilization that thrived on that planet before it lost most of its atmosphere.

¶A force exists in the cosmos, hitherto unperceived, that controls time and causes spinning bodies, such as the planets Earth, Saturn and Jupiter, to be heart-shaped.

According to an account in the Aug. 28 issue of Sovietskaya Rossiya, a nuclear explosion was first proposed in 1950 as an explanation for the "Tungus Wonder" of 1908.

An expedition of the Soviet Academy of Sciences visited the site last year. In August of this year a dozen scientists and senior students from universities and institutes at Tomsk made a second study.

From The New York Times, Oct. 3, 1960 and reprinted with their kind permission.

They found that the radioactivity of plants at the center of the explosion site was from 50 to 100 per cent higher than

Frances Gaston 9 years old

Push Pin Monthly Graphic

on the edge of the area of destruction, at a distance of twenty to twenty-five miles in all directions. There was a sharp drop in radioactivity some six miles from the center point.

Some of the rock and earth samples also showed abnormally high radioactivity. The Tungus explosion has long been a subject of speculation.

According to earlier accounts a few inhabitants of this sub-Arctic region saw a huge fire-ball fall from the sky. The explosion that followed leveled 700 to 800 sq. mi. of forest.

As described by H. H. Nininger in his book, "Out of the Sky," a great "fountain-like" cloud soared into the stratosphere. Barographs as far away as London recorded the pressure wave.

What puzzled scientists who reached the site later was the absence of a great hole in the ground or any fragments typical of meteorites. There were many small craters within

Evelyn Roon 8 years old

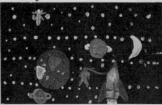
Helen Pietovetsky 9 years old

3,000 feet of the center and tiny globules of nickel-iron imbedded in bed rock fused by the explosion.

It was suggested that a swarm of small meteorites had exploded and vaporized on impact. But it was estimated that they would have had to weigh a total of 40,000 tons to produce the observed effects.

Felix Lopez 10 years old

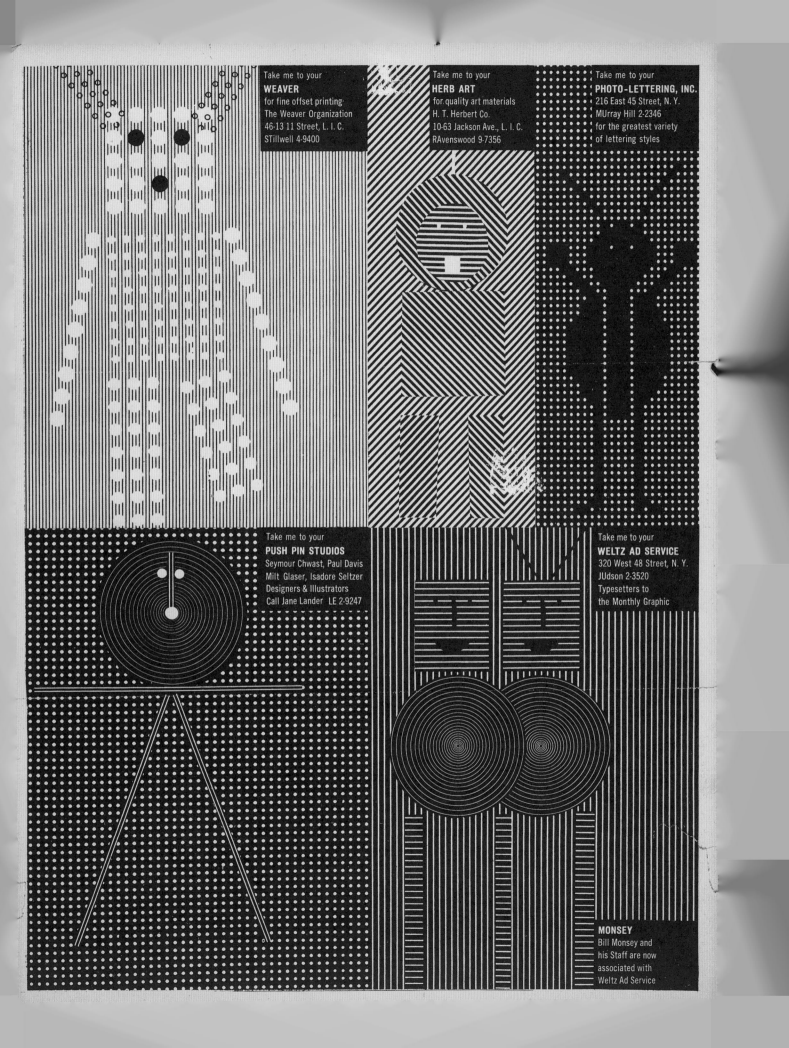

ENGLISH ROYALTY: HOW THEY DIED

NUMBER
27

1960

King William I died of rupture and fever in 1087; Henry I died of disease in 1135; Henry II died of grief in 1189; Richard I was killed by an arrow in 1199. Paul Davis and Isadore Seltzer illustrated these and other royal fatalities.

Richard III: Killed in Battle in 1485

Henry VIII: Died of Ulcerated Leg 1547

Edward VI: Died of Consumption in 1553

Edward III: Died of Grief at the Death of His Son in 1377

Richard II: Died of Consumption in 1399	
Henry IV: Died of Apoplexy in 1413	
Henry V: Died of Pleurisy in 1422	
Edward IV: Died of Ague in 1483	
Edward V: Smothered in 1483	
Henry VII: Died of Consumption in 1509	
Mary: Died of Smallpox in 1558	
Henry VI: Murdered in 1461	

THE CIRCUS

NUMBER

28

1960

Here are more of Glaser's gestural drawings that he suggests may be the best example of the genre he produced at that time. He transformed the black-and-white drawing into what was known as a split-fountain chromatic color or rainbow effect with the help of Push Pin's willing printer.

inhabitant of the United States of America to visit the circus at least twice a year, with the stipulation that each visitor must spend (willy-nilly) not less than half an hour in the menagerie, I believe that, throughout the entire country, four out of five hospitals, jails and insane-asylums would close down. It is my hunch that, as an immediate result of this simple legislation, hundreds of cripples—lame, halt and blind—would toss their infirmities to the winds, thousands of ill-starred homes would break into paeans of rejoicing—and millions of psychoanalysts would be thrown out of employment.

For the benefit of any disciple of Freud

hance to peruse the above
hereby whisper that my own
elephant. And what, genle
Vanity Fair, may your to-
case you aren't sure, or think
any, I counsel you to take the
ain for whatever city the cir-
ppen to occupy (unless you

are so fortunate as to have it with you at
the moment). Above all, don't be satisfied with a trip to some mere zoo; for zoos
—poor, placid, colourless things that they
are—completely lack that outrageous intensity which makes the circus menagerie
unique as a curative institution and en-
dows the denizens of that institution with

a fourth or fifth-dimensional significance
for the neuroses.

By this time, surely, my worthy readers have doubtless decided that I myself
am a salaried member of that branch of
the circus which comprises "the strange
people". Although this is an error—although I am neither a Missing Link nor

a Fat Lady nor yet an Ambassador from
Mars—I may mention that I feel highly
complimented at being mistaken for one
or all of these prodigies. For (in my opinion) happy is that writer, who, in the
course of his lifetime, succeeds in making
a dozen persons react to his personality as
genuinely or vividly as millions react,

75

76

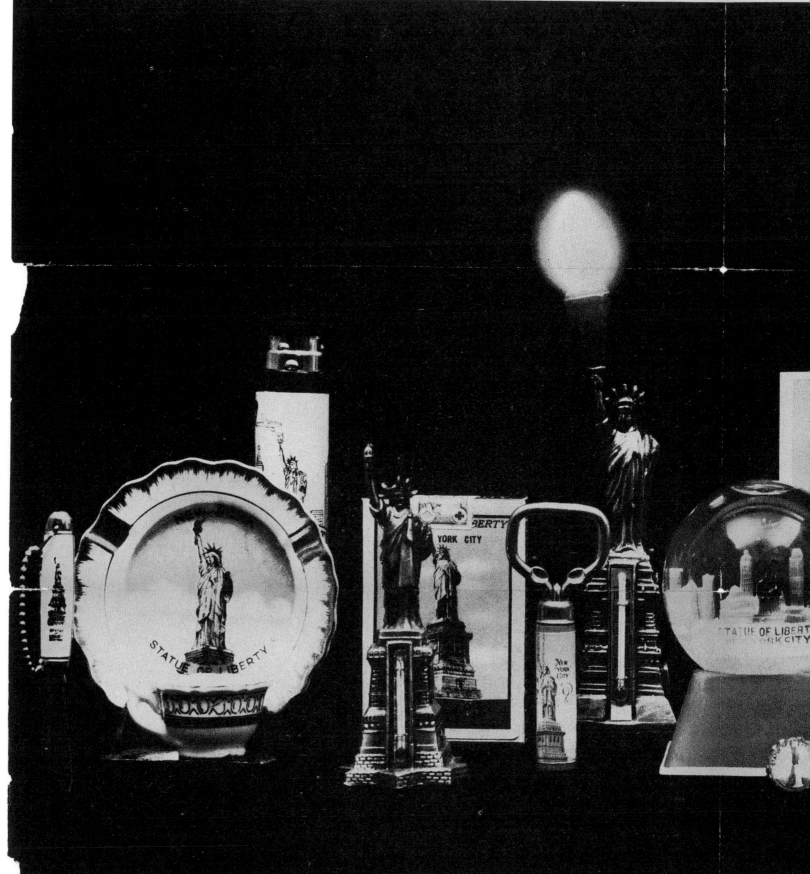

Political malfeasance was not an
issue that every design studio addressed
back then, but it was a burning one
for Push Pin, especially during the
1960 election. This front page was
an early 1900s text supporting
"honest graft," by George
Washington Plunkitt.
At that time,
Chwast and Glaser saw
little difference between
Nixon and Kennedy
and so produced a button
that was a composite of
both candidates.

WIN WITH JICK.

THE PUSH PIN Monthly Graphic. NUMBER 29

HONEST GRAFT

A
CALENDAR
1961
NUMBER
30
1960

This Christmas issue was actually a calendar for the following year featuring drawings by the Push Pin members. The decorative background pattern shown here was taken from the wrap-around cover.

78

January		February		March	
1	Sunday	1	Wednesday	1	Wednesday
2	Monday	2	Thursday	2	Thursday
3	Tuesday	3	Friday	3	Friday
4	Wednesday	4	Saturday	4	Saturday
5	Thursday	5	Sunday	5	Sunday
6	Friday	6	Monday	6	Monday
7	Saturday	7	Tuesday	7	Tuesday
8	Sunday	8	Wednesday	8	Wednesday
9	Monday	9	Thursday	9	Thursday
10	Tuesday	10	Friday	10	Friday
11	Wednesday	11	Saturday	11	Saturday
12	Thursday	12	Sunday	12	Sunday
13	Friday	13	Monday	13	Monday
14	Saturday	14	Tuesday	14	Tuesday
15	Sunday	15	Wednesday	15	Wednesday
16	Monday	16	Thursday	16	Thursday
17	Tuesday	17	Friday	17	Friday
18	Wednesday	18	Saturday	18	Saturday
19	Thursday	19	Sunday	19	Sunday
20	Friday	20	Monday	20	Monday
21	Saturday	21	Tuesday	21	Tuesday
22	Sunday	22	Wednesday	22	Wednesday
23	Monday	23	Thursday	23	Thursday
24	Tuesday	24	Friday	24	Friday
25	Wednesday	25	Saturday	25	Saturday
26	Thursday	26	Sunday	26	Sunday
27	Friday	27	Monday	27	Monday
28	Saturday	28	Tuesday	28	Tuesday
29	Sunday			29	Wednesday
30	Monday			30	Thursday
31	Tuesday			31	Friday

Chwast enjoyed visually interpreting nursery rhymes. This issue was devoted to some well-known ones culled from the Oxford collection and illustrated in black-and-white woodcut to give it, as Chwast notes, a "graphic, not childlike, edge."

80

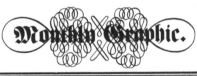

NUMBER 31/THE PUSH PIN *Monthly Graphic.* ELEVEN NURSERY RHYMES

A man in the wilderness asked me,
How many strawberries grow in the sea?
I answered him, as I thought good,
As many as red herrings grow in the wood.

Oh, mother,
I shall be married to
Mr. Punchinello,
To Mr. Punch,
To Mr. Joe,
To Mr. Nell,
To Mr. Lo,
Mr. Punch, Mr. Joe,
Mr. Nell, Mr. Lo,
To Mr. Punchinello.

There was a king, and he had three daughters,
And they all lived in a basin of water;
The basin bended, my story's ended.
If the basin had been stronger,
My story would have been longer.

Oh, the brave old Duke of York,   He had ten thousand men;   He marched them up to the top of the hill,   And he marched them down again.   And when they were up, they were up,   And when they were down, they were down,   And when they were only half way up,   They were neither up nor down.

S Chwast

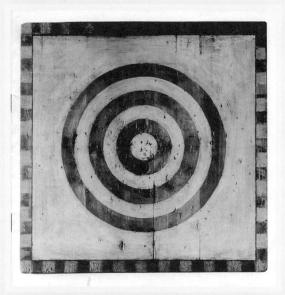

THE PUSH PIN

Monthly Graphic.

NUMBER 32

© 1961 by The Push Pin Studios

114 East 31 Street, New York 16, LE 2-9247

Subscription: $2.50 for 12 issues.

Canada and Foreign: $3.50

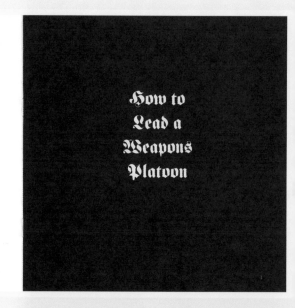

How to Lead a Weapons Platoon

82

POINT ONE. Our first point is to select targets and possible targets for each section. The company has been given a mission in the battalion attack order. The weapons platoon mission is to support the company by fire. The company will attack by fire and maneuver—the rifle platoons will maneuver, the weapons platoon will fire.

Where should this fire be placed to do the company the most good and the enemy the most harm? If it were possible to see all of the enemy positions, the job of keeping him in his hole would be comparatively simple. Normally, however, the enemy can't be seen. You know he's out there; what you have to do is to figure out where he is most likely to be. If you were in his place, where would you put your automatic weapons, your riflemen? After answering these questions to the best of his ability, the platoon leader should try to pick up any odd or suspicious terrain features. There is not enough ammunition to span an objective from flank to flank, so the fire must be concentrated on points where the enemy is likely to be.

POINT TWO. Terrain to the front should be examined for anything that might mask observation for the mortar. Observation is the keynote of attachment or non-attachment of the mortars. If it is possible to gain observation over the entire company or zone of action, then the weapons platoon leader should recommend that mortars be fired as a section from one central OP. If the zone of one of the leading platoons is masked, and the terrain looks as if observation could be obtained from the route the platoon will take, then a mortar squad should be attached to that platoon. The weapons platoon leader must make a decision in this case. It is necessary for this reason that he know something of the company commander's plan of attack.

Davis developed his influential illustrative style based on primitive German wooden targets. By distressing the wood, he made these look as though they were, in fact, used as real targets. Davis's version of the Boston Massacre also humorously included the likenesses of Chwast, Glaser, Seltzer, and Myrna Mushkin (Davis's future wife).

POINT THREE. *The 57-mm recoilless guns may be fired as a section or attached to the rifle platoons. It is most likely that they will be attached to the rifle platoons where they can assist them against machine gun nests, pillboxes, light armored vehicles, etc. (On numerous known occasions, well-directed close-in shots by this weapon have accounted for even heavy armored vehicles.) If observation is good, however, these guns may be massed, in order to place a large volume of fire quickly on the targets. One thing is certain though; they cannot remain in one location long because of back-blast. For the same reason, they should not be placed near the machine guns or the mortars because they will invite unnecessary enemy fire on all weapons in the vicinity.*

When selecting positions for these guns, the weapons platoon leader must consider enemy action. The enemy won't stand by idly; he will start tossing things in the

platoon's direction. The usual means of control within the sections will be by voice or by hand and arm signals. Therefore, the weapons will have to be spaced so that one mortar or artillery shell will not knock out the entire section. Try to keep the weapons about fifty yards apart, depending on the type of terrain.

Consider the three types of positions to be selected for the weapons—primary, alternate and supplementary. A primary position is the best available position from which a gun can most effectively fire its primary mission. An alternate position is a position, also covering the primary mission, to which a gun may move when the primary position becomes untenable. Alternate positions must always be selected when a gun is put into a firing position. A supplementary position is one from which the gun can fire a secondary mission, and should have the same characteristics as a primary position. Alternate positions should also be selected for these supplementary positions.

83

POINT FOUR. *The reconnaissance must also deal with the selection of off-carrier positions for the weapons carriers. Positions for the carriers must be selected to provide protection from the flat trajectory fire and concealment from the air.*

These points are followed by the weapons platoon leader in making recommendations to the company commander for the employment of his platoon in the attack. The company commander will not always accept his recommendations. However, they will normally be accepted as given, if practicable.

From THE ARMY OFFICER'S GUIDE by Col. Paul D. Harkins, U.S. Army, and Philip Harkins. Copyright 1951, by McGraw-Hill Book Company, Inc.

Push Pin Studios
Design and illustration
114 E. 31 St., N.Y., LExington 2-9247
Miss Jane Lander represents Seymour Chwast,
Paul Davis, Milton Glaser, Isadore Seltzer

84

THE COUNT AND THE CUCUMBERS. The Count had not ridden very far when something fragile and white a-flutter in the nearby vegetable garden caused him to check his horse. He studied the garden intently. It made a charming picture, with its rows of pleasant fruit trees and its brilliant vegetable beds. Here a bald-headed cabbage seemed to be meditating the way an old man does on grave matters like Life and Death and Destiny. Yonder a slender yellow bean, its pods entwined with the green tresses of the carrots, was to be seen, and shafts of golden-tasseled corn. Over there

KAPUSTA KISZONA NA WINIE
(Sauerkraut in Wine)
2 lbs. sauerkraut
1 cup dry white wine
1 heaping tbs. butter
1 medium onion, blanched
  and grated
salt and pepper to taste

2 tsp. flour
½ tsp. Maggi or Kitchen
  Bouquet
sugar to taste

Squeeze kraut as dry as possible.

Simmer in a heavy casserole,

tightly covered, with wine, butter, onion, and seasoning. Stir frequently. After about 30 minutes, dust with flour, add Maggi extract and sugar to taste, and mix thoroughly. Allow to cook uncovered for about 5 minutes more. Serves 6.

JOSEPH CONRAD: MY RETURN TO CRACOW. On this journey of ours, which for me was essentially not a progress, but a retracing of footsteps on a road travelled before, I had no beacons to look for in Germany. I had never lingered in that land which, on the whole, is so singularly barren of memorable manifestations of generous sympathies and magnanimous impulses. An ineradicable, invincible, provincialism of envy and vanity clings to the forms of its thought like a frowsy garment. Even while yet very young I turned my eyes away from it instinctively as from a threatening phantom. I believe that children and dogs have, in their innocence, a special power of perception as far as spectral apparitions and coming misfortunes are concerned.

I let myself be carried through Germany as if it were through pure space, without sights, without sounds. No whisper of the war reached my voluntary abstraction. And perhaps not so very voluntary after all! Each of us is a fascinating spectacle to himself, and I had to watch my own personality returning from another world, as it were, to revisit the glimpses of old moons. Considering the condition of humanity, I am, perhaps, not so much to blame for giving up to that preoccupation. We prize the sensation of our continuity, and we can only capture it in that way. By watching.

Glaser and his wife, Shirley, found a collection of elaborate graphic cutouts while they were traveling in Poland. He thought (correctly) that the cutouts would make a striking cover on the *Graphic* without any modification except their arrangement on the page.

85

POCZTA POLSKA

25 halerzy 25

THE PUSH PIN

Monthly Graphic.

NUMBER 33

© 1961 by The Push Pin Studios

114 East 31 Street, New York 16, t.e. 2-9247

Subscription: $2.50 for 12 issues.

Canada and Foreign: $3.50

Glaser and his wife, Shirley, found a collection of elaborate graphic cutouts while they were traveling in Poland. He thought (correctly) that the cutouts would make a striking cover on the *Graphic* without any modification except their arrangement on the page.

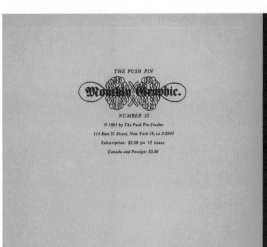

THE PUSH PIN

Monthly Graphic.

NUMBER 33

© 1961 by The Push Pin Studios

114 East 31 Street, New York 16, LE 2-9247

Subscription: $2.50 for 12 issues.

Canada and Foreign: $3.50

Chwast routinely trolled through moldy old newspapers for historical oddities. For this issue, news items from the twenties allowed Seltzer an opportunity to play with vintage graphic forms. The cover art was printed on coated paper and tipped onto the newsprint covers.

THE PUSH PIN

Monthly Graphic.

NUMBER 34

©1961 by The Push Pin Studios
114 East 31 Street, New York 16, LE 2-9247
Subscription: $2.50 for 12 issues.
Canada and Foreign: $3.50

MOTHERS COMPLAIN

Modern Girls "Vamp" Their Sons at Petting Parties.

The boys of today must be protected from the girl "vamp" and if standards of young people are to be raised the boys must do it, said Janet Richards of Washington, at a meeting in the home of Mrs. Otto H. Kahn at 1100 Fifth Avenue yesterday. Miss Richards discussed the girl of today and she said that although she had not seen much of the petting parties which are talked of so much, she had heard enough to realize that some girls were deliberate vamps.

"I have recently been told by the mothers of five sons of some of their problems," said Miss Richards, "and they told me that the most serious thing I had to face was the saving of their sons from the girl 'vamp.'

"These boys have gone to their mothers," said Miss Richards, and said: "Mother, it is so hard for me to be decent and live up to the standards you have set me, and to always keep in mind the loveliness and purity of girls. How can I do it with this cheek dancing, and if I pull away they call me a prude. And when I take a girl home in the way that you have told me is the proper fashion she is not satisfied."

Miss Richards said that she was trying to get some of the boys to band together to raise the standards of the set in which they move, in which the girl "petter" holds sway.

"These girls are a small percentage of the whole, and there are not enough of them to condemn them all," she said, "but it is sad to think that the girls are setting such standards for the boys." Middle-aged people, who remember the old-fashioned girl, must interfere in the young people's affairs, she said, and help to restore them to wholesome standards.

February 17, 1922

CARRY RUM UNDER WAISTS

Women Bootleggers in Massachusetts Town Use Novel Containers.

PEABODY, Mass. Feb. 15—Women bootleggers are plying their trade here, wearing moonshine containers made for wear under their waists, Chief of Police M. H. Grady said today. He showed in court a copper tank, constructed like a baseball catcher's chest protector, seized with a still in a raid on the home of Mrs. Annie Shanaway, who was fined $50 for keeping liquor for sale.

Chief Grady explained that if an order for moonshine was received, the container, which holds a gallon, was filled and strapped to the body of the bootlegger, who was able to go into the streets with it for delivery without detection.

February 16, 1922

TO EXHIBIT CARVED BEAN.

"Christus de Profundis" to Be Shown to Aid Fund for Shrine.

The carving of "Christus de Profundus" on a bean will be placed on public display tomorrow in the reception room of the Aeolian Company, 29 West Forty-second Street, it was announced yesterday by Mrs. H. Willis McFadden and Mrs. Oliver Harriman.

A booth will be erected in the reception room and the carving will be viewed through a magnifying glass. A small fee will be charged. The proceeds will go to a fund for the construction of a shrine in which the carving will find a permanent place.

Similar exhibitions of the bean will be made throughout the country.

April 3, 1921

ANOTHER
HOLIDAY
ISSUE

NUMBER
35

1961

With this issue, the *Monthly Graphic* changed its name to the *Push Pin Graphic*. It was ostensibly the same venue for experimentation but on a less frequent basis. The drawings here were by Paul Davis and Glaser.

CRADLE SONG

Slowly   JOHANNES BRAHMS

Lul-la - by and good - night, With ros - es be - dight, With lil - ies be - decked, Is ba - by's wee bed; Lay thee down now and rest, may thy slum - ber be blest, Lay thee down now and rest, May thy slum - ber be blest.

In the manner of issue number 34, Chwast found quirky stories from newspapers of the thirties and illustrated them in his noir-inspired woodcut style. The last piece of art shown on page 92 was based on a photo of Mussolini and other officials. The cover art was again printed on coated stock and tipped onto the newsprint.

90

NUMBER 36

© 1962 by The Push Pin Studios
114 East 31 Street, New York 16, LE 2-9247
Subscription: $2.50 a year, published bi-monthly
Canada and Foreign: $3.50

MOB OF GIRLS ANSWER "WORLD" AD—THEY DRAW LOTS FOR LONE JOB

There are many ways of getting a job, but the blue ribbon for the most unusual way goes to Miss Isabel Iskowitz of 139 Norfolk Street. She won her job on a raffle.

David Kirchenberg of 1193 Broadway advertised in the want ad columns of The World last Thursday for a stenographer. The job would pay $12 a week. Arriving at his office Friday morning a few minutes after 9 he found the entrance to the building blockaded. Hundreds of young girls thronged about the entrance and filled the street.

The landlord of the building, who had received several telephone calls; also arrived at this time. In a frenzy he beseeched Mr. Kirchenberg to get rid of the mob. Mr. Kirchenberg promised to do so, and, gaining his own office, opened the doors to admit applicants. Then the trouble began.

Literally hundreds of girls surged into the office. The railing was torn down, tables overturned and Mr. Kirchenberg, a small, natty little man, was almost trampled underfoot. Extricating himself he climbed on a chair and urged that the girls get into the hall and he would interview them. But to no avail.

"Give us a chance, give us a chance," they kept shouting.

Then one of the girls with sporting blood in her veins had an idea.

"Raffle the job off," she suggested. The idea took like wildfire. Several of the girls pitched in and made up about five hundred numbers with duplicates. The lucky number, 42, was drawn by Miss Isabel Iskowitz. And just to prove that they were good sports the other girls left cheering the winner. *January 13, 1931*

HITLER DENIES INTENT OF WAR

Aim Is Defense Only, He Says, Citing Lessons of 1918—Covets No Colonies

LONDON, Aug. 6 (AP)—Chancellor Hitler told Ward Price in an exclusive interview published today in the London Mail that "if it rests with Germany, war will not come again."

"This country has a more profound impression than any other of the evils war causes," the Chancellor said.

"Ninety-five per cent of the members of our national administration have had personal experience with the horrors of war and know that it is not an adventure but a ghastly catastrophe.

"It is the disciplined conviction of the Nazi movement that war can benefit nobody, but only bring about general ruin. Nineteen-eighteen was a lesson and a warning for us."

Only in Self Defense

"Germany's present problems could not be settled by war," the Reichfuehrer added. "Her claims upon Europe do not involve risk of such a disaster.

"We ask only that our present frontiers shall be maintained," he said, "and, believe me, we shall never fight again except in self defense."

Herr Hitler said he had repeatedly assured France that once the Saar question is settled there would be no further territorial differences between Germany and France. He said Germany had further proved her peaceful intentions by completing a pact with Poland.

Alluding to a statement in London of acting Prime Minister Stanley Baldwin last week that Britain's frontier was on the Rhine, the Chancellor said:—

"Maybe French statesmen will go further and say that France must defend herself on the River Oder; or Russia might claim her line of defense was the Danube."

"Unless England attacks us," he said, "we shall never have a conflict with England, on the Rhine or anywhere else. We want nothing from England." *August 6, 1934*

RUDOLPH FRIML QUOTES NAPOLEON VIA OUIJA BOARD

Predicts Hitler's Defeat, Chopin and Herbert Help Composer With His Work

BY WILLIAM BLOETH

Rudolf Friml, who has managed, unlike most composers, to stay in the upper income brackets for well over 30 years, is on one of his infrequent visits to town. He stopped long enough at his suite in the St. Moritz today to narrow the source of his inspiration down to:

1. The Ouija board.
2. Rhythmic sounds like water in a shower, the clack of a train's wheels on the rail splits, etc.
3. Long walks in the park, and
4. Omniscient spirits who predetermine a man's success or failure.

In short, according to Composer Friml, "a composer cannot labor."

Helpful Spirits

"It amuses me very much to see the movie version of a composer laboring for a chord," said Mr. Friml. He added that he usually devotes "not more than five minutes" in the actual composing and made it obvious that all of his sources he leans most heavily on the Ouija board.

"I really don't want to take the Ouija board too seriously," he explains, "but it is decidedly interesting.

"I talk on the board to Chopin (in French) and Victor Herbert—why, Herbert once gave me five notes and I played them on a piano and everyone said it really was Victor Herbert.

"I have a Polish poet who talks to me in rhymes—everything in rhymes. One he gave me was:

"May I know
Why I long for you?
Maybe because
I love you so."

Napoleon on Hitler

"When I talk about war I get big people like President Wilson. I got Napoleon the other day. I was told Germany was going to lose—was going to be destroyed. He told me in French.

"I knew the war would start September 2, and it did." *November 3, 1939*

COMPOSITE BEAUTY FIGURES

Lester Gaba's new manikins, which made their debut yesterday in Altman's window, are the composite figures of thirteen famous women, embodying the best features of each. Mrs. F. D. Roosevelt's height, Ruth St. Denis' carriage, Gloria Vanderbilt's poise, Myrna Loy's hair, Princess Ketto Mikeladze's coloring, Gertrude Lawrence's nose, Mary Taylor's cheekbones, Tilly Losch's hands, Rosamond Pinchot's chin, Elsa Maxwell's feet, Renee de Marco's figure and the eyes of both Garbo and Mrs. Byron Foy have been utilized in women. *March 2, 1937*

WHITESIDE PROTESTS IN COURT AT SHOW GIRLS GIGGLING AT HIM

Ethel Jane Walker, chorus girl, has been wont to sweep, at the lead of some of the girl friends, into the lobby of the Taft Hotel with a look-it-here-everybody air and, with knowing nods and giggles, point at Norman Whiteside, it was said today in and outside of West Side Court, where Miss Walker was arraigned on a disorderly conduct charge.

Miss Walker would whisper something—Mr. Whiteside said he could only guess what—and the girls would scream with laughter and hoot.

Mr. Whiteside, wealthy, of prominent lineage, an aviation enthusiast, former treasurer of the National Credit Corp., and who at the present moment, is writing a book about the folly of failure, did not like this form of attention-calling a bit.

He had a sinking feeling that the girls hooted and shook with glee, because, he said, Miss Walker announced something similar to:—

"There's a big honey that could be fleeced."

Mr. Whiteside said later the Taft lobby incidents followed a $50,000 breach of promise suit against him by Miss Walker.

April 11, 1933

BERLIN, Nov. 1. (UP) — The Propaganda Ministry today banned the sale of picture postcards showing Adolf Hitler and Benito Mussolini together over the caption, "Feuhrer and Duce have decided—Peace!" The Ministry also banned the seals bearing the inscription "Adolf Hitler, our peace leader."

November 1, 1939

PLAIN BROWN WRAPPER

THE COURTEZAN OLYMPIA

NUMBER

37

1962

This issue (wrapped in plain brown paper on preceding page) was based on Édouard Manet's notorious painting of a prostitute, *Olympia*. Glaser's favorite page (opposite) derives in part from Henri Matisse, but it also represents another direction in drawing for him that builds on complexity and reduction. Davis (right), Chwast, and Seltzer did the other illustrations.

94

Paul Davis

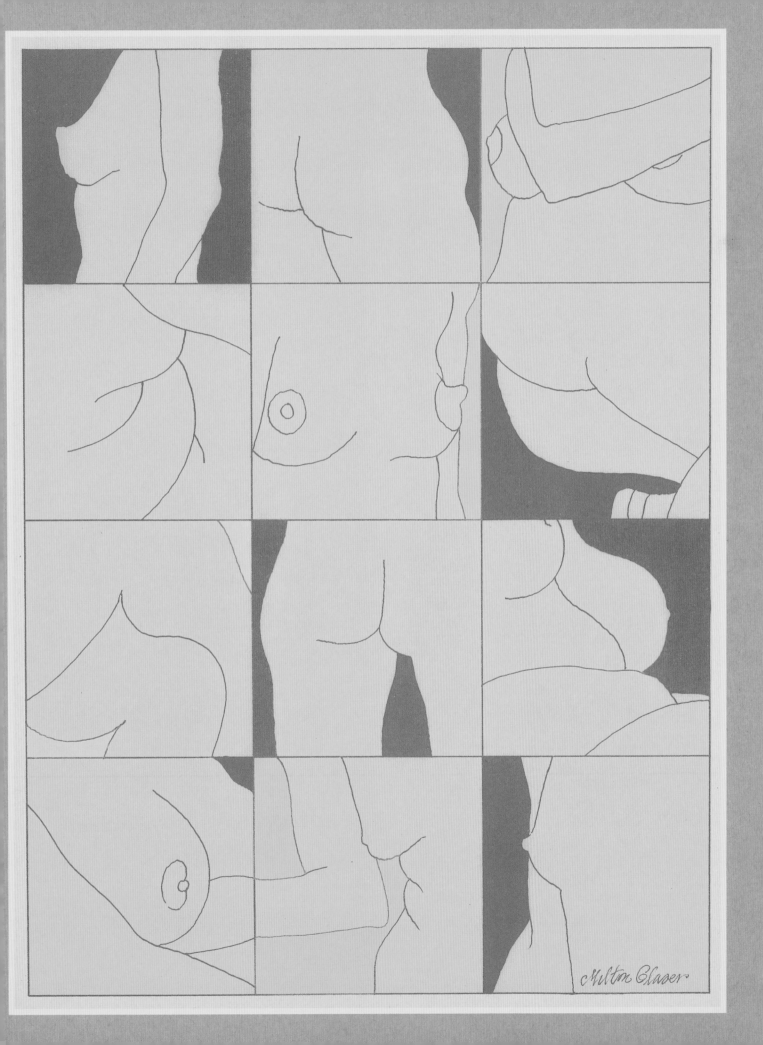

95

This is another of Glaser's drawing experiments using heavily textured paper. He says he was very interested in Georges Seurat at the time. The typography was a mix of Victorian slab serifs.

NUMBER THIRTY EIGHT

Push Pin Graphic.

© 1962 by The Push Pin Studios, Inc., 114 East 31 Street, New York 16, LE 2-0247 Subscription $2.50 a year, published bi-monthly Canada and Foreign: $3.50

1. HOW MANY SORTS OF DIET THERE BE.

There be especially three sorts of Diets; a full Diet, a moderate Diet, and a thin Diet. The first increaseth flesh, spirits, and humours, the second repaireth early them that were lost, and third lesseneth them all for a time, to preserve life. Full Diet is proper unto them which be young, growing, strong, lusty, and able through their good constitution to endure much exercise. Moderate Diet is fittest for persons of a middle health, whose estate of body is neither perfectly strong nor over-weak. Thin Diets are never to be used, especially in the strictest kind, but where violent diseases (caused either of fulness or corruption) have the predominancy wherein how much the body wanteth food, so much the sickness wanteth his tyrannical vigor.

2. OF THE TIMES ORDER AND MANNER OF EATING

Mince or chaw your meat finely, eat leisurely, swallow advisedly, and sit upright with your body for an hours space or less (howsoever some affect it) nay it is rather hurtful unless it be confirmed by long custom, or made more tolerable by reason of some pastime, game or discourse to refresh the mind.

3. LAST OF ALL, CONCERNING THE ORDER OF TAKING OF MEATS

The first course in old times was called *frigida mensa*, the cold service; because nothing but Oisters, Lettice, Spinache, cold salades, cold water and cold sauces were then set on the table; which order was clean altered in Plutarchs time, for they began their meals with wine, hot pottage, black or peppered broth, and hot meat, ending them with Lettice and Porcelane to suppress vapours and procure sleep; which example is diligently to be followed of cold stomachs, as the other is to be imitated of them which are over hot.

Likewise that the most nourishing meat is first to be eaten, that ancient Proverb ratifieth *Ab ovo ad mala*; from the eg to the Apples; wherefore I utterly mislike our English custome, where Pheasant, Partridge and Plover are last served, and meats of hard concoction and less good nourishment sent before them. As for fruit (if it be not astringent, so tart apples, pears, soure-plums, quinces, medlars, cervines, cornels, wardens, soure pomgranates, and all meats made of them) it should be eaten last.

Contrariwise all sweet and moist fruit (as ripe melons, gourds, cucumbers, pompions, old and sweet apples, sweet pomgranates, sweet oranges) and all things either fatty, light, liquid and thin of substance, and easie of concoction, should be first eaten, unless we be subject to great fluxes of the belly, or cholerick dispositions of stomach, and then the contrary course is most warrantable. For if slippery and light meats went formost into hot stomachs, they would either be burnt before the grosser were concocted, or at the least, cause all to slip downwards over-soon, by making the lower mouth of the stomach too too slippery. And verily I think that this is the best reason, wherewithall to maintain our English custome, in eating biefe and motton formost before foul and fish; unless the reason drawn from use and custome may seem more forcible.

Finally let me add one thing more, and then an end of this treatise; namely that if our breakfast be of liquid and supping meats, our dinner moist and of boiled meats, and our supper chiefly of roasted meats, a very good order is observed therein, agreeable both to art and the natures of most men.

Health Improvement; or, Rules Comprising the Nature, Method, and Manner of Preparing all sorts of Food used in this Nation. Written by Thomas Moffett, Doctor in Physick. London, 1655.

FASTWEIGH

Paul Anderson 390 lbs.

BRILLAT-SAVARIN LEANNESS AND ITS CURE

Every thin woman wishes to be stouter. This is a wish we have heard expressed a thousand times. It is, therefore, with the intention of rendering a last homage to that all-powerful sex that we shall now endeavor to replace by flesh and blood those appurtenances of silk or cotton which we behold so profusely displayed in the show windows, which shock the virtuous-minded passer-by and bring the reality almost visibly before him. Now, the whole secret for a thin lady to acquire a little embonpoint lies in a nutshell. It consists in a suitable *regime*. She must learn how to select and how to eat her food. We shall, therefore, endeavor to point out the system which ladies ought to follow who wish to become more plump, or, to use the more elegant term, who are desirous of acquiring "the rounded limb and the graceful curve."

GENERAL RULE.—Eat a quantity of fresh bread—the same day's baking—and do not throw away the crumb. Before eight A.M., when in bed, take a basin of soup (*potage au pain or aux pates*), not too much, or, if you prefer it, a cup of good chocolate. Breakfast at eleven and fresh eggs, boiled or poached, *petit pates*, cutlets, or anything else; but eggs are essential. A cup of coffee will not hurt. After breakfast take a little exercise. Go shopping or call on a friend, sit and chat, and walk home again. At dinner, eat as much soup, meat, and fish as you like, but do not omit to eat the rice with the fowl, macaroni, sweet pastry, cream etc. At dessert, savory biscuits, babas, and other farinaceous preparations which contain eggs and sugar. This diet may seem limited but it is capable of great variation, and comprises the whole animal kingdom. Drink beer by preference; otherwise Bordeaux or wine from the South of France. Avoid acids except salad, which gladdens the heart. Eat sugar with your fruit, if it admits of it. Do not take baths too cold; breath the fresh air of the country as often as you can; eat plenty of grapes when in season; do not fatigue yourself by dancing at a ball.

THE ANTI-CORPULENCY BELT

Every anti-corpulent system ought to be accompanied by a precautionary step. It consists in wearing, day and night, a belt round the stomach, which can gradually be tightened. To prove the necessity of this it must be considered that the spine, which is one of the mainstays of the internal machine, is firm and inflexible; hence, it results that any excess of weight thrown upon the bowels during a state of corpulency makes them deviate from the vertical line; they fall upon the various tissues of which the skin of the stomach consists, and as they have the power of expansion to an almost indefinite extent, there might be sufficient strength left for them to retract when the effort of expansion diminished, unless assisted by mechanical means, which, acting upon the spine itself, had become an antagonist, and reestablished the equilibrium. Thus, a belt such as we have described produces a double effect: it prevents the bowels from encroaching too much upon it, and it gives the necessary power of contraction when the weight diminishes. This belt should never be taken off; otherwise the good done during the day will be cancelled in the night. Moreover, it is not uncomfortable, and a man soon gets accustomed to it.

From The Handbook of Dining; or, Corpulency and Leanness Scientifically Considered by Anthelme Brillat-Savarin, 1865.

Milton Glaser

DR. GEORGE HARROP'S BANANA DIET

	Monday	Tuesday	Wednesday	Thursday	Friday
Breakfast:	1 BANANA black coffee	½ glass orange juice 1 poached egg 1 piece raisin toast black coffee	1 BANANA black coffee	½ glass apple juice 1 toasted corn muffin 1 pat butter black coffee	1 BANANA
Lunch:	1 BANANA 1 glass milk	1 BANANA black coffee	1 BANANA 1 glass milk	1 BANANA black coffee	1 BANANA 1 glass milk
Tea:	1 BANANA		1 BANANA		1 BANANA
Dinner:	1 BANANA sliced with 1/3 cup milk and cream half and half	1 cup buillon ¼ lb lean broiled steak 4 medium-sized broiled mushrooms ½ cup lettuce with tomato slices (½ *tomato*) lemon dressing ½ cup sliced pineapple	1 BANANA *(same as Monday)*	4 medium-sized shrimp 2 tablespoons catsup ½ broiled chicken 6 small boiled onions carrot and celery sticks ½ pear *(water pack)*	1 BANANA *(same as Monday)*
Late Supper:	1 BANANA		1 BANANA		1 BANANA Introduced in the 1930's by Dr. George Harrop of Johns Hopkins Hospital.

MANYA KAHN'S GRAPE DIET

	Monday	Tuesday	Wednesday	Thursday	Friday
Breakfast:	GRAPES (one-half pound)	GRAPES	1 sliced orange 1 soft-boiled egg protein toast (*1 slice*) black coffee or Sanka	GRAPES	honeydew melon (a small slice) 1 soft-boiled egg protein toast (*1 slice*) black coffee or Sanka
Lunch:	GRAPES	GRAPES	GRAPES	broiled lean hamburger lettuce and tomatoes (lemon juice dressing)	GRAPES
Tea:	GRAPES	GRAPES			
Dinner:	GRAPES	GRAPES	vegetable juice lean roast beef cucumber salad (lemon juice dressing) half melon tea with lemon	half grapefruit half broiled chicken lettuce salad (lemon juice dressing) baked apple with honey tea with lemon	tomato juice broiled halibut cole slaw fresh fruit tea with lemon
Late Supper:	GRAPES	GRAPES			Reprinted with the permission of Manya Kahn, famed specialist in scientific weight control, posture correction face-and-figure rejuvenation.

THE SUBJECT WAS LOVE

NUMBER

39

1962

Chwast made his monoprint of the flower lady (below) by rolling printer's ink on stiff paper, placing a sheet of paper over it, and drawing on top of the paper. Voilá, the image is on the reverse side. Also in this issue Davis finesses his signature style.

HOLIDAY ISSUE OF THE **Push Pin Graphic.** NUMBER THIRTY-NINE

Seymour Chwast

How well to break a lance, you'll gain great praise;
You'll be much loved if you're expert in arms...
'Tis advantageous that a bachelor
Should be expert in playing flute or viol;
By this and dancing he'll advance his cause.
    "Let no one think that you are miserly,
For such a reputation causes grief;
It is most fitting that a lover wise
Should give more freely from his treasury
Than any common simpleton or sot.
Naught of the lore of love the miser knows,
Whom giving does not please. From avarice
The one who wishes to progress in love
Must guard himself full well; for any swain
Who for a pleasant glance or winsome smile
Has given his heart entirely away
Ought well, after so rich a gift, his goods
Willingly to offer and bestow.
    "Now shortly I'll review what I have said,
For best remembered are things briefly told:
Whoever wishes to make Love his lord
Must courteous be and wholly void of pride,
Gracious and merry, and in giving free.
    "Next I enjoin as penance, night and day,
Without repentance, that you think on Love,
Forever keeping ceaselessly in mind
The happy hour which has such joy in store.
That you may be a lover tried and true,
My wish and will are that your heart be fixed
In one sole place whence it can not depart
But whole and undivided there remain;
For no half hearted service pleases me.
He who in many a place bestows his heart
Has but a little part to leave in each;
But of that may I never have a doubt
Who his whole heart deposits in one place.
When you have given your heart, then lend it not;
To lend what one has given is scandalous.
Unconditionally one should make
His gift, and thus a greater merit gain.
The bounty of a thing that's merely lent
Is paid for with a mere return of thanks;
But great should be guerdon of free gift.
Give, then, not only freely but with grace;
For debonairly given gift is best.
Things given grudgingly are nothing worth at all."

THE WISDOM OF GUTAMA: ILLUSION AND LOVE from *Siddhartha* by Hermann Hesse, translated by Hilda Rosner, © 1951 by New Directions. Reprinted by permission of New Directions, publishers. ROME, MAY 14, 1904; TO LOVE IS DIFFICULT from *Letters to A Young Poet* by Rainer Maria Rilke, translated by M. D. Herter Norton, © 1934, 1954 by W. W. Norton & Company, Inc., New York. PROGRESSIVE DEMOCRACY AND LOVE from *Selected Writings of Juan Ramón Jiménez*, translated from the Spanish by H. R. Hays, reprinted by permission of the publishers, Farrar, Straus & Company, Inc., © 1957 by Juan Ramón Jiménez. THE LOVER LEARNS THE COMMANDMENTS OF LOVE from *The Romance of The Rose* by Guillaume de Lorris and Jean de Meun, 13th century, translated by Harry W. Robbins, © 1962 by Florence W. Robbins, E. P. Dutton, Inc., New York.

Chwast and Glaser used any curious text for the *Graphic*, like this on the act of walking by Henry David Thoreau. Through their recasting and reinvention they wanted to transform whatever they touched into something more than it was. And this was the epitome of postmodernism before the term was coined.

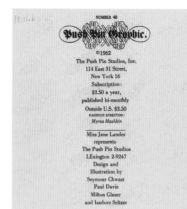

NUMBER 40

Push Pin Graphic.

©1962
The Push Pin Studios, Inc.
114 East 31 Street,
New York 16
Subscription:
$2.50 a year,
published bi-monthly
Outside U.S. $3.50
FASHION DIRECTOR:
Myrna Mushkin

Miss Jane Lander
represents
The Push Pin Studios
LExington 2-9247
Design and
Illustration by
Seymour Chwast
Paul Davis
Milton Glaser
and Isadore Seltzer

I have met with but one or two persons in the course of my life who understood the art of Walking, that is, of taking walks—who had a genius, so to speak, for *sauntering:* which word is beautifully derived "from idle people who roved about the country, in the Middle Ages, and asked charity, under pretense of going *à la Sainte Terre,*" to the Holy Land, till the children exclaimed, "There goes a *Sainte-Terrer,*" a Saunterer, a Holy-Lander. They who never go to the Holy Land in their walks, as they pretend, are indeed mere idlers and vagabonds; but they who do go there are saunterers in the good sense, such as I mean. Some, however, would derive the word from *sans terre,* without land or home, which, therefore, in the good sense, will mean, having no particular home, but equally at home everywhere. For this is the secret of successful sauntering. He who sits still in a house all the time may be the greatest vagrant of all; but the saunterer, in the good sense, is no more vagrant than the meandering river, which is all the while sedulously seeking the shortest course to the sea. But I prefer the first, which, indeed, is the most probable derivation. For every walk is a sort of crusade, preached by some Peter the Hermit in us, to go forth and reconquer this Holy Land from the hands of the Infidels. It is true, we are but faint-hearted crusaders,

even the walkers, nowadays, who undertake no persevering, never-ending enterprises. Our expeditions are but tours, and come round again at evening to the old hearth-side from which we set out. Half the walk is but retracing our steps. We should go forth on the shortest walk, perchance, in the spirit of undying adventure, never to return—prepared to send back our embalmed hearts only as relics to our desolate kingdoms. If you are ready to leave father and mother, and brother and sister, and wife and child and friends, and never see them again—if you have paid your debts, and made your will, and settled all your affairs, and are a free man, then you are ready for a walk. To come down to my own experience, my companion and I, for I sometimes have a companion, take pleasure in fancying ourselves knights of a new, or rather an old, order—not Equestrians or Chevaliers, not Ritters or Riders, but Walkers, a still more ancient and honorable class, I trust. The chivalric and heroic spirit which once belonged to the Rider seems now to reside in, or perchance to have subsided into, the Walker—not the Knight, but Walker, Errant. He is a sort of fourth estate, outside of Church and State and People. We have felt that we almost alone hereabouts practiced this noble art; though, to tell the truth, at least, if their own assertions are

to be received, most of my townsmen would fain walk sometimes,

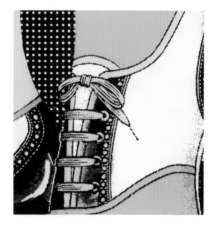

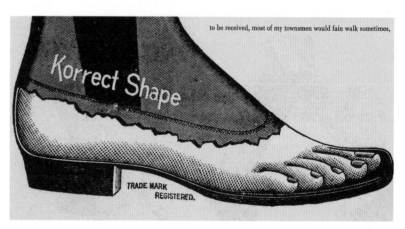

Korrect Shape

TRADE MARK
REGISTERED.

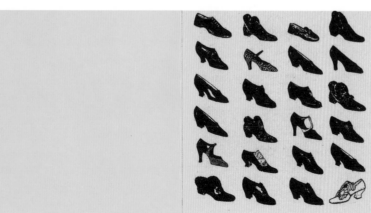

as I do, but they cannot. No wealth can buy the requisite leisure, freedom, and independence which are the capital in this profession. It comes only by the grace of God. It requires a direct dispensation from Heaven to become a walker. You must be born into the family of the Walkers. *Ambulator nascitur, non fit.* Some of my townsmen, it is true, can remember and have described to me some walks which they took ten years ago, in which they were so blessed as to lose themselves for half an hour in the woods; but I know very well that they have confined themselves to the highway ever since, whatever pretensions they may make to belong to this select class. No doubt they were elevated for a moment as by the reminiscence of a previous state of existence, when even they were foresters and outlaws. I think that I cannot preserve my health and spirits, unless I spend four hours a day at least—and it is commonly more than that—sauntering through the woods and over the hills and fields, absolutely free from all wordly engagements. You may safely say, a penny for your thoughts, or a thousand pounds. When sometimes I am reminded that the mechanics and shopkeepers stay in their shops not only all the forenoon, but all the afternoon too, sitting with crossed legs, so many of them, as if legs were made to sit upon, and not to stand or walk upon — I think that they deserve some credit for not having all committed suicide long ago. I, who cannot stay in my chamber for a single day without acquiring some rust, and when sometimes I have stolen forth for a walk at the eleventh hour or four o'clock in the afternoon, too late to redeem the day, when the shades of night were already beginning to be mingled with the daylight, have felt as if I had committed some sin to be atoned for — I confess that I am astonished at the power of endurance, to say nothing of the moral insensibility, of my neighbors who confine themselves to shops and offices the whole day for weeks and months, aye, and years almost together. I know not what manner of stuff they are of — sitting there now at three o'clock in the afternoon, as if it were three o'clock in the morning. Bonaparte may talk of the three-o'clock-in-the-morning courage, but it is nothing to the courage which can sit down cheerfully at this hour in the afternoon over against one's self whom you have known all the morning, to starve out a garrison to whom you are bound by such strong ties of sympathy. I wonder that about this time, or say between four and five o'clock in the afternoon, too late for the morning papers and too early for the evening ones, there is not a general explosion heard up and down the street,

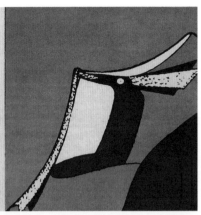

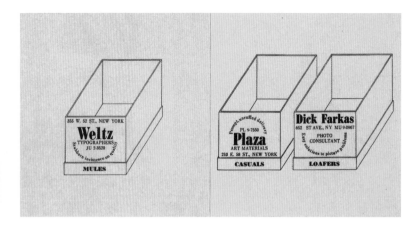

scattering a legion of antiquated and house-bred notions and whims to the four winds for an airing — and so the evil cure itself.

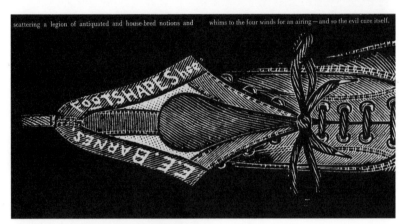

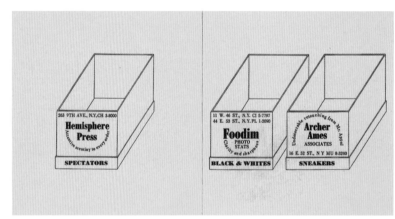

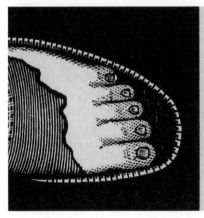

How womankind, who are confined to the house still more than men, stand it I do not know; but I have ground to suspect that most of them do not *stand* it at all. When, early in a summer afternoon, we have been shaking the dust of the village from the skirts of our garments, making haste past those houses with purely Doric or Gothic fronts, which have such an air of repose about them, my companion whispers that probably about these times their occupants are all gone to bed. Then it is that I appreciate the beauty and the glory of architecture, which itself never turns in, but forever stands out and erect, keeping watch over the slumberers. No doubt temperament, and, above all, age, have a good deal to do with it. As a man grows older, his ability to sit still and follow indoor occupations increases. He grows vespertinal in his habits as the evening of life approaches, till at last he comes forth only just before sundown, and gets all the walk that he requires in half an hour. But the walking of which I speak has nothing in it akin to taking exercise, as it is called, as the sick take medicine at stated hours — as the swinging of dumbbells or chairs; but is itself the enterprise and adventure of the day. If you would get exercise, go in search of the springs of life. Think of a man's swinging dumbbells for his health, when those springs are

with finer tissues of self-respect and heroism, whose touch thrills the heart, than the languid fingers of idleness. That is mere sentimentality that lies abed by day and thinks itself white, far from the tan and callus of experiences. When we walk, we naturally go to the fields and woods: what would become of us, if we walked only in a garden or a mall? Even some sects of philosophers have felt the necessity of importing the woods to themselves, since they did not go to the woods. "They planted groves and walks of Platanes," where they took *subdiales ambulationes* in porticos open to the air...My vicinity affords many good walks; and though for so many years I have walked almost every day, and sometimes for several days together, I have not yet exhausted them. An absolutely new prospect is a great happiness, and I can still get this any afternoon. Two or three hours' walking will carry me to as strange a country as I expect ever to see. A single farmhouse which I had not seen before is sometimes as good as the dominions of the King of Dahomey. There is in fact a sort of harmony discoverable between the capabilities of the landscape within a circle of ten miles' radius, or the limits of an afternoon walk, and the threescore years and ten of human life. It will never become quite familiar to you.

From an essay by Henry David Thoreau on Walking.

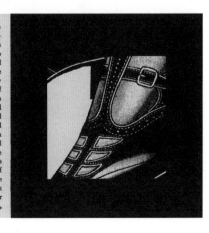

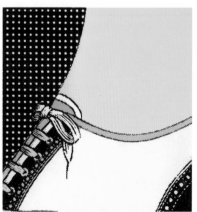

EMOTIONAL INVOLVEMENT

NUMBER
41

1963

This number with the text "Emotional Involvement" by Ralph R. Freenson, M.D., is what Glaser calls "a little experiment with die-cut flower imagery." It was a decidedly complex tour de force in that the image changes with the turning of every page.

personal, human part of the relationship has become a gadget—a gadget-like replaceable thing. If this person doesn't fill that purpose and it's worn out—like you change a car every few years, so you change the person every few years. And this is how you go on.

Now,—all these examples have to do with my subject of emotional involvement or univolvement. And when you look at this now a little more intently, which I now propose to do after these many examples—what am I really describing? What is involvement? What is this emotional involvement? It has to do with the care or concern or regard or interest in human beings. It has to do with relatedness to people. Obviously care, concern is derived from love in its broadest sense, in its perhaps most sublimated sense, if you will. Because caring and concerning—being concerned, has to do with the non-sexual, non-romantic part of a relationship. You can care for someone you love. That's marvelous. You could also care for someone in whom you are not interested, sexually or romantically—and that's also marvelous. Or another order of relationship. And this is what involvement refers to: it means you recognize that every human being is a unique individual and that you can discriminate and distinguish between them, and they are not interchangeable. There's a difference between sweetheart and friend and acquaintances or enemies. They're not all the same and you do not behave the same way to them. You don't call your wife honey and your enemy honey. There's a difference. And you do not expose yourself or talk in the same way to your enemy as you talk to your wife, or your dear friend, or the casual acquaintance. It is the most flabbergasting thing to see people who have the ability — if you want to call it — to talk to the milkman or

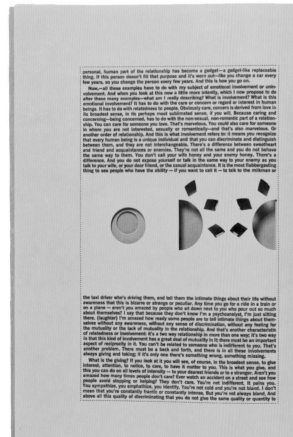

the taxi driver who's driving them, and tell them the intimate things about their life without awareness that this is bizarre or strange or peculiar. Any time you go for a ride in a train or on a plane – aren't you amazed by people who sit down next to you who pour out so much about themselves? I say that because they don't know I'm a psychoanalyst, I'm just sitting there. (laughter) I'm amazed how ready some people are to tell intimate things about themselves without any awareness, without any sense of discrimination, without any feeling for the mutuality or the lack of mutuality in the relationship. And that's another characteristic of relatedness or involvement: it's a two way relationship in more than one way; it's two way in that this kind of involvement has a great deal of mutuality in it; there must be an important aspect of reciprocity in it. You can't be related to someone who is indifferent to you. That's another problem. There must be a back and forth, and there is in all these involvements always giving and taking; it's only one there's something wrong, something missing.

What is the giving? If you look at it you will see, of course, in the broadest sense, to give interest, attention, to notice, to care, to have it matter to you. This is what you give, and this you can do on all levels of intensity – to your dearest friends or to a stranger. Aren't you amazed how many times people don't care? Ever watch an accident on a street and see how people avoid stopping or helping? They don't care. You're not indifferent, it pains you. You sympathize, you empathize, you identify. You're not cold and you're not bland. I don't mean that you're constantly frantic or constantly intense. But you're not always bland, And above all this quality of discriminating that you do not give the same quality or quantity to

everybody. It matters who they are; not in terms of snobbishness as to who they are, but in terms of what they mean to you and also what you can do for them. This kind of caring brings with it the capacity that you will be concerned for someone else even when it makes you uncomfortable. I mention it because so many people are ready to be helpful when it's convenient, but are so unready to be helpful when it's uncomfortable or inconvenient or painful; so I mention precisely that: care when it hurts you, when it bothers you; to subordinate your own needs and to sacrifice your own pleasure for the care of someone who means something to you. That means, yes, when you're on vacation or on Saturday night too — to be concerned. This giving has another meaning too, and it means a willingness of experience, the willingness to have another person participate with you in what's happening — both painful and pleasurable, both; not only tell the good things, but also the bad things. And the willingness to bear the bad news and the grief, but also the willingness to share the joys, of course. Again, this has to do with personal communication. It's intimate in the sense that you are dealing here not only with events but what did you feel? — above all, what did you imagine? What did you fantasy? And the greatest intimacy comes from the sharing of fantasies and imagination with another human being. Of course, this is terribly revealing; this makes you terribly vulnerable, for these are the parts of you that are most precious and you hate to show unless you feel it is a risk worth taking because you can be so hurt; nothing can hurt more than exposing a fantasy, something you imagined, to another human being and have them ridicule it or misunderstand it, or be indifferent.

This sharing has also to do with a willingness to be hurt and to have a relationship endure even if you are hurt. Emotional involvement means that someone is a friend even though he was nasty to you or mean or cruel or angry or thoughtless; and yet, you can remember when he wasn't or other qualities, and you're not willing to discard the whole relationship because of it. You're willing to endure pain for someone who matters to you. This, I think, is a very important ingredient of emotional involvement. Sure it means a willingness to understand; but it also means a willingness to be misunderstood at times. It is based, as you can see, on some kind of trust to this other human being. And you will immediately say to me, and I immediately think of it: well, trust! — you go around trusting and you're going to get hurt. These are the suckers. And it is true. The biggest trusters in the world are the biggest suckers in the world. They're the gullible ones, they're the credulous ones. But let me tell you, by and large, they are far more happy than the cynical ones and the suspicious ones. Do you know any suckers? Think about it. They've usually had a lot of good experiences — I'll get into that later. (laughter)

But the other part of this involvement has to do with being willing to take — and I say it in a peculiar way: being willing to take. But I want it emphasized that there are some people who are quite ready to give but have great difficulty in taking, which limits the involvement and limits the mutuality and is a problem. It has to have both in it, And there must be this willingness to give the other one the pleasure of giving you. You see what the ones who don't take don't realize. They're not being noble, they're not being abstinent, but they're

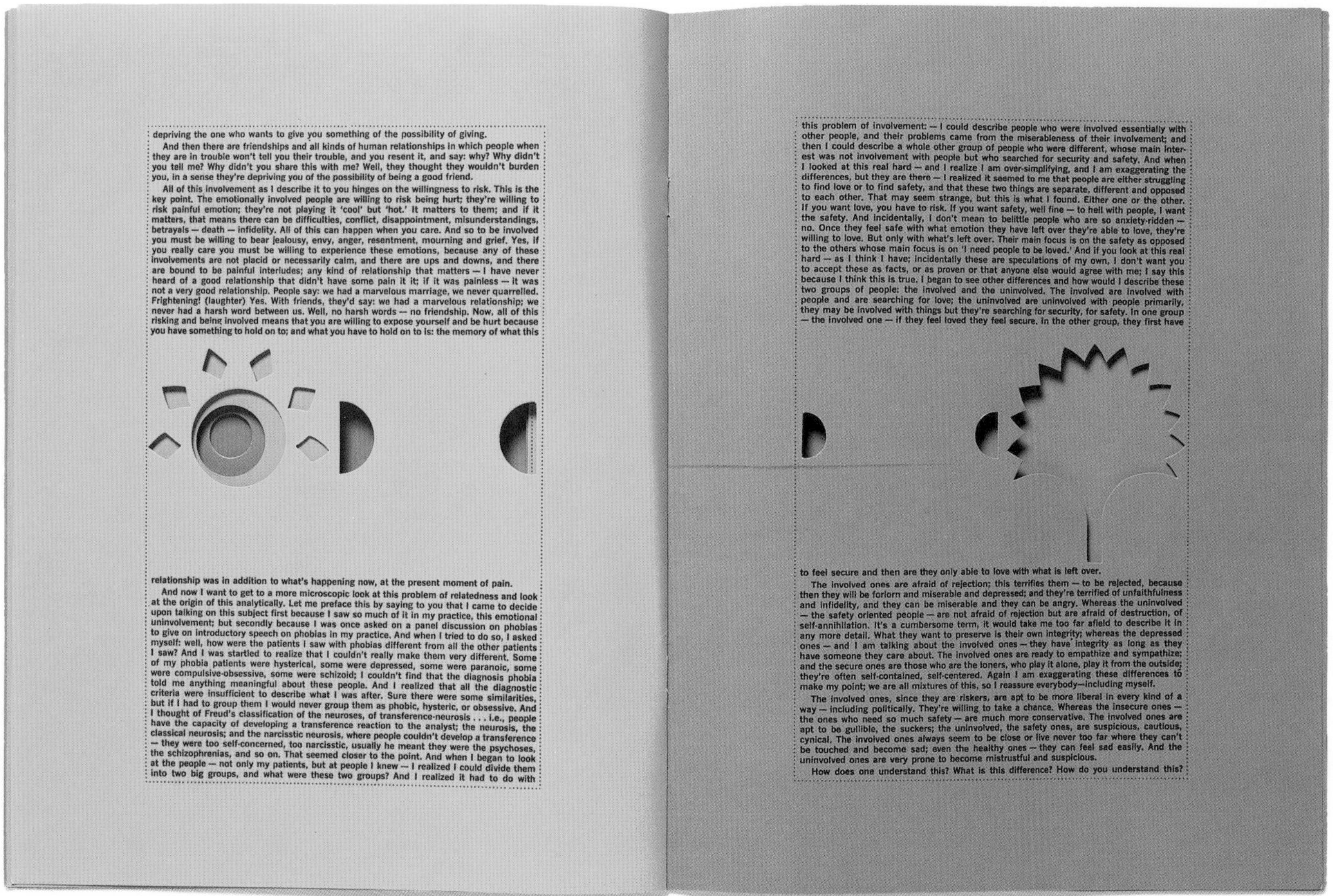
depriving the one who wants to give you something of the possibility of giving.
And then there are friendships and all kinds of human relationships in which people when they are in trouble won't tell you their trouble, and you resent it, and say: why? Why didn't you tell me? Why didn't you share this with me? Well, they thought they wouldn't burden you, in a sense they're depriving you of the possibility of being a good friend.
All of this involvement as I describe it to you hinges on the willingness to risk. This is the key point. The emotionally involved people are willing to risk being hurt; they're willing to risk painful emotion; they're not playing it 'cool' but 'hot.' It matters to them; and if it matters, that means there can be difficulties, conflict, disappointment, misunderstandings, betrayals — death — infidelity. All of this can happen when you care. And so to be involved you must be willing to bear jealousy, envy, anger, resentment, mourning and grief. Yes, if you really care you must be willing to experience these emotions, because any of these involvements are not placid or necessarily calm, and there are ups and downs, and there are bound to be painful interludes; any kind of relationship that matters — I have never heard of a good relationship that didn't have some pain it it; if it was painless — it was not a very good relationship. People say: we had a marvelous marriage, we never quarrelled. Frightening! (laughter) Yes. With friends, they'd say: we had a marvelous relationship; we never had a harsh word between us. Well, no harsh words — no friendship. Now, all of this risking and being involved means that you are willing to expose yourself and be hurt because you have something to hold on to; and what you have to hold on to is: the memory of what this
relationship was in addition to what's happening now, at the present moment of pain.
And now I want to get to a more microscopic look at this problem of relatedness and look at the origin of this analytically. Let me preface this by saying to you that I came to decide upon talking on this subject first because I saw so much of it in my practice, this emotional uninvolvement; but secondly because I was once asked on a panel discussion on phobias to give on introductory speech on phobias in my practice. And when I tried to do so, I asked myself: well, how were the patients I saw with phobias different from all the other patients I saw? And I was startled to realize that I couldn't really make them very different. Some of my phobia patients were hysterical, some were depressed, some were paranoic, some were compulsive-obsessive, some were schizoid; I couldn't find that the diagnosis phobia told me anything meaningful about these people. And I realized that all the diagnostic criteria were insufficient to describe what I was after. Sure there were some similarities, but if I had to group them I would never group them as phobic, hysteric, or obsessive. And I thought of Freud's classification of the neuroses, of transference-neurosis . . . i.e., people have the capacity of developing a transference reaction to the analyst; the neurosis, the classical neurosis; and the narcisstic neurosis, where people couldn't develop a transference — they were too self-concerned, too narcisstic, usually he meant they were the psychoses, the schizophrenias, and so on. That seemed closer to the point. And when I began to look at the people — not only my patients, but at people I knew — I realized I could divide them into two big groups, and what were these two groups? And I realized it had to do with
this problem of involvement: — I could describe people who were involved essentially with other people, and their problems came from the miserableness of their involvement; and then I could describe a whole other group of people who were different, whose main interest was not involvement with people but who searched for security and safety. And when I looked at this real hard — and I realize I am over-simplifying, and I am exaggerating the differences, but they are there — I realized it seemed to me that people are either struggling to find love or to find safety, and that these two things are separate, different and opposed to each other. That may seem strange, but this is what I found. Either one or the other. If you want love, you have to risk. If you want safety, well fine — to hell with people, I want the safety. And incidentally, I don't mean to belittle people who are so anxiety-ridden — no. Once they feel safe with what emotion they have left over they're able to love, they're willing to love. But only with what's left over. Their main focus is on the safety as opposed to the others whose main focus is on 'I need people to be loved.' And if you look at this real hard — as I think I have; incidentally these are speculations of my own, I don't want you to accept these as facts, or as proven or that anyone else would agree with me; I say this because I think this is true. I began to see other differences and how would I describe these two groups of people: the involved and the uninvolved. The involved are involved with people and are searching for love; the uninvolved are uninvolved with people primarily, they may be involved with things but they're searching for security, for safety. In one group — the involved one — if they feel loved they feel secure. In the other group, they first have
to feel secure and then are they only able to love with what is left over.
The involved ones are afraid of rejection; this terrifies them — to be rejected, because then they will be forlorn and miserable and depressed; and they're terrified of unfaithfulness and infidelity, and they can be miserable and they can be angry. Whereas the uninvolved — the safety oriented people — are not afraid of rejection but are afraid of destruction, of self-annihilation. It's a cumbersome term, it would take me too far afield to describe it in any more detail. What they want to preserve is their own integrity; whereas the depressed ones — and I am talking about the involved ones — they have integrity as long as they have someone they care about. The involved ones are ready to empathize and sympathize; and the secure ones are those who are the loners, who play it alone, play it from the outside; they're often self-contained, self-centered. Again I am exaggerating these differences to make my point; we are all mixtures of this, so I reassure everybody—including myself.
The involved ones, since they are riskers, are apt to be more liberal in every kind of a way — including politically. They're willing to take a chance. Whereas the insecure ones — the ones who need so much safety — are much more conservative. The involved ones are apt to be gullible, the suckers; the uninvolved, the safety ones, are suspicious, cautious, cynical. The involved ones always seem to be close or live never too far where they can't be touched and become sad; even the healthy ones — they can feel sad easily. And the uninvolved ones are very prone to become mistrustful and suspicious.
How does one understand this? What is this difference? How do you understand this?

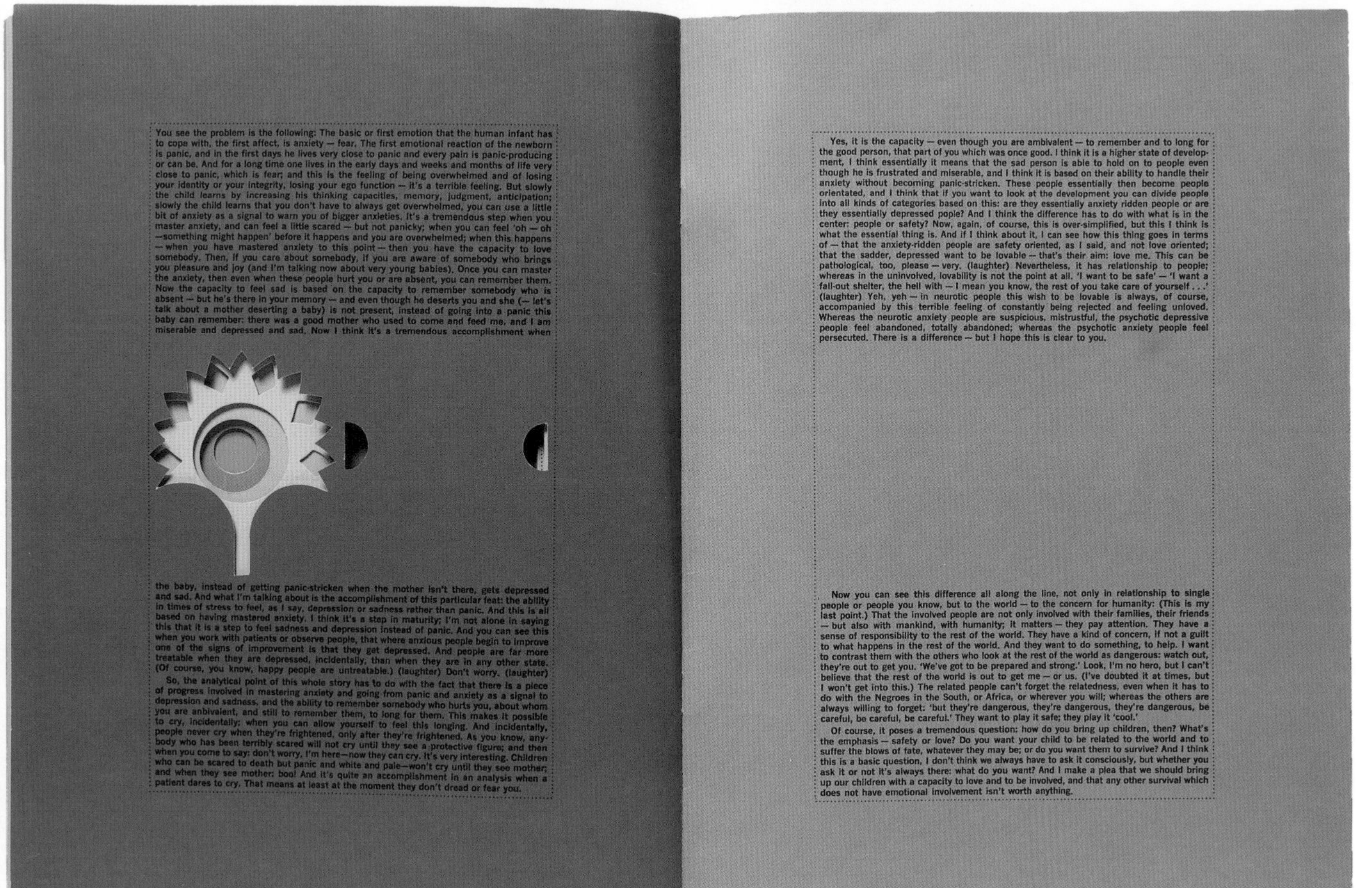
You see the problem is the following: The basic or first emotion that the human infant has to cope with, the first affect, is anxiety — fear. The first emotional reaction of the newborn is panic, and in the first days he lives very close to panic and every pain is panic-producing or can be. And for a long time one lives in the early days and weeks and months of life very close to panic, which is fear; and this is the feeling of being overwhelmed and of losing your identity or your integrity, losing your ego function — it's a terrible feeling. But slowly the child learns by increasing his thinking capacities, memory, judgment, anticipation; slowly the child learns that you don't have to always get overwhelmed, you can use a little bit of anxiety as a signal to warn you of bigger anxieties. It's a tremendous step when you master anxiety, and can feel a little scared — but not panicky; when you can feel 'oh — oh —something might happen' before it happens and you are overwhelmed; when this happens — when you have mastered anxiety to this point — then you have the capacity to love somebody. Then, if you care about somebody, if you are aware of somebody who brings you pleasure and joy (and I'm talking now about very young babies). Once you can master the anxiety, then even when these people hurt you or are absent, you can remember them. Now the capacity to feel sad is based on the capacity to remember somebody who is absent — but he's there in your memory — and even though he deserts you and she (— let's talk about a mother deserting a baby) is not present, instead of going into a panic this baby can remember: there was a good mother who used to come and feed me, and I am miserable and depressed and sad. Now I think it's a tremendous accomplishment when
the baby, instead of getting panic-stricken when the mother isn't there, gets depressed and sad. And what I'm talking about is the accomplishment of this particular feat: the ability in times of stress to feel, as I say, depression or sadness rather than panic. And this is all based on having mastered anxiety. I think it's a step in maturity; I'm not alone in saying this that it is a step to feel sadness and depression instead of panic. And you can see this when you work with patients or observe people, that where anxious people begin to improve one of the signs of improvement is that they get depressed. And people are far more treatable when they are depressed, incidentally, than when they are in any other state. (Of course, you know, happy people are untreatable.) (laughter) Don't worry. (laughter)
So, the analytical point of this whole story has to do with the fact that there is a piece of progress involved in mastering anxiety and going from panic and anxiety as a signal to depression and sadness, and the ability to remember somebody who hurts you, about whom you are anbivalent, and still to remember them, to long for them. This makes it possible to cry, incidentally; when you can allow yourself to feel this longing. And incidentally, people never cry when they're frightened, only after they're frightened. As you know, anybody who has been terribly scared will not cry until they see a protective figure; and then when you come to say: don't worry, I'm here—now they can cry. It's very interesting. Children who can be scared to death but panic and white and pale—won't cry until they see mother; and when they see mother: boo! And it's quite an accomplishment in an analysis when a patient dares to cry. That means at least at the moment they don't dread or fear you.
Yes, it is the capacity — even though you are ambivalent — to remember and to long for the good person, that part of you which was once good. I think it is a higher state of development, I think essentially it means that the sad person is able to hold on to people even though he is frustrated and miserable, and I think it is based on their ability to handle their anxiety without becoming panic-stricken. These people essentially then become people orientated, and I think that if you want to look at the development you can divide people into all kinds of categories based on this: are they essentially anxiety ridden people or are they essentially depressed pople? And I think the difference has to do with what is in the center: people or safety? Now, again, of course, this is over-simplified, but this I think is what the essential thing is. And if I think about it, I can see how this thing goes in terms of — that the anxiety-ridden people are safety oriented, as I said, and not love oriented; that the sadder, depressed want to be lovable — that's their aim: love me. This can be pathological, too, please — very. (laughter) Nevertheless, it has relationship to people; whereas in the uninvolved, lovability is not the point at all. 'I want to be safe' — 'I want a fall-out shelter, the hell with — I mean you know, the rest of you take care of yourself . . .' (laughter) Yeh, yeh — in neurotic people this wish to be lovable is always, of course, accompanied by this terrible feeling of constantly being rejected and feeling unloved. Whereas the neurotic anxiety people are suspicious, mistrustful, the psychotic depressive people feel abandoned, totally abandoned; whereas the psychotic anxiety people feel persecuted. There is a difference — but I hope this is clear to you.
Now you can see this difference all along the line, not only in relationship to single people or people you know, but to the world — to the concern for humanity: (This is my last point.) That the involved people are not only involved with their families, their friends — but also with mankind, with humanity; it matters — they pay attention. They have a sense of responsibility to the rest of the world. They have a kind of concern, if not a guilt to what happens in the rest of the world. And they want to do something, to help. I want to contrast them with the others who look at the rest of the world as dangerous: watch out, they're out to get you. 'We've got to be prepared and strong.' Look, I'm no hero, but I can't believe that the rest of the world is out to get me — or us. (I've doubted it at times, but I won't get into this.) The related people can't forget the relatedness, even when it has to do with the Negroes in the South, or Africa, or wherever you will; whereas the others are always willing to forget: 'but they're dangerous, they're dangerous, they're dangerous, be careful, be careful, be careful.' They want to play it safe; they play it 'cool.'
Of course, it poses a tremendous question: how do you bring up children, then? What's the emphasis — safety or love? Do you want your child to be related to the world and to suffer the blows of fate, whatever they may be; or do you want them to survive? And I think this is a basic question, I don't think we always have to ask it consciously, but whether you ask it or not it's always there: what do you want? And I make a plea that we should bring up our children with a capacity to love and to be involved, and that any other survival which does not have emotional involvement isn't worth anything.

DIARY OF A MADMAN

NUMBER
42
1963

In this issue about madness Chwast employed surrealist photomontage and collage, popularized in the twenties, to great advantage in the sixties, a period when surrealism was being adopted (in large part thanks to Paul Davis) in the mainstream of American illustration.

THE DIARY OF A MADMAN
Number 42
Push Pin Graphic

October 3

An extraordinary thing happened today. I got up rather late, and when Marva brought my boots, I asked her the time. Hearing that ten had struck quite a while before, I dressed in a hurry. I must say I'd as soon have skipped the office altogether, knowing the sour look the Chief of my Division would give me. For a long time now he has been telling me: "How come, my man, you're always in such a muddle? Sometimes you dart around like a house on fire, and get your work in such a tangle the Devil himself couldn't put it straight; you're likely to start a new heading with a small letter and give no date or reference number." The vicious old crane! He must envy me for sitting in the Director's room and sharpening his quills. So I wouldn't have gone to the office if not in hopes of seeing the cashier and trying to get even a small advance on my salary out of the Jew. What a creature he is! The Last Judgment will come before you'll get a month's pay out of him in advance. Even if there's a dire emergency, you can beg till something bursts inside you; he won't give in, the hoary monster. Yet at home his own cook slaps him around. Everyone knows that. I see no advantage in working in our department. No side benefits whatever. It's not like working, say, for the City Administration or in the Justice Department. There you may see someone nesting in a corner and scribbling away. He may be wearing a shabby coat and have a snout that you'd want to spit at. But then, just take a look at the summer house he rents! And don't even think of offering him a gilt china cup: this, he'd say, may be all right for a doctor. But he—he must have a pair of horses maybe, or a carriage, or a beaver fur—300 rubles' worth or so. And he looks so quiet and sounds so deferential and polite: "Would you," he'll say, "be so kind as to lend me your penknife to sharpen my quill, if you please." But he'll strip a petitioner naked, except perhaps for his shirt. On the other hand, though, to work in our department carries more prestige. The people of the City Administration have never dreamt of such cleanliness. Then we have red mahogany tables and our superiors always address us politely. Yes, if it weren't for the prestige, I confess I'd have left the department long ago.

I put on my old overcoat and, as it was pouring rain, took my umbrella. The streets were quite deserted except for some peasant women, their skirts thrown over their heads, a few merchants under umbrellas, and a coachman here and there. As for decent people there was only our kind, the civil-service clerk, squelching along. I saw him at a street crossing. And as soon as I saw him I said to myself: "You're not on your way to the office, my man. You're after that one trotting ahead over there and it's her legs you're staring at." What a rogue your civil servant is! When it comes to such matters, he can take on an army officer any day. He'll try to pick up anything under a bonnet. I was passing by a store, thinking about all this, when a carriage stopped in front of it. I recognized it at once: it belonged to the Director of our Department, himself. But, I thought, he cannot possibly need anything here—it must be his daughter. I pressed myself against the wall. The footman opened the carriage door and she fluttered out like a little bird. Ah, how she looked around, first right, then left, how her eyes and eyebrows flashed past me!…Oh God, I'm lost, lost forever. And why did she have to drive out in the pouring rain? Try and deny after that, that women have a passion for clothing. She did not recognize me. Besides, I was trying to hide myself; my coat was quite stained and out of fashion too. Nowadays, they are wearing long collars on their coats while I had two very short ones, one on top of the other. Her lap dog was too slow to get into the store while the door was open and had to stay in the street. I know this little dog. She's called Madgie. Then, a minute or so later, I heard a thin little voice: "Hello, Madgie." I'll be damned! Who's that talking? I turned around and saw two ladies walking under their umbrellas: one old, the other young and pretty. But they had already passed when I heard again, just next to me: "You ought to be ashamed, Madgie!" What on earth was going on? I

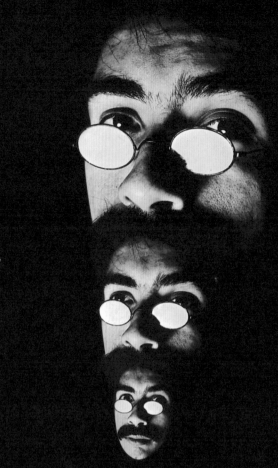

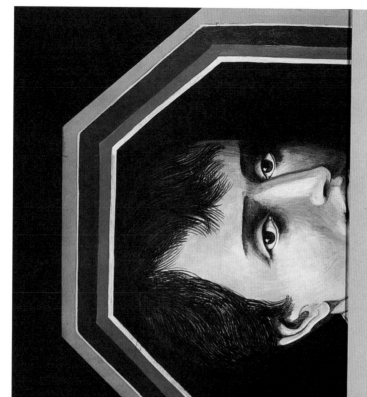

WAR, SEX, AND HISTORY

NUMBER

43

1963

This issue is devoted to the rhetoric of sex and war with a text (excerpted from a talk by Guy Endore before the 1962 graduating class of the University of California at Los Angeles) discussing, in one fell swoop, Achilles, Oscar Wilde, Marquis de Sade, and Adolf Hitler. Seltzer's illustrations of Napoleon and de Sade form a gatefold with text and ads printed on an insert.

WAR YES, SEX NO.

women of France than this bloody tyrant from whose recruiters upwards of half a million boys were hiding out in the forests because their womenfolk did not want them to go to war and to death.

But this murderer of millions has been forgiven. Poets without number have sung his praise, town after town in France has its street named Napoleon or Bonaparte. He lies in a tomb such as no writer, no artist, no scientist in the world has ever had erected over his bones. And his works and his deeds are celebrated in thousands of books of which not one is suppressed or locked away. And one may well wonder if his counterpart of today, Hitler, will not someday have his equal in monuments too. But Sade? No, Sade will never be forgiven. There are no Sade streets, no Sade monuments, and there never will be any. And his books are in jail today as his body was years ago. As recently as 1950, nearly a century and a half after his death, the Parisian publisher of a small edition of one of Sade's works was fined and the entire lot was ordered burnt.

So vile is still the name of Sade that when Eichmann, a year ago, was much in the news, reporter after reporter spoke of him as a sadist. But Eichmann killed millions, whereas Sade never killed anyone. Should not Eichmann have been called Napoleonic rather than sadistic? No one even thought of such a thing. It would have been ridiculous. The word Napoleonic would have suggested something big and glorious and praise-worthy. Even the psychoanalysts, the people to whom we sometimes look for a solution of our sexual neuroses, speak of Eichmann in terms such as anal-sadistic. Why not anal-Napoleonic? Isn't it clear that even in the ranks of these truth-seekers, the old taboos somehow manage to perpetuate themselves? But what else can one feel but revulsion for the Marquis de Sade, this demoniac man, who seriously proposed during the early days of the French revolution that the state should build huge brothels in which every female of France, from little girls to old women, should be required to prostitute themselves to any man? And similarly that all males, from little boys to grey-haired gentlemen, should be available for whatever desires a woman might have. Isn't that a frightful project? That the state should built palaces of fornication and perversion? That the whole nation should be converted into one huge brothel? Truly such an idea is unforgiveable.

And yet, at this very moment, is not our whole country, our whole globe, being turned into a military fortress? And is that not quite all right to many people? And are not many of our most important public figures, such as the scientist Edward Teller, going up and down our land advocating that the government should build vast underground shelters, two hundred feet below the surface of the earth, to accommodate every man and woman and child of our cities? That such places would be called shelters cannot alter the fact that they would really be gigantic dungeons, and that their existence would entitle and release our leaders to be even more intransigent in their demands and more reckless in their rattling of atom bomb threats than ever.

Have these people who dream of putting the whole human

race into prison thereby become social outcasts? T... not. Come to think of it, I would rather see the natio... into a brothel than into a prison. But that's hardly... I simply marvel that the one is considered respec... the other disgraceful; that the one, involving sex, ... into your Special Collections, while the other, involvi... remains available to all, and even to children; that ... remain a criminal, and that the others may even ... our heroes. That's how it is in our world. German ger... quickly forgiven and become respected functionarie... forces of Nato. They are only murderers, not sex fien... still sleeps not far from Lenin, in the Kremlin instea... Square. Mussolini's son does not seem to have found... sary to seek death on the battlefield in order to clo... name, and Krupp still runs his gigantic steel mills. ... world's statesmen, who, just a few years after ma... gigantic war, have brought us to an even worse p... of being buried alive or being buried dead, are still fur... to the applause of billions. There's nothing unclean ab... Indeed one is tempted to suggest that the man who ... off the whole human race will without a doubt be man's ... hero, with but one problem, that of a lack of survivor... him due credit.

Is there no way of breaking this bloody enchantme... which we live? Cannot we have two beginnings as ... two ends? Alfred North Whitehead in his Harvard ... on symbolism, said: "The art of a free society consist... the maintenance of the symbolic codes; and secondly... lessness of revision, to secure that the code shall ser... purposes which satisfy an enlightened reason. Those ... which cannot combine reverence to their symbols w... dom of revision must ultimately decay either from ... or from slow atrophy of a life stifled by useless sh... Whitehead wrote this in 1927, before we realized ... world is more likely to end with a bang than a wh... do not know what the symbols may be to which we m... in order to save ourselves at this late date. But I do th... we shall have to find them or else perish. I don't think... have found them yet. But I'm looking for them, dow... in your stacks of bookshelves, and you will know i... should run across them, for I shall give a great big... and lay another egg, and claim it all for myself.

Perhaps in that great day when we really beat our ... into ploughshares, you librarians will put your militar... in Special Collections and your sex books on the open ... All except the Marquis de Sade's works. I'm afraid ... matter how you change your symbols that man's bo... always be too shocking. I wouldn't want my children t... a school where such books were readily accessible. A... wouldn't either. That's how we human beings are. Tha... your card catalogue is as it is. And that's why this ... animals seems headed for doom.

From a talk given by Guy Endore before the graduating cla... School of Library Service, University of California at Los... Friday, May 25, 1962. Copyright 1963 by Guy Endore. Used... mission of Barthold Fles, Literary Agent.

EIGHTEEN MAXIMS

NUMBER 44

1964

Comprising maxims by Oscar Wilde,
La Rochefoucauld, and Franz Kafka,
this issue addressed Push Pin's
concerns about ethics or righteousness
(and occasionally self-righteousness)
in the world.

18 Maxims

OSCAR WILDE

1
Experience
is the name everyone gives
to their mistakes.

2
Conscience and cowardice
are really the same things.

3
What is a cynic? A man who
knows the price of everything,
and the value of nothing.

5
In this world there are only
two tragedies. One is not getting
what one wants, and the
other is getting it.

6
The only way
to get rid of a temptation
is to yield to it.

4
It is through Art, and through Art only,
that we can realize our perfection;
through Art and Art only
that we can shield ourselves
from the sordid perils of actual existence.

LA ROCHEFOUCAULD

7
One is almost always bored
by the very people one is not
permitted to find boring

8
Generally we praise with enthusiasm
only those who admire us.

9
Mediocre minds
usually condemn all that is
beyond their comprehension.

10
If vanity does not overturn
the virtues entirely,
at least it shakes them up.

12
One does not give praise
except to profit by it.

11
Sometimes one is happier
being deceived by that which one loves
than learning the truth.

LA ROCHEFOUCAULD

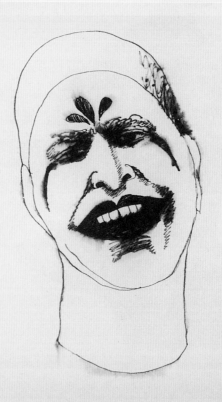

17
In the fight between you and
the world back the world.

13
The martyrs do not under-
estimate the body; they cause
it to be elevated on the cross.
In that they are at one with
their enemies.

14
Intercourse with human beings
seduces one to self-contemplation.

15
Some deny the existence of
misery by pointing to the sun;
he denies the existence of the
sun by pointing to misery.

16
It is conceivable that Alexander
the Great, in spite of the martial
successes of his early days, in
spite of the excellent army that
he had trained, in spite of the
power he felt within him to
change the world, might have
remained standing on the bank
of the Hellespont and never out
of indecision, not out of infirmity
of will, but because of the
mere weight of his own body.

18
A first sign of nascent knowledge
is the desire for death. This life
seems unendurable, any other
unattainable. One is no longer
ashamed of wishing to die; one
prays to be conducted from the
old cell that one hates into a new
one that one has yet to hate.
There is in this a vestige of faith
that during the change the
Master may chance to walk
along the corridor, contemplate
the prisoner, and say: "You
must not lock up this one
again. He is to come to me."

THINGS THAT FLY

NUMBER
45

1964

Chwast was intrigued with the transformation of images from one form to another unique entity. In this case conventional artwork could be made into a functional yet unconventional kite (complete with instructions on how to make it).

112

ADVERTISEMENTS

Snipe (snīp), *n.* [ME. snype, of Scand. origin.] Any of certain limicoline birds (genus *Capella*) related to the woodcocks and frequenting bogs and marshes, and highly valued game. *v.i.* snipe at your contemporaries but see their work first in CA MAGAZINE. 809 San Antonio, Palo Alto, Calif. $12 a year, bi-monthly, $14 foreign.

Swallow (swŏl'ō), *n.* [AS. swealwe, swalewe, swalwe.] *Zool.* Any of a family (Hirundinidae) of small long-winged passerine birds noted for their graceful flight and regular migrations. Swallows occur in all parts of the world except New Zealand and polar regions. *v.t.* Don't *swallow* those stories. See for yourself that PLAZA ART MATERIALS has the most complete stock anywhere. 210 East 58 St., New York, PL 9-7550.

Lark (lärk), *n.* [AS. Lawerce, laferce.] Any of numerous singing birds (family Alaudidae). esp. the skylark. They are found chiefly in Europe, Asia and Northern Africa. *Colloq.* On a *lark*, try FOODIM for photostats. You'll be satisfied. 44 East 53 St., New York, PL 1-2090, or 11 West 46 St., CI 5-7797.

WHITE-THROATED SWIFT.

Swift (swĭft), *n.* Any of a family (Apodidae) of small, plainly colored birds allied to the hummingbirds and goatsuckers, but superficially resembling swallows. The common American species (*Chaetura pelagica*) is called *chimney swift* from its habits of nesting and roosting in disused chimneys. Common usage: *swift* and sure is the typography from WELTZ AD SERVICE, 355 West 52 St., New York, JU 2-3520, typesetters to the Push Pin Graphic.

Rail (rāl), *n.* [F. rale, fr. OF. ralle, raale.] Any of numerous small preocial wading birds (family Rallidae, subfamily Rallinae) structurally related to the cranes, and prized as game birds. *v.i.* rail against imperfection. Let ARCHER AMES ASSOCIATES retouch those photos. Call Leon Appel at 40 East 49 St., New York, MU 8-2340.

WOOD DUCK.

Duck (dŭk), *n.* [AS. *duce*.] Any of various swimming birds (family Antidae) having short neck and legs, and a somewhat depressed body. The *sea ducks*, which chiefly frequent salt water, constitute a subfamily (fuligulinae, the duck family). *v.t.* Don't try to *duck* your printing problems. Take them directly to ASTORIA PRESS, 324 East 24 St., New York, MU 3-8607, printers to the Push Pin Graphic.

Flicker (flĭk' ẽr), *n.* [Perh. imitative.] A woodpecker (*Colaptes Auratus*) of eastern North America, with a black crescent on the breast, a red nape, white rump, and yellow shafts to the tail and wing feathers. Example: See hundreds of type styles in the *flicker* of an eye at PHOTO-LETTERING, Inc., 216 East 45 St., New York, MU 2-2346.

YELLOW-BREASTED CHAT.

STONECHAT.

Chat (chăt), *n.* Any of several oscine birds so called from their notes, esp. of the genus *Saxicola*, including the European *stonechat* and *whinchat* (see these terms), and in America the genus *Icteria*, which includes the yellow-breasted chat (*I.V. virens*) and the Pacific coast long-tailed chat (*I.V. logicauda*). *i.v.* Come in and *chat* with Stuart Q. Hyatt,, representing Seymour Chwast, Milton Glaser and Isadore Seltzer of PUSH PIN STUDIOS, 114 East 31 St., New York, LE 2-9247.

113

HOW TO BUILD A BASIC KITE

You will need two thin sticks or dowel rods, a large piece of paper, strong string or fishing cord, and glue or paste. Make cross stick shorter than upright, glue at ⅓-length of upright. Reinforce by winding string around joint Ⓐ. Cut notches in the ends of the sticks and fit with string around the frame, winding extra string around each notch for strength Ⓑ. Lay kite frame on paper, which should be large enough for edges to overlap the string outline. Cut to shape of kite, fold edges over string and paste down securely Ⓒ. To make bridle, measure a length of string equal to the two short sides of the kite, and tie it across the exposed crosspiece; this should be slack Ⓓ. Measure a length of string equal to the upright, allowing a little extra to meet the slack of the cross string Ⓔ. Tie bridle strings together with another string at the point where they cross, and attach long kite line at same point Ⓕ. Then take a length of string for the tail, tie paper or cloth bows on it, and attach to bottom of the upright Ⓖ. When the tail is the proper weight, it will keep the kite from diving or falling.

FOLLIES

NUMBER

46

1964

A friend told Glaser and his wife about an odd performer appearing at a seedy nightclub in Greenwich Village. His name was Tiny Tim. Glaser asked him if he would record some songs for an issue on the Follies and took him to a recording studio for half an hour, where they made a floppy record (inserted into the *Graphic*). It was the first time this soon-to-be pop star had ever recorded. Glaser then did a series whereby he experimented with dot screens overlapping the drawings.

114

necessary to enjoy its delights and with an escort who was rich, handsome, and her husband.

|T|hey must both have tried to recapture the love or infatuation, call it what you will, they had felt for one another at their first meeting. After a dinner at which she did little more than toy with her food and drink an abundance of champagne she left for a tour of Montmartre, fiercely gay, singing, drinking as if she had but one night to live. As dawn was breaking over the Sacre Coeur basilica, which would be filled with worshipers in a scant few hours, Olive returned to their apartment in the Ritz. Her nerves frayed from her night of excitement and her despair, she recklessly, and probably mistaking them for sleeping medicine, poured into her slim hand a number of bichloride tablets. Filling a glass from the silver-plated faucet, she popped them into her mouth. They didn't bring the sleep she craved or the oblivion she probably wanted more than anything else in the world at that moment; they brought instead an agony not obliterated until her death four days later. A doctor from the American Hospital in Neuilly was hastily summoned by Jack Pickford when he heard Olive's screams and found her on the bathroom floor. With a McKees Rocks outlook on life, Olive said to the doctor merely: "Well, doctor, Paris has got me."

There was a time when meadow, grove, and stream, the earth, and every common sight, to me did seem

Apparelled in celestial light, the glory and the freshness of a dream.

Glaser was always playing with several conceptual ideas at once. These images of a bouncing ball change page-for-page in flipbook fashion, rendered as a mosaicked puzzle for textural purposes. Push Pin members imagined famous and notorious people as children.

116

It is not now as it hath been of yore; turn wheresoe'er I may,

By night or day, the things which I have seen I now can see no more. *William Wordsworth*

Adam and Eve in the garden
Studying the beauty of nature;
The devil jumped out of a Brussel sprout
And hit Eve in the eye with a tater.
Girl, 10, Oxford

Good King Wenceslas
Knocked a bobby senseless,
Right in the middle of
Marks and Spencer's.
Girl, 12, Swansea

Queenie, Queenie Caroline,
Dipped her hair in turpentine;
Turpentine to make it shine,
Queenie, Queenie Caroline.
Girl, 9, Amnesley

Mr. Ross, he thinks he's boss,
Because he's the owner of the H. P. Sauce.
Girl, 12, Aberdeen

Julius Caesar,
The Roman geezer,
Squashed his wife with a
lemon squeezer.
Boy, 9, Birmingham

Mary Jane went to Spain
In a chocolate aeroplane;
The door fell in and she fell out
And landed on a chimney spout.
Girl, 10, Penrith

Matthew, Mark, Luke and John,
Went to bed with their trousers on.
Mark cried out in the middle of the night,
Oh, my trousers are too tight!
Boy, 11, London

In fourteen hundred and ninety-two
Columbus sailed the ocean blue;
He lost his yacht, the clumsy clot,
That was a good one, was it not?
Girl, 13, Aberdeen

Masculine, Feminine, Neuter,
I went for a ride on my scooter,
I bumped into the Queen
And said, Sorry old bean,
I forgot to toot-toot on my tooter.
Boy, 9, Hindhead

A
BOY
OF
EGYPT

He was convinced that the world ended to the right of him with the canal, which was only a few paces away from where he stood . . . and why not? For he could not appreciate the width of this canal, nor could he reckon that this expanse was so narrow that any active youth could jump from one bank to the other. Nor could he imagine that there was human, animal and vegetable life on the other side of the canal just as much as there was on his side; nor could he calculate that a grown man could wade across this canal in flood without the water reaching up to his armpits; nor did he conjecture that from time to time there was no water in it. Then it would become a long ditch in which boys played and searched in the soft mud for such little fishes as had been left behind, and so had died when the water had been cut off.

None of these things did he ponder, and only

WAR
GAMES
FOR
KIDS

There has been a "dramatic upsurge in the popularity of war gaming," according to a current how-to-do-it called "How To Play War Games in Miniature." A new board game called "Risk" is a product of Parker Brothers, Inc., manufacturer of "Monopoly," the real-estate trading game and best-seller since 1935. "Risk" is a game of world conquest in which the players range themselves around a somewhat distorted map of the world (China has dwindled to about the size of Australia, and Russia has ceased to exist altogether). By casting dice, drawing cards and so advancing or withdrawing armies, the players strive to subjugate the world. The instruction booklet declares the object of the game is "to occupy every territory on the board, and in so doing, eliminate the other players."

Creative Playthings, Inc., is offering a "family game" called "Diplomacy" in which the progress of armies across a map of the world is assisted by "secret plotting" and "rumor spreading." The Milton Bradley Company's entry is called "Stratego." A key role is played by assassination. ("Even the 'Marshal', the highest-ranking piece, has a weakness in that the lowly 'Spy' can remove him from the game.") The instructions insist, "Stratego . . . is not a war game," then go on to describe "bombs which blow up and remove any attacking piece."

The Avalon Hill Company's "Tactics II" is a "full-scale war game." Players are urged to unleash a nuclear holocaust, with atomic and hy-

drogen bombs and a choice of sophisticated delivery systems. According to the rules, artillery can shoot atomic (fission) bombs a distance of four squares, destroying all personnel and structures on the square they land on; rockets may be used to dispatch a hydrogen (fusion) weapon a distance of seven squares, devastating 16 squares where they fall; and ICBM's can deliver a thermonuclear warhead "the full length and width of the map-board," coming very close to achieving in one fell swoop the object of the game, which is "to eliminate all opponents."

In the Milton Bradley Company's "Summit — The Top-Level Game of Global Strategy," exchange of nuclear missiles is high-mindedly excluded, and the instructions merely encourage the players to exchange threats ("use 'threats' of military strength as weapons for domination, or retaliation to others' 'threats' ").

"Combat!", manufactured by the Ideal Toy Corporation, has four-color illustrations of battle action, to get players into the fighting spirit, and such hotsip-directions as: "A player landing on a space occupied by any opponent must yell COMBAT!" "Combat" is adapted to the weekly ABC-TV war-story program of the same name, and thus provides an opportunity to re-experience each televised "Combat!" over and over.

Some new games, like "Gettysburg," "Waterloo" and "Afrika Korps," are advertised as history lessons. The Avalon Hill Company's "Afrika Korps" begins with a token representation of the war in North Africa as it was "on the night of March 31, 1941 [when] Rommel launched the first of many brilliant offensives that earned him the famed title —'The Desert Fox'." The game ends in August,

TEENS AND BIKERS ON CARS

NUMBER 48

1965

For this homage to car songs, Chwast teamed up with photographer Alan Vogel to interpret such classics as "Teen Angel," "Hot Rod USA," and others. The issue also introduced Chwast and Glaser's shaded and shadowed novelty lettering.

Hot Rod U. S. A.

Don't you know
They're shuttin' 'em down
In ev'ry town
In the U. S. A.
They're drivin' old woodies up in Salt Lake City
Hot Rod, U. S. A.
And strippin' 'em down, now, they sure look pretty
Hot Rod U. S. A.
They're racing all over, even out on the Coast, now
Give it a try, you're gonna dig it the most, now
Hot Rod U. S. A.
They're building deuce coupes out in Old Cincinnati,
Hot Rod, U. S. A.
Pulling out flat-heads, and dropping in Caddies,
They're breaking track records out in Abilene,
Burnin' up the quarter mile in New Orleans
Hot Rod U. S. A.
Summer's almost here, we'll have some fun, fun, fun now
Hot Rod U. S. A.
Jump in your car, and take a trophy run now,
Hot Rod, U. S. A.
The whole thing started back in sixty-three
With Jan and Dean, the Beach Boys and me
Hot Rod U. S. A.
Winding out in old L. A. now
Run 'em thru' to Frisco Bay now
Shut 'em down in Philly, P. A. now,
All around, you can hear 'em say
They're shuttin' 'em down
In ev'ry town in the U. S. A.

Photographs Allen Vogel

USED
STOP
EXTRA

119

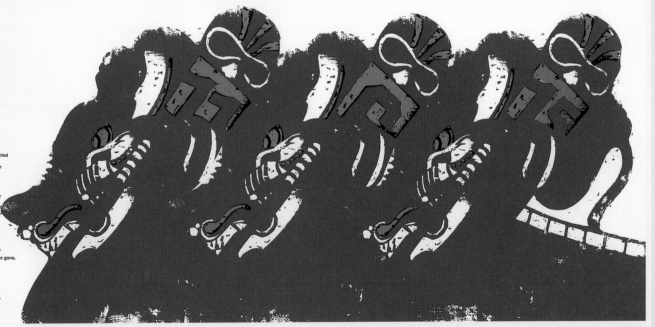

Teen Angel

That fateful night the car was stalled
Upon the railroad track
I pulled you out and we were safe
But you went running back.
TEEN ANGEL, can you hear me
TEEN ANGEL, can you see me
Are you somewhere up above
And am I still your own true love?
What was it you were looking for
That took your life that night
They said they found my
    high school ring
Clutched in your fingers tight.
TEEN ANGEL, can you hear me
TEEN ANGEL, can you see me
Are you somewhere up above
And am I still your own true love?
Just sweet sixteen and now you're gone,
They've taken you away
I'll never kiss your lips again,
They buried you today.
TEEN ANGEL, can you hear me
TEEN ANGEL, can you see me
Are you somewhere up above
And am I still your own true love?
TEEN ANGEL, TEEN ANGEL,
Answer me, please . . .

THE
MEANING OF
DREAMS

NUMBER
49

1965

The format for this "inspiring guide" was influenced by vintage fortune-telling and magic-trick booklets usually sold in the back of comics. The text came from one such booklet. The deco motif was Chwast's signature "Roxie Style." The illustrations were by Glaser, Chwast, and James McMullan.

THE WAY TO BIGGER AND BETTER VISIONS

A MEDIUM OF YOUR OWN

Voodoo from A to Z

Up-to-date Book of Revelations

A Useful and Inspiring Guide
to the Mysterious Wisdom of the Unconscious

NUMBER 49

Push Pin Graphic.

DREAM BOOK

ANIMALS.   5

If a lover dreams of
various animals it signifies
that he will soon wed.

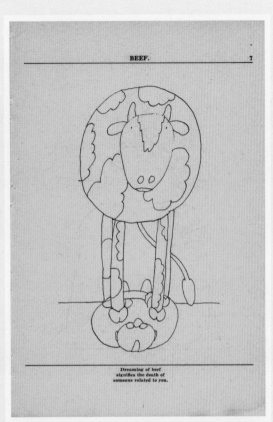

BEEF.   7

Dreaming of beef
signifies the death of
someone related to you.

8   BREAST.

To dream of
having a large breast
denotes losing a mate.

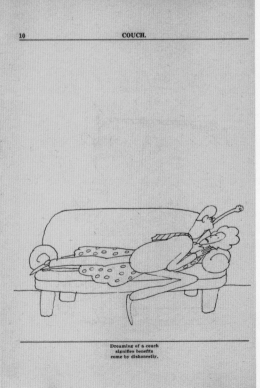

10   COUCH.

Dreaming of a couch
signifies benefits
come by dishonestly.

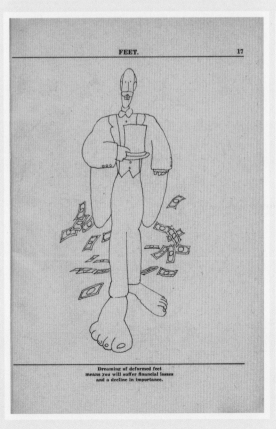

FEET.   17

Dreaming of deformed feet
means you will suffer financial losses
and a decline in importance.

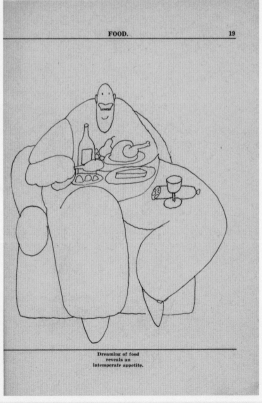

FOOD.   19

Dreaming of food
reveals an
intemperate appetite.

ICE. 23

To dream of ice
signifies endurance and mastery
of your environment.

24 JOCKEY.

To dream of a jockey
foretells good
luck to a gambling man.

26 KING.

To dream of being
a king foretells travelling
to strange climes.

28 LEOPARD.

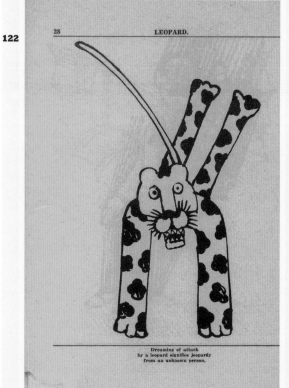

Dreaming of attack
by a leopard signifies jeopardy
from an unknown person.

LION. 29

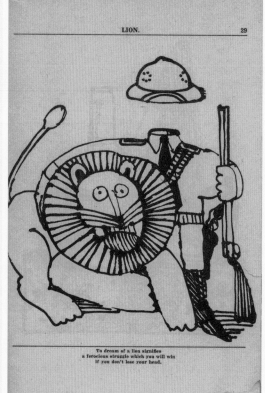

To dream of a lion signifies
a ferocious struggle which you will win
if you don't lose your head.

NOISE. 33

Dreaming of noise
denotes that someone will give you
something you do not want.

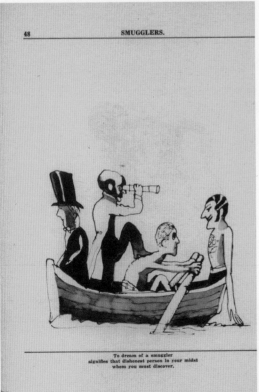

To ride signifies that you
will indulge your pleasures
at the expense of your reputation.

Hearing a rooster
denotes that you are the subject
of malicious gossip.

Dreaming of a seamstress
means happiness for you. Dreaming of sewing
yourself signifies a brief problem.

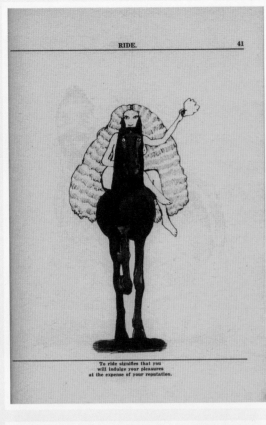

To dream of a smuggler
signifies that dishonest person in your midst
whom you must discover.

Riding in a taxicab
signifies a brief but happy
respite.

Dreaming of undressing
before other people indicates that you
are living a loose life.

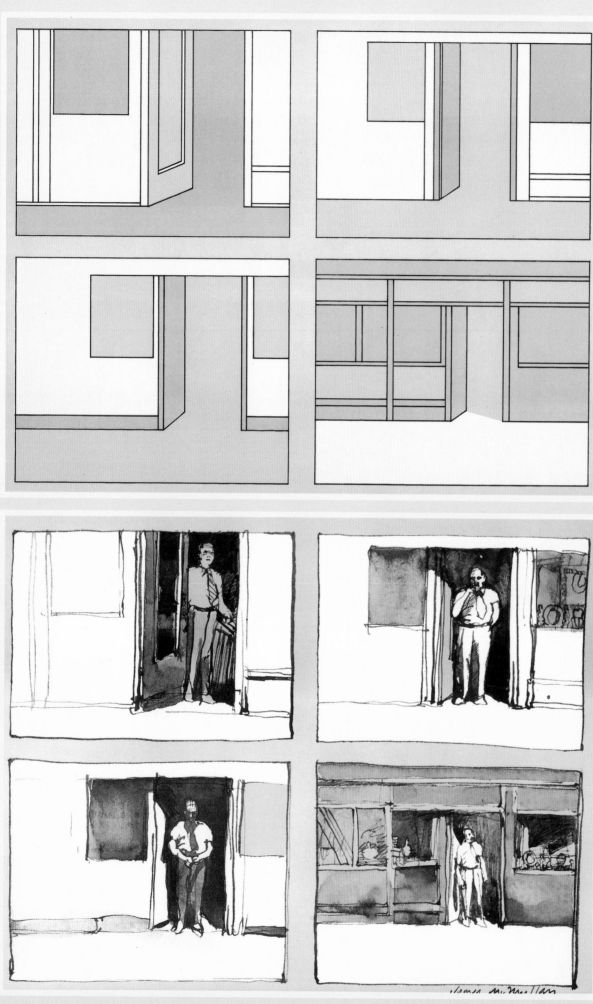

McMullan's illustrations were inspired by Jane Jacobs's "The Uses of Sidewalks: Contact" from *The Death and Life of Great American Cities*, an essay that promoted the virtues of life in urban environs.

The uses of sidewalks: contact

Reformers have long observed city people loitering on busy corners, hanging around in candy stores and bars and drinking soda pop on stoops, and have passed a judgment, the gist of which is: "This is deplorable! If these people had decent homes and a more private or bosky outdoor place, they wouldn't be on the street!"

This judgment represents a profound misunderstanding of cities. It makes no more sense than to drop in at a testimonial banquet in a hotel and conclude that if these people had wives who could cook, they would give their parties at home.

The point of both the testimonial banquet and the social life of city sidewalks is precisely that they are public. They bring together people who do not know each other in an intimate, private social fashion and in most cases do not care to know each other in that fashion.

Nobody can keep open house in a great city. Nobody wants to. And yet if interesting, useful and significant contacts among the people of cities are confined to acquaintanceships suitable for private life, the city becomes stultified. Cities are full of people with whom, from your viewpoint, or mine, or any other individual's, a certain degree of contact is useful or enjoyable; but you do not want them in your hair. And they do not want you in theirs either.

In speaking about city sidewalk safety, I mentioned how necessary it is that there should be, in the brains behind the eyes on the street, an almost unconscious assumption of general street support when the chips are down—when a citizen has to choose, for instance, whether he will take responsibility, or abdicate it, in combating barbarism or protecting strangers. There is a short word for this assumption of support: trust. The trust of a city street is formed over time from many, many little

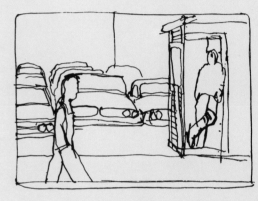

time to time I would make my pickups.* As a result of engaging in this messenger work, I have since become automatically the sidewalk public character on petition strategy. Before long, for instance, Mr. Fox at the liquor store was consulting me, as he wrapped up my bottle, on how we could get the city to remove a long abandoned and dangerous eyesore, a closed-up comfort station near his corner. If I would undertake to compose the petitions and find the effective way of presenting them to City Hall, he proposed, he and his partners would undertake to have them printed, circulated and picked up. Soon the stores round about had comfort station removal petitions. Our street by now has many public experts on petition tactics, including the children.

Not only do public characters spread the news and learn the news at retail, so to speak. They connect with each other and thus spread word wholesale, in effect.

A sidewalk life, so far as I can observe, arises out of no mysterious qualities or talents for it in this or that type of population. It arises only where the concrete, tangible facilities it requires are present. These happen to be the same facilities, in the same abundance and ubiquity, that are required for cultivating sidewalk safety. If they are absent, public sidewalk contacts are absent too.

The well-off have many ways of assuaging needs for which poorer people may depend much on sidewalk life—from hearing of jobs to being recognized by the headwaiter. But nevertheless, many of the rich or near-rich in cities appear to appreciate sidewalk life as much as anybody. At any rate, they pay enormous rents to move into areas with an exuberant and varied sidewalk life. They actually crowd out the middle class and the poor in lively areas like Yorkville or Greenwich Village in New York, or Telegraph Hill just off the North Beach

* This, by the way, is an efficient device, accomplishing with a fraction of the effort what would be a mountainous task door to door. It also makes more public conservation and opinion than door-to-door visits.

streets of San Francisco. They capriciously desert, after only a few decades of fashion at most, the monotonous streets of "quiet residential areas" and leave them to the less fortunate. Talk to residents of Georgetown in the District of Columbia and by the second or third sentence at least you will begin to hear rhapsodies about the charming restaurants, "more good restaurants than in all the rest of the city put together," the uniqueness and friendliness of the stores, the pleasures of running into people when doing errands at the next corner—and nothing but pride over the fact that Georgetown has become a specialty shopping district for its whole metropolitan area. The city area, rich or poor or in between, harmed by an interesting sidewalk life and plentiful sidewalk contacts has yet to be found.

Efficiency of public sidewalk characters declines drastically if too much burden is put upon them. A store, for example, can reach a turnover in its contacts, or potential contacts, which is so large and so superficial that it is socially useless. An example of this can be seen at the candy and newspaper store owned by the housing cooperative of Corlears Hook on New York's Lower East Side. This planned project store replaces perhaps forty superficially similar stores which were wiped out (without compensation to their proprietors) on that project site and the adjoining sites. The place is a mill. Its clerks are so busy making change and screaming ineffectual imprecations at rowdies that they never hear anything except "I want that." This, or utter disinterest, is the usual atmosphere where shopping center planning or repressive zoning artificially contrives commercial monopolies for city neighborhoods. A store like this would fail economically if it had competition. Meantime, although monopoly insures the financial success planned for it, it fails the city socially.

Sidewalk public contact and sidewalk public safety, taken together, bear directly on our country's most serious social problem—segregation and racial discrimination.

I do not mean to imply that a city's planning and

design, or its types of streets and street life, can automatically overcome segregation and discrimination. Too many other kinds of effort are also required to right these injustices.

But I do mean to say that to build and to rebuild big cities whose sidewalks are unsafe and whose people must settle for sharing much or nothing, can make it *much harder* for American cities to overcome discrimination no matter how much effort is expended.

Considering the amount of prejudice and fear that accompany discrimination and bolster it, overcoming residential discrimination is just that much harder if people feel unsafe on their sidewalks anyway. Overcoming residential discrimination comes hard where people have no means of keeping a civilized public life on a basically dignified public footing, and their private lives on a private footing.

To be sure, token model housing integration schemes here and there can be achieved in city areas handicapped by danger and by lack of public life—achieved by applying great effort and settling for abnormal (abnormal for cities) choosiness among new neighbors. This is an evasion of the size of the task and its urgency.

The tolerance, the room for great differences among neighbors—differences that often go far deeper than differences in color—which are possible and normal in intensely urban life, but which are so foreign to suburbs and pseudosuburbs, are possible and normal only when streets of great cities have built-in equipment allowing strangers to dwell in peace together in civilized but essentially dignified and reserved terms.

THE
FILM
PIONEER

NUMBER
51

1967

Glaser had become interested in pioneer filmmaker Georges Méliès after seeing several films in Paris at the Cinémathêque during the 1950s. This issue reflected his continued fascination with cinema.

HOMAGE TO GEORGES MÉLIÈS

G. MELIES
STAR ★ FILM
PARIS

126

movies were like life
life was like a dream
movies were like the theatre of life and dreams
thus for Méliès
everything was equal and inter-changeable
allergy . . . allegory
telescope . . . microscope
light . . . delight
cinder . . . cinderella
canteloupe . . . envelope
focus . . . and focus hocus.

Méliès was the first manufacturer of a dream factory.
The after-image left from seeing his films
reminds me always of distant hotels filled
with endless rooms and phantoms
a flickering chronicle of men and women
who are traveling in another land.

In his movie factory he stuffed 1200 films into 18 years
he created the first movie studio in the world
he created the first movie spectacles
building elaborate sets, elaborate machinery to
produce his illusions
he built his own camera
developed his own film
he was painter, draughtsman, technician, inventor,
magician, actor, metaphysician, showman
he was an image-alchemist, working in the two dimensions of
light and shadow
reality-surreality
time and its displacement
motion and stopping motion

a man whose visions wave like a flag
in the early history of motion pictures.

Hooray for Georges Méliès

hooray for all magic movies
that in their mystery cast spells and move
the furniture of the mind about

that in their spectacle and prophecy
give us a poet's leverage to lift us to
a new position
that will get us to the fantastic, to visual rites
of proto-story, myth, discovery
and insight.

There is very little magic left in movies.
The spectacles of the mind's eye that began
with Georges Méliès
have been replaced with commercial glass.

Georges Méliès was instinctively right
life is illusional
movies illustrate this.

2

GEORGE
MÉLIÈS
THE
JULES
VERNE
OF THE
CINEMA
BY
MERRITT
CRAWFORD
CINEMA
THE
MAGAZINE
OF
PHOTOPLAY
OCTOBER
1930

The career of Georges Méliès, aptly described by his countrymen in years past as "le Jules Verne du Cinema," forms an epic in the history of the motion picture, in many respects more amazing, and certainly more tragical than any of the masterpieces of dramatic and fantastic cinematography that for nearly two decades made the name of Méliès and of his productions, Star Films pre-eminent in two hemispheres, wherever motion pictures were shown.

Méliès may be said to have been the first man who really had a true conception of the motion picture as

THREE POSTERS

NUMBER
52

1967

Push Pin was caught up with, and helped influence, the colorful psychedelic fashions of the late sixties. This issue consisted of three faux "advertising" posters with slogans on the front and texts on the verso side. Chwast, Glaser, and McMullan interpreted the drug-induced style in their own ways. Chwast's devilish image illustrated Canto XVIII of Dante's *Inferno*.

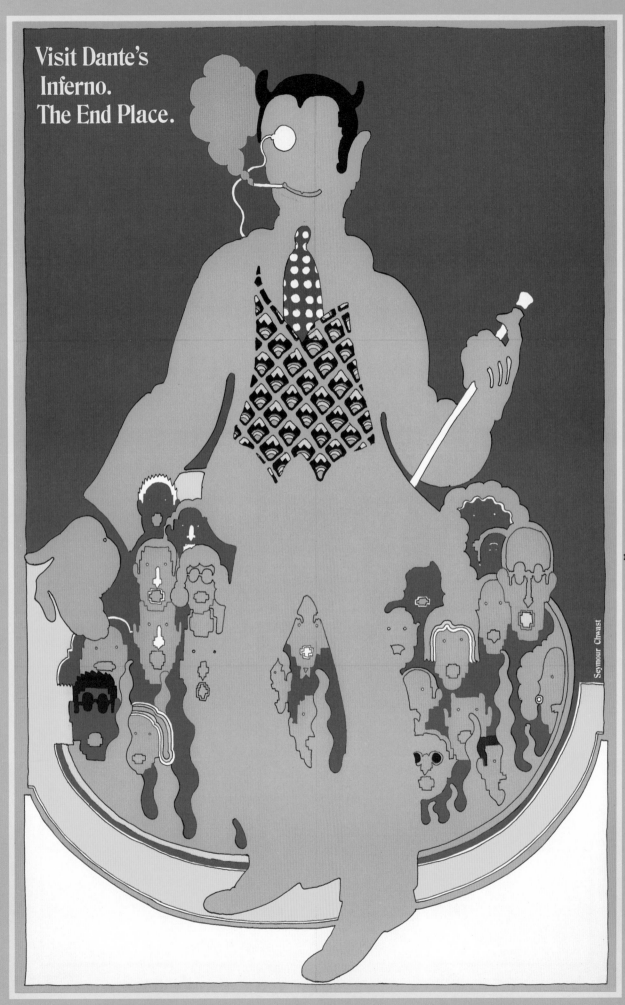

Chew, Chew, Baby

NUTRITION AND HEALTH

NUMBER

53

1967

To illustrate an excerpt from "The Nuts Among the Berries" by Ronald M. Deutsch, about odd eating habits, Chwast forsook his raw woodcut style for a more cooked and refined outline method filled with flat color, which ultimately became one of his distinctive editorial methods.

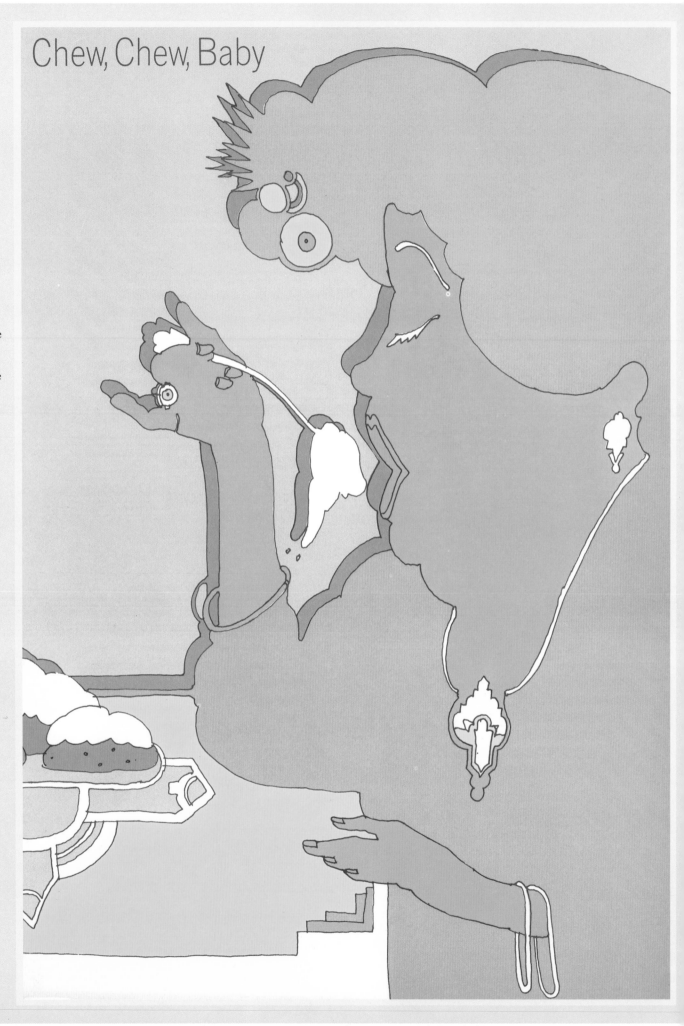

In the days of Horace Fletcher's ascendancy
there was rather a bad pun current to the
effect that whatever the scientific value
of his ideas, they certainly had teeth in them.
The raillery is as simple and direct
as Fletcher's philosophy itself.
For Horace Fletcher stands as the high priest
of mastication, of ideas about eating so clear
and so easy to understand that they fastened
firmly in the minds of millions.
Make no mistake, unlike many of his
colleagues in the health-through-eating field,
Fletcher at one point drew to him some
of the soundest and most influential
public-health support of his time, which was
the turn of the century. Many a distinguished
physician and physiologist, finding germs of
truth in Fletcher's battle cry, misconstruing
the evidence of their own senses and
experiments, flocked to his banner.
He was given earnest and effective backing
by elements from Yale University to the
Ladies' Home Journal. His reputation and
influence were international.
In 1909, for example, the *Ladies' Home
Journal* crowned its September issue with an
article by Fletcher, explaining his thinking,
and the *Journal* editors introduced it thus:
"Fletcherism has become a fact. Ten years
ago it was laughed at. Today the most
famous men of science indorse it and teach
its principles. Scientific leaders at
Cambridge University; University of Turin,
Italy; University of Berne, Switzerland;
Université de la Sorbonne, France; the
Universities of Berlin, Brussels and
St. Petersburg . . . as well as Harvard, Yale
and Johns Hopkins . . . all indorse Fletcherism
and teach its principles. The honorary degree
of M.A. has been conferred upon him
at Dartmouth. Professor William James
of Harvard and Professors Fisher and
Chittenden, of Yale, have indorsed his
principles. Chautauqua made him its lecturer
on Vital Economics. It has been established
that more than 200,000 families in America
are living according to Fletcherism.
It is no longer a question of doubt that of all
the many current movements for sane
eating and living, Mr. Fletcher and his
principles have emerged at the very front."
These are pretty strong words, and the
Ladies' Home Journal was not entirely alone
in using them. Virtually every important
magazine of the time took note of Horace
Fletcher and ended, though sometimes
grudgingly, by conceding that he had
something. It is easy to believe that the *Journal*
reader, studying this issue and the subsequent
one, rose before her family with that bright
cheery look with which the American *mater
familias* presents new ideas to her brood
and enunciated, "Let us Fletcherize."

Push Pin Graphic

Number 53 ©1967 The Push Pin Studios, Inc.
207 East 32nd Street, New York 10016.
Subscription: $3.50 six issues. Outside U.S. $5.00.

SOUTHERN
JUSTICE

NUMBER

54

1967

Chwast supported the civil rights
movement and its young martyrs.
For this issue (see insert, page 16)
he published songs and images of the
Old South juxtaposed as a counterpoint
to photographs of activists (plus Emmitt
Louis Till, an innocent teenager)
killed by white racists. The entire issue
was a bold commentary on the doctrine
of "separate but equal" that prefigured
the landmark civil rights legislation
enacted during Lyndon B. Johnson's
administration. Push Pin's members
supported (and worked for) civil rights,
yet this unique and poignant *Graphic*
was one of the rare political statements
made by a graphic design studio
at that time.

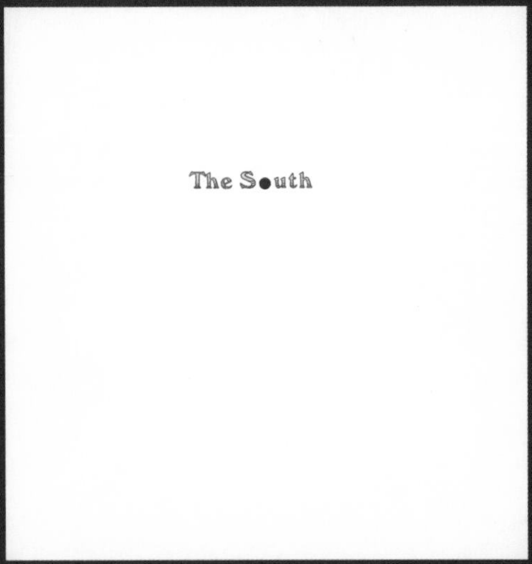

The South

twin er
and shame as
failure are the
s anger, and no
a, such indirect
ill hatred.
ay- The struggl
ind is not betweer
ced country and thos
un- merely a neurotic
ing outward of a d
struggle, a strug
ns' gratitude ar
try and their
able moral o
th success

p. 8

VIOLENCE AND THE AMERICAN DREAM

NUMBER

55

1969

This collage involved torn pages with actual die-cuts and photographs of tears so that one wouldn't know if something has a real tear or a photographic one— Glaser has always been interested in illusion as some of his later work suggests. To add to the complexity, he reprinted the missing parts of the text (caused by the die-cuts) on translucent vellum cover wrap so that the reader could replace the missing parts and read the entire text.

Violence and the American Dream

u or demotion
.t our dispensabil-
among all people we
.ath the most.
.ourse fear death. What is
.ut the American fear is our
attempt to evade and dis-
Success and guilt are still fuse
country, and guilt always le
.ar of death. Moreover, a peo
.sy supplying the banquet of
.nere is little time to dine
scarcely enjoy the pass'
There is nothing stran

p. 6

nate and th
which to
stuff of
Th
ste
r

r.
by .
rever.
ense   only to
uman   an actual i
e that   naive to ass
thers.   and justice a
ary is   Albert Szer
most   "Science, B
font   tions," has a
o;   "In their
g   mals ha
            claws
            Th
p. 10

I have chosen the rather threadbare, slightly tired title, "Violence and the American Dream," in the hope that it might arouse in the reader something of the fatigue, the nervous exhaustion hovering between despair and rage that seems to afflict America. We are a tense and very tired people, and one senses a fearful expectancy in the air, as if people were listening to inner voices, faint premonitions of savage release. The entire country seems to be engaged in silent dialogue. And given the forces tearing at this country, we should hardly have expected it to be otherwise.

There are times, and this is one, when civilization is too stern and indiscriminate in its punishment, when even cherry orchards meet the axe of change, when society demands that man relinquish too much of his baser self, when merely to keep ahead of the ravages of change requires a strength, patience, courage and idealism that tries the best of men and is beyond most, when self-pity stalks the man and anger is used to keep down and disguise tears of frustration. At such times, society is like the sea invading a sand castle at high tide; it threatens to overwhelm the individual's defenses and to obliterate his frail dreams. At such times, when the public

life impinges too heavily on the private one, people come to hate civilization.

Torn between the conflicting demands of moral idealism and personal ambition, Americans are beginning to hate the country that demands a difficult choice. Could we have hoped for anything else? A society that will not stand still long enough for a man to see his sunflower seed go to flower; that despite its great idealism, so glorifies youth, beauty and success that it constantly reproaches a man for failing and growing old; that incessantly reminds him in advertisement after advertisement that his best is not good enough— such a society can hardly hope to command great love and that deep rooted commitment to her well-being that transcends cynicism and shallow self-interest. Only self-satisfaction, a very shabby substitute for contentment, is possible in such a society; only greed and rapacity masquerading as public service can thrive in such a soil. And to further both, we have refined Orwellian newspeak until it is the language of the land.

Thus we have a governor who in vetoing a bill permitting open primaries, mouths inanities to the effect that such a bill adds "nothing to the democratic process. It is, in fact, an infringement

on the rights of certain individuals." This behavior passes for leadership in the state of California. And we have industries which, in their greed for quick profits and easy disposal of wastes, so pollute the rivers and lakes of this country that Max Edwards, an assistant Secretary of the Interior, was forced to warn us that if something is not done we will soon have to drink water someone else flushed down the drain.

People behaving in such insidious ways do not love this country; they love an abstraction, a set of platitudes, a charade. They have succumbed to the embittering and morally corrupting need to succeed; and having climbed the ladder of success, they now want to kick it down. And yet these are the very people who so trumpet patriotism that many good and decent men can scarcely bring themselves to declare their love of country. When scoundrels take refuge in patriotism, sensitive men slink away in shame.

What is so frightening about this "new patriotism," is not that "the lady doth protest too much"; it is that outpourings of this sort mask an inner dissolution, just as they did in Germany forty years ago. The peculiar kind of "new patriotism" being manifested by people in the

135

1

to material goods is bound to breed massive insecurity in its people. As people acquire new debts and come to depend on affluence and success for more and more of their happiness, they develop a commensurate sense of helplessness and anxiety. They are no longer masters of their own destiny, no longer free men, but slaves to circumstance and to their own clownish material lusts.

This is a nation divided with itself, humane and compassionate but with an underlying barbarism and ferocity—a ferocity which is the result of emotional exhaustion and frustration. A society which exalts competition over cooperation, which measures people's worth by their productivity instead of by their humanity, which believes that a fat bank account is a greater blessing to the world than a slender book of poems —such a society demands so much creative and emotional self-sacrifice from its citizens that it breeds a murderous and diffuse rage, a rage waiting only for another person's claim to justice in order to explode. A country surely has lost its way when for the sake of increasing the Gross National Product and creating demand, it is willing

in advertisement after advertisement to create such helpless rage and terror. A country which glorifies the creation of frustration in its citizens is suffering from an unconscious death wish. For one of the oldest psychological equations is that frustration breeds aggression. The violence in this country is the inevitable product of artificially created frustrations, frustrations which are unrecognizable, unacceptable and unappeasable.

The central paradox in America today is that it is proper, even desirable to be dissatisfied with one's drapes, one's car, even one's mate, but it is not acceptable, even traitorous, to be unhappy with the moral condition of one's country. It is apparently acceptable, even expected, that one's heart will ache at being deprived of a new plaything, but let one feel sick at heart and outraged at the profligacy, misplaced priorities and dishonesty of this country, at its callous indifference toward the poor, at its brutality toward its minorities, and one is called a weeper or a dissenter. There is something radically wrong with a country that is more concerned with decor than with human dignity, that dismisses unselfish con-

cern as do-goodism and moral men kooks or crypto-commies. When mo action becomes a reproach to men, g and selfishness have reached an in erable and explosive level.

A society which so little prepares citizens for failure while almost ins ing a sense of it by the fierceness of competition, is like our governm sending marines into the battle to H without knowing the difference betwe outgoing and incoming mortars — it defective in a fundamental way and w not long command the allegiance of people. These Czechoslo otions of im tence e floating fea a result of ima ined with t it will breeding ground he also kn attach society can long surv would s gas cha and unacknowledg conte e terror s tell ms from ou going on in this coun W uccess and our those who love th things. Thoreau e who hate it—that survival sometime projection, a mirr people can do wi eper, more person earned this elemen le between Ame ica people need s d deep love for th coun o, but it does hatred for her har implac only thing emands. For she d mands bo aterial pr and morality. T drama being acted out in the stree

Each spread here was a study in good and evil. Glaser says the two forms were very similar but had a slight shift that "made you pay attention." Illustrations included those of Fatty Arbuckle (Chwast, opposite bottom), Aimee Semple McPherson (Hedda Johnson, top), Mata Hari (Barry Zaid, opposite top), and François de Sade (Glaser, bottom).

138

GOOD & BAD

Aimee Semple McPherson

She began her career as an evangelist and healer with her first marriage at seventeen, to a Pentecostal preacher. Aimee Semple McPherson made the rounds of religious circuits in Canada and America's backwoods, and even went to China and Australia to save souls. In 1921 she arrived in Los Angeles, where combining her skills in theater and her sincere belief in her divine powers, she presented incredible tableaux illustrating her sermons. Her Angelus Temple was complete with crystal doors, an enormous dome, huge stage and a seating capacity of over 5,000. It was built by the millions who revered and adored her and considered her the nation's number one Hellseeker.

Aimee Semple McPherson

On May 18, 1926 Aimee disappeared from a lonely beach in a shroud of mystery. Many thought that she'd drowned and a great deal of money was raised for her memorial fund and never returned; even after she turned up on June 27th with an extraordinary tale of kidnapping and torture. There seemed to be evidence that she'd been on an amorous spree and that a criminal hoax had been perpetrated. A trial ensued, but ended abruptly when the District Attorney unexplainedly moved for her acquittal. All told, she'd been involved in fifty five law suits, many connected with tax evasion charges. After the trial her life slipped into oblivion and she died in an obscure hotel room, alone.

Hedda Johnson

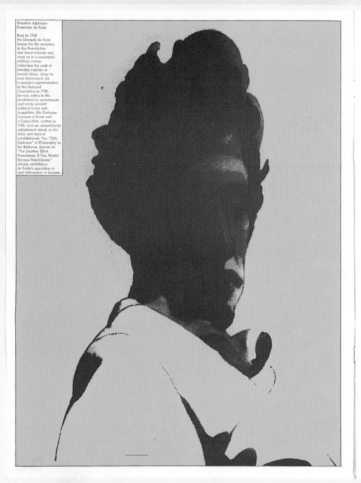

Donatien Alphonse François de Sade

Born in 1740 the Marquis de Sade began his life studying in the Benedictine and Jesuit schools and went on to a successful military career, achieving the rank of cavalry captain at twenty three, when he was discharged. As a people's representative to the National Convention in 1790, he was active in the revolutionary government and wrote several political tracts and pamphlets. His Dialogue between a Priest and a Dying Man, written in 1782, was an astonishingly enlightened attack on the deity and clerical establishment. The "Fifth Dialogue" of Philosophy in the Bedroom, known as "Yet Another Effort, Frenchmen, If You Would Become Republicans" clearly symbolizes de Sade's opposition to and abhorrence of fascism.

Donatien Alphonse François de Sade

On October 29, 1763, five months after his marriage, de Sade is sent to prison for the first time. He is charged with committing excesses in a brothel which he frequented. He is released in a few months but continues to be involved in various scandals and incidents with other women. In 1768 he is accused of flogging and, in general, abusing a young pastry cook's assistant and again goes to prison briefly. In 1772 he is found guilty of poisoning and sodomy and sentenced to death. He escapes and in June of 1778 a High Court nullifies the sentence on insufficient evidence but orders new investigations of allegations of perjurary and libertinage. De Sade's imprisonment and release continued until 1801 when he was finally incarcerated for the rest of his life. He died in 1814 at Charenton Prison.

Milton Glaser

Margaretha Geertruida Zelle (Mata Hari)

Born in 1876, the daughter of a middle class Dutch family in Leeuwarden, Holland, Margaretha Geertruida Zelle did not seem destined for the exotic life she led. After her marriage to Major John MacLeod in 1895, she lived in Java where he was stationed and was generally considered a good wife and mother. Seven years later they were back in Holland and legally separated. In 1905 Margaretha performed at the private salon of Mme. Kireievsky, a prominent singer, and was an instant success. It was at this time that she changed her name to Mata Hari, which is Malay for "eye of the day." She was praised for her authenticity and knowledge of oriental dancing and greatly admired. Among her followers were Massenet and Puccini; and her performance of a ballet in the third act of Massenet's opera Le Roi de Lahore in 1906 established Mata Hari as a serious artist.

Margaretha Geertruida Zelle (Mata Hari)

During divorce proceedings against her in 1906 Mata Hari lost custody of her daughter Non and was declared an unfit mother. Later that year she became the mistress of Lieutenant Kiepert, a German officer. He was one of many military lovers with whom she was involved over the next ten years. By the time war broke out in Europe, Mata Hari's funds were very low, so that early in 1916 when Captain Ladoux, Chief of the French Intelligence Service asked her to help France, she agreed, but insisted on being paid for her services. Captain von Kalle, Chief of German Intelligence in Madrid, was a very close associate of hers and at her subsequent trial in Paris it was brought out that their frequent meetings resulted in Germany paying her 20,000 francs for services rendered. She was found guilty of espionage against France and executed at Vincennes, October 15, 1917.

Barry Zaid

Roscoe (Fatty) Arbuckle

Typical of many of the popular comics in the early 1900's, "Fatty" Arbuckle was also larger and more colorful than life. His obesity, which amounted to 350 pounds, made his extreme agility and dexterity hilariously funny. He was an appealing innocent, always running into misfortune but winning the heroine in the end. The various roles he portrayed, such as the Keystone cop, the bumbling country boy, and the bottom sized lady, were considered the essence of good clean Mack Sennett slapstick and brought great joy to millions of Americans.

Roscoe (Fatty) Arbuckle

On September 5, 1921, in the St. Francis Hotel in San Francisco, a twenty three year old starlet named Virginia Rappe moaned the words, "I'm dying, I'm dying," and ended Fatty Arbuckle's career. She died four days later of peritonitis following a rupture of the bladder and Fatty Arbuckle stood accused of manslaughter. According to several witnesses who were members of Arbuckle's party, he and Miss Rappe were alone together for half an hour in a locked room. They further testified that when Arbuckle emerged he was drunk and in a bathrobe. The girl was naked and in pain, her clothes in shreds. After two mistrials due to hung juries, Fatty was acquitted by a third jury; but his career was already wrecked by public opinion and a professional blacklisting.

Seymour Chwast

Master & Dog

WHY PEOPLE KEEP DOGS

NUMBER
57

1972

Chwast broadened his range of techniques in this issue devoted to canines—from the linear (with color fill) cover to the woodcut bulldog, papier-mâché and watercolor hounds, and monoprint of a blind man and his trusty guide dog. The text by Konrad Lorenz was on the relationship between people and dogs.

ADVERTI

ISEMENTS

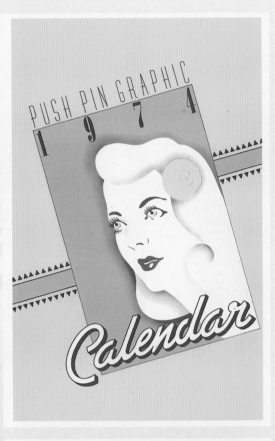

PUSH PIN GRAPHIC
1974
Calendar

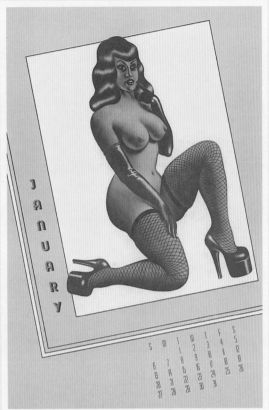

JANUARY

October

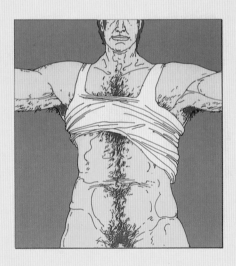

JUNE

SEPTEMBER

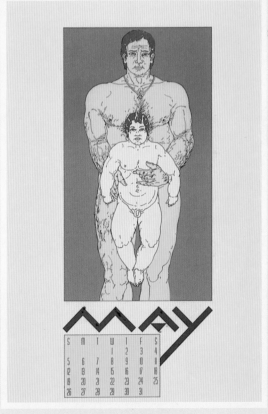

MAY

March

S	M	T	W	T	F	S
					1	2
3	4	5	6	7	8	9
10	11	12	13	14	15	16
17	18	19	20	21	22	23
24/31	25	26	27	28	29	30

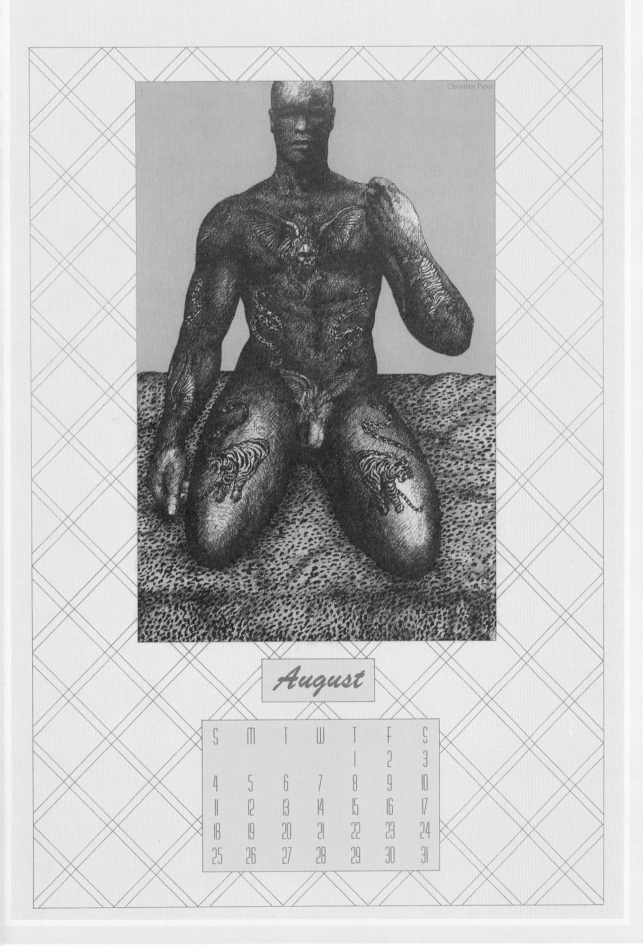

145

LITERARY MASTERS

NUMBER

59

1974

Glaser was a big fan of
Franz Kafka's novels and stories.
"His was a convincing view of the
world that I found compelling."
Philip Roth was also interested in
East European prewar fiction generally
and had written an essay on Kafka in
particular. Glaser had done some
designs for Roth's book jackets through
the years and asked him if he could
republish the Kafka essay in this issue
of the *Push Pin Graphic*.
This is one of Glaser's favorite issues,
in part because the wash drawings
shown in this facsimile, derived from
photographs in his personal collection,
"seem to be fresher and more
spontaneous than much of my work
of this period," he says.

"I always wanted you
to admire my fasting"; or,
looking at Kafka
Philip Roth

To the students
of English 275,
University of
Pennsylvania,
Fall, 1972

1

"I always wanted you to admire my fasting," said the hunger artist. "We do admire it," said the overseer, affably. "But you shouldn't admire it," said the hunger artist. "Well then we don't admire it," said the overseer, "but why shouldn't we admire it?" "Because I have to fast, I can't help it," said the hunger artist. "What a fellow you are," said the overseer, "and why can't you help it?" "Because," said the hunger artist, lifting his head a little and speaking, with his lips pursed, as if for a kiss, right into the overseer's ear, so that no syllable might be lost, "because I couldn't find the food I liked. If I had found it, believe me, I should have made no fuss and stuffed myself like you or anyone else." These were his last words, but in his dimming eyes remained the firm though no longer proud persuasion that he was still continuing to fast.

I am looking, as I write of Kafka, at the photograph taken of him at the age of forty (my age)—it is 1924, as sweet and hopeful a year as he may ever have known as a man, and the year of his death. His face is sharp and skeletal, a burrower's face: pronounced cheekbones made even more conspicuous by the absence of sideburns; the ears shaped and angled on his head like angel wings; an intense, creaturely gaze of startled composure—enormous fears, enormous control; a black towel of Levantine hair pulled close around the skull the only sensuous feature; there is a familiar Jewish flare in the bridge of the nose, the nose itself is long and weighted slightly at the tip—the nose of half the Jewish boys who were my friends in high school. Skulls chiseled like this one were shoveled by the thousands from the ovens; had he lived, his would have been among them, along with the skulls of his three younger sisters. Of course it is no more horrifying to think of Franz Kafka in Auschwitz than to think of anyone in Auschwitz—to paraphrase Tolstoy, it is just horrifying in its own way. But he died too soon for the holocaust. Had he lived, perhaps he would have escaped with his good friend and great advocate Max Brod, who eventually found refuge in Palestine, a citizen of Israel until his death there in 1970. But *Kafka* escaping? It seems unlikely for one so fascinated by entrapment and careers that culminate in anguished death. Still, there is Karl Rossman, his American greenhorn. Having imagined Karl's escape to America and his mixed luck here, could not Kafka have found a way to execute an escape for himself? The New School for Social Research in New York becoming *his* Great Nature Theater of Oklahoma? Or perhaps through the influence of Thomas Mann, a position in the German department at Princeton . . . But then had Kafka lived it is not at all certain that the books of his which Mann celebrated from *his* refuge in New Jersey would ever have been published; eventually Kafka might either have destroyed those manuscripts that he had once bid Max Brod to dispose of at his death, or, at the least, continued to keep them his secret. The Jewish refugee arriving in America in 1938 would not then have been Mann's "religious humorist," but a frail and bookish fifty-five-year-old bachelor, formerly a lawyer for a government insurance firm in Prague, retired on a pension in Berlin at the time of Hitler's rise to power—an author, yes, but of a few eccentric stories, mostly about animals, stories no one in America had ever heard of and only a handful in Europe had read; a homeless K., but without K.'s willfulness and purpose, a homeless Karl, but without Karl's youthful spirit and resilience; just a Jew lucky enough to have escaped with his life, in his possession a suitcase containing some clothes, some family photos, some Prague mementos, and the manuscripts, still unpublished and in pieces, of *Amerika, The Trail, The Castle,* and (stranger things happen) three more fragmented novels, no less remarkable than the bizarre masterworks that he keeps to himself out of Oedipal timidity, perfectionist madness, and insatiable longings for solitude and spiritual purity.

July, 1923: eleven months before he will die in a Vienna sanatorium, Kafka somehow finds the resolve to leave Prague and his father's home for good. Never before has he even remotely succeeded in living apart, independent of his mother, his sisters and his father, nor has he been a writer other than in those few hours when he is not working in the legal department of the Workers' Accident Insurance Office in Prague; since taking his law degree at the university, he has been by all reports the most dutiful and scrupulous of employees, though he finds the work tedious and enervating. But in June of 1923—having some months earlier been pensioned from his job because of his illness—he meets a young Jewish girl of nineteen at a seaside resort in Germany, Dora Dymant, an employee at the vacation camp of the Jewish People's Home of Berlin. Dora has left her Orthodox Polish family to make a life of her own (at half Kafka's age); she and Kafka—who has just turned forty—fall in love ... Kafka has by now been engaged to two somewhat more conventional Jewish girls—twice to one of them—hectic, anguished engagements wrecked largely by his fears. "I am mentally incapable of marrying," he writes his father in the forty-five-page letter he gave to his mother to deliver, "... the moment I make up my mind to marry I can no longer sleep, my head burns day and night, life can no longer be called life." He explains why. "Marrying is barred to me," he tells his father, "because it is your domain. Sometimes I imagine the map of the world spread out and you stretched diagonally across it. And I feel as if I could consider living in only those regions that either are not covered by you or are not within your reach. And in keeping with the conception I have of your magnitude, these are not many and not very comforting regions—and marriage is not among them." The letter explaining what is wrong between this father and this son is dated November, 1919; the mother thought it best not even to deliver it, perhaps for lack of courage, probably, like the son, for lack of hope.

During the following two years Kafka attempts to wage an affair with Milena Jesenská-Pollak, an intense young woman of twenty-four who has translated a few of his stories into Czech and is most unhappily married in Vienna; his affair with Milena, conducted feverishly, but by and large through the mails, is even more demoralizing to Kafka than the fearsome engagements to the nice Jewish girls. They aroused only the paterfamilias longings that he dared not indulge, longings inhibited by his exaggerated awe of his father—"spellbound," says Brod, "in the family circle"—and the hypnotic spell of his own solitude; but the Czech Milena, impetuous, frenetic, indifferent to conventional restraints, a woman of appetite and anger, arouses more elemental yearnings and more elemental fears. According to a Prague critic, Rio Preisner, Milena was "psychopathic"; according to Margaret Buber-Neumann, who lived two years beside her in the German concentration camp where Milena died following a kidney operation in 1944, she was powerfully sane, extraordinarily humane and courageous. Milena's obituary for Kafka was the only one of consequence to appear in the Prague press; the prose is strong, so are the claims she makes for Kafka's accomplishment. She is still only in her twenties, the dead man is hardly known as a writer beyond his small circle of friends—yet Milena writes, "His knowledge of the world was exceptional and deep, and he was a deep and exceptional world in himself ... (He had) a delicacy of feeling bordering on the miraculous and a mental clarity that was terrifyingly uncompromising, and in turn he loaded on to his illness the whole burden of his mental fear of life ... He wrote the most important books in recent German literature." One can imagine this vibrant young woman stretched diagonally across the bed, as awesome to Kafka as his own father spread out across the map of the world. His letters to her are disjointed, unlike anything else of his in print; the word fear, frequently emphasized, appears on page after page. "We are both married, you in Vienna, I to my Fear in Prague." He yearns to lay his head upon her breast; he calls her "Mother Milena"; during at least one of their two brief rendezvous, he is hopelessly impotent. At last he has to tell her to leave him be, an edict that Milena honors though it leaves her hollow with grief. "Do not write," Kafka tells her, "and let us not see each other; I ask you only to quietly fulfill this request of mine; only on those conditions is survival possible for me; everything else continues the process of destruction."

Then in the early summer of 1923, during a visit to his sister who is vacationing with her children by the Baltic Sea, he finds young Dora Dymant, and within a month Franz Kafka has gone off to live with her in two rooms in a suburb of Berlin, out of reach at last of the "claws" of Prague and home. How can it be? How can he, in his illness, have accomplished so swiftly and decisively the leave-taking that was so beyond him in his healthiest days? The impassioned letter-writer who could equivocate interminably about which train to catch to Vienna to meet with Milena (if he should meet with her for the weekend at all); the bourgeois suitor in the high collar, who, during his drawn-out agony of an engagement with the proper Fraulein Bauer, secretly draws up a memorandum for himself, countering the arguments "for" marriage with the arguments "against"; the poet of the ungraspable and the unresolved, whose belief in the immovable barrier separating the wish from its realization is at the heart of his excruciating visions of defeat, the Kafka whose fictions refute every easy, touching, humanish daydream of salvation and justice and fulfillment with densely imagined counter-dreams that mock all solutions and escapes—this Kafka, escapes! Overnight! K. penetrates the Castle walls—Joseph K. evades his indictment—"a breaking away from it altogether, a mode of living completely outside the jurisdiction of the court.'' Yes, the possibility of which Joseph K. has just a glimmering in the Cathedral, but can neither fathom nor effectuate—''not . . . some influential manipulation of the case, but . . . a circumvention of it''—Kafka realizes in the last year of his life.

Was it Dora Dymant or was it death that pointed the new way? Perhaps it could not have been one without the other. We know that the ''illusory emptiness'' at which K. gazed upon first entering the village and looking up through the mist and the darkness to the Castle was no more vast and incomprehensible than was the idea of himself as husband and father to the young Kafka; but now it seems the prospect of a Dora forever, of a wife, home, and children everlasting, is no longer the terrifying, bewildering prospect it would once have been, for now ''everlasting'' is undoubtedly not much more than a matter of months. Yes, the dying Kafka is determined to marry, and writes to Dora's Orthodox father for his daughter's hand. But the imminent death that has resolved all contradictions and uncertainties in Kafka is the very obstacle placed in his path by the young girl's father. The request of Franz Kafka, a dying man, to bind to him in his invalidism Dora Dymant, a healthy young girl, is—denied!

If there is not one father standing in Kafka's way, there is another—and, to be sure, another beyond him. Dora's father, writes Max Brod in his biography of Kafka, ''set off with (Kafka's) letter to consult the man he honored most, whose authority counted more than anything else for him, the 'Gerer Rebbe.' The rabbi read the letter, put it to one side, and said nothing more than the single syllable, 'No.' '' *No*. Klamm himself could have been no more abrupt—or any more removed from the petitioner. *No*. In its harsh finality, as telling and inescapable as the curselike threat delivered by his father to Georg Bendemann, that thwarted fiancé: ''Just take your bride on your arm and try getting in my way. I'll sweep her from your very side, you don't know how!'' *No*. Thou shalt not have, say the fathers, and Kafka agrees that he shall not. The habit of obedience and renunciation; also his own distaste for the diseased and reverence for strength, appetite, and health. '' 'Well, clear this out now!' said the overseer, and they buried the hunger artist, straw and all. Into the cage they put a young panther. Even the most insensitive felt it refreshing to see this wild creature leaping around the cage that had so long been dreary. The panther was all right. The food he liked was brought him without hesitation by the attendants; he seemed not even to miss his freedom; his noble body, furnished almost to the bursting point with all that it needed, seemed to carry freedom around with it too; somewhere in his jaws it seemed to lurk; and the joy of life streamed with such ardent passion from his throat that for the onlookers it was not easy to stand the shock of it. But they braced themselves, crowded around the cage, and did not want

ever to move away.'' So no is no; he knew as much himself. A healthy young girl of nineteen cannot, *should* not, be given in matrimony to a sickly man twice her age, who spits up blood (''I sentence you,'' cries Georg Bendemann's father, ''to death by drowning!'') and shakes in his bed with fevers and chills. What sort of un-Kafka-like dream had Kafka been dreaming?

And those nine months spent with Dora have still other ''Kafkaesque'' elements: a fierce winter in quarters inadequately heated; the inflation that makes a pittance of his own meager pension, and sends into the streets of Berlin the hungry and needy whose sufferings, says Dora, turn Kafka ''ash-gray''; and his tubercular lungs, flesh transformed and punished. Dora cares as devotedly and tenderly for the diseased writer as does Gregor Samsa's sister for her brother, the bug. Gregor's sister plays the violin so beautifully that Gregor ''felt as if the way were opening before him to the unknown nourishment he craved''; he dreams, in his condition, of sending his gifted sister to the Conservatory! Dora's music is Hebrew, which she reads aloud to Kafka, and with such skill that, according to Brod, ''Franz recognized her dramatic talent; on his advice and under his direction she later educated herself in the art...''

Only Kafka is hardly vermin to Dora Dymant, *or to himself*. Away from Prague and his father's home, Kafka, in his fortieth year, seems at last to have been delivered from the self-loathing, the self-doubt, and those guilt-ridden impulses to dependence and self-effacement that had nearly driven him mad throughout his twenties and thirties; all at once he seems to have shed the pervasive sense of hopeless despair that informs the great punitive fantasies of *The Trial*, ''The Penal Colony,'' and ''The Metamorphosis.'' Years earlier, in Prague, he had directed Max Brod to destroy all his papers, including three unpublished novels, upon his death; now, in Berlin, when Brod introduces him to a German publisher interested in his work, Kafka consents to the publication of a volume of four stories, and consents, says Brod, ''without much need of long arguments to persuade him.'' With Dora to help, he diligently resumes his study of Hebrew; despite his illness and the harsh winter, he travels to the Berlin Academy for Jewish Studies to attend a series of lectures on the Talmud — a very different Kafka from the estranged melancholic who once wrote in his diary, ''What have I in common with the Jews? I have hardly anything in common with myself and should stand very quietly in a corner, content that I can breathe.'' And to further mark the change, there is ease and happiness with a woman: with this young and adoring companion, he is playful, he is pedagogical, and one would guess, in light of his illness (*and* his happiness), he is chaste. If not a husband (such as he had striven to be to the conventional Fraulein Bauer), if not a lover (as he struggled hopelessly to be with Milena), he would seem to have become something no less mir-

aculous in his scheme of things: a father, a kind of father to this sisterly, mothering daughter. *As Franz Kafka awoke one morning from uneasy dreams he found himself transformed in his bed into a father, a writer and a Jew.*

"**I have completed** the construction of my burrow," begins the long, exquisite, and tedious story that he wrote that winter in Berlin, "and it seems to be successful. . . . Just the place where, according to my calculations, the Castle Keep should be, the soil was very loose and sandy and had literally to be hammered and pounded into a firm state to serve as a wall for the beautifully vaulted chamber. But for such tasks the only tool I possess is my forehead. So I had to run with my forehead thousands and thousands of times, for whole days and nights, against the ground, and I was glad when the blood came, for that was proof that the walls were beginning to harden; in that way, as everybody must admit, I richly paid for my Castle Keep." "The Burrow" is the story of an animal with a keen sense of peril whose life is organized around the principle of defense, and whose deepest longings are for security and serenity; with teeth and claws—*and* forehead—the burrower constructs an elaborate and ingeniously intricate system of underground chambers and corridors that are designed to afford it some peace of mind; however, while this burrow does succeed in reducing the sense of danger from without, its maintenance and protection are equally fraught with anxiety: "these anxieties are different from ordinary ones, prouder, richer in content, often long repressed, but in their destructive effects they are perhaps much the same as the anxieties that existence in the outer world gives rise to." The story (whose ending is lost) terminates with the burrower fixated upon distant subterranean noises that cause it "to assume the existence of a great beast," itself burrowing in the direction of the Castle Keep.

Another grim tale of entrapment, and of obsession so absolute that no distinction is possible between character and predicament. Yet this fiction imagined in the last "happy" months of his life is touched with a spirit of personal reconciliation and sardonic self-acceptance, with a tolerance for one's own brand of madness, that is not apparent in "The Metamorphosis"; the piercing masochistic irony of the early animal story—as of "The Judgment" and *The Trial*—has given way here to a critique of the self and its preoccupations that, though bordering on mockery, no longer seeks to resolve itself in images of the uttermost humiliation and defeat . . . But there is more here than a metaphor for the insanely defended ego, whose striving for invulnerability produces a defensive system that must in its turn become the object of perpetual concern—there is also a very unromantic and hard-headed fable about how and why art is made, a portrait of the artist in all his ingenuity, anxiety, isolation, dissatisfaction, relentlessness, obsessiveness, secretive-

ness, paranoia, and self-addiction, a portrait of the magical thinker at the end of his tether, Kafka's Prospero . . . It is an infinitely suggestive story, this story of life in a hole. For, finally, remember the proximity of Dora Dymant during the months that Kafka was at work on "The Burrow" in the two underheated rooms that was their illicit home. Certainly a dreamer like Kafka need never have entered the young girl's body for her tender presence to kindle in him a fantasy of a hidden orifice that promises "satisfied desire," "achieved ambition," and "profound slumber," but that once penetrated and in one's possession, arouses the most terrifying and heartbreaking fears of retribution and loss. "For the rest I try to unriddle the beast's plans. Is it on its wanderings, or is it working on its own burrow? If it is on its wanderings then perhaps an understanding with it might be possible. If it should really break through to the burrow I shall give it some of my stores and it will go on its way again. It will go on its way again, a fine story! Lying in my heap of earth I can naturally dream of all sorts of things, even of an understanding with the beast, though I know well enough that no such thing can happen, and that at the instant when we see each other, more, at the moment when we merely guess at each other's presence, we shall blindly bare our claws and teeth . . ."

He died of tuberculosis of the lungs and the larynx a month short of his forty-first birthday, June 3, 1924. Dora, inconsolable, whispers for days afterward, "My love, my love, my good one . . ."

2

1942. I am nine; my Hebrew school teacher, Dr. Kafka, is fifty-nine. To the little boys who must attend his "four-to-five" class each afternoon, he is known—in part because of his remote and melancholy foreignness, but largely because we vent on him our resentment at having to learn an ancient calligraphy at the very hour we should be out screaming our heads off on the ballfield—he is known as Dr. Kishka. Named, I confess, by me. His sour breath, spiced with intestinal juices by five in the afternoon, makes the Yiddish word for "insides" particularly telling, I think. Cruel, yes, but in truth I would have cut out my tongue had I ever imagined the name would become legend. A coddled child, I do not yet think of myself as persuasive, nor, quite yet, as a literary force in the world. My jokes don't hurt, how could they, I'm so adorable. And if you don't believe me, just ask my family and the teachers in school. Already at nine, one foot in Harvard, the other in the Catskills. Little Borscht Belt comic that I am outside the classroom, I amuse my friends Schlossman and Ratner on the dark walk home from Hebrew school with an imitation of Kishka, his precise and finicky professorial manner, his German accent, his cough, his gloom. "Doctor *Kishka!*" cries Schlossman, and hurls himself savagely against the newsstand that belongs to the candy store owner whom Schlossman drives just a little crazier each night. "Doctor Franz — Doctor Franz — Doctor Franz — *Kishka!*" screams Ratner, and my chubby little friend who lives upstairs from me on nothing but chocolate milk and Mallomars does not stop laughing until, as is his wont (his mother has asked me "to keep an eye on him" for just this reason), he wets his pants. Schlossman takes the occasion of Ratner's humiliation to pull the little boy's paper out of his notebook and wave it in the air—it is the assignment Dr. Kafka has just returned to us, graded; we were told to make up an alphabet of our own, out of straight lines and curved lines and dots. "That is all an alphabet is," he had explained. "That is all Hebrew is. That is all English is. Straight lines and curved lines and dots." Ratner's alphabet, for which he received a C, looks like twenty-six skulls strung in a row. I received my A for a curlicued alphabet inspired largely (as Dr. Kafka would seem to have surmised from his comment at the top of the page) by the number eight. Schlossman received an F for forgetting even to do it—and a lot he seems to care, too. He is content—he is *overjoyed*—with things as they are. Just waving a piece of paper in the air, and screaming, "*Kishka! Kishka!*" makes him deliriously happy. We should all be so lucky.

At home, alone in the glow of my goose-necked "desk" lamp (plugged after dinner into an outlet in the kitchen, my study) the vision of our refugee teacher, sticklike in a fraying three-piece blue suit, is no longer very funny—particularly after the entire beginner's Hebrew class, of which I am the most studious member, takes the name "Kishka" to its heart. My guilt awakens redemptive fantasies of heroism. I have them often about "the Jews in Europe." I must save him. If not me, who? The demonic Schlossman? The babyish Ratner? And if not now, when? For I have learned in the ensuing weeks that Dr. Kafka lives in "a room" in the house of an elderly Jewish lady on the shabby lower stretch of Avon Avenue, where the trolley still runs, and the poorest of Newark's Negroes shuffle meekly up and down the street, for all they seem to know still back in Mississippi. A *room*. And *there!* My family's apartment is no palace, but it is ours at least, so long as we pay thirty-eight-fifty a month in rent; and though our neighbors are not rich, they refuse to be poor and they refuse to be meek. Tears of shame and sorrow in my eyes, I rush into the living room to tell my parents what I have heard (though not that I heard it during a quick game of "aces up" played a minute before class against the synagogue's rear wall—worse, played directly beneath a stained glass window embossed with the names of the dead): "My Hebrew teacher lives in a *room.*"

My parents go much further than I could imagine anybody going in the real world. Invite him to dinner, my mother says. *Here?* Of course here—Friday night; I'm sure he can stand a home-cooked meal and a little pleasant company. Meanwhile my father gets on the phone to call my Aunt Rhoda, who lives with my grandmother and tends her and her potted plants in the apartment house at the corner of our street. For nearly two decades now my father has been introducing my mother's forty-year-old "baby" sister to the Jewish bachelors and widowers of New Jersey. No luck so far. Aunt Rhoda, an "interior decorator" in the dry goods department of "The Big Bear," a mammoth merchandise and produce market in industrial Elizabeth, wears falsies (this information by way of my older brother) and sheer frilly blouses, and family lore has it that she spends hours in the bathroom every day applying powders and sweeping her stiffish hair up into a dramatic pile on her head; but despite all this dash and display, she is, in my father's words, "still afraid of the facts of life." He, however, is undaunted, and administers therapy regularly and gratis: "Let 'em squeeze ya, Rhoda—it *feels* good!" I am his flesh and blood, I can reconcile myself to such scandalous talk in our kitchen—*but what will Dr. Kafka think?* Oh, but it's too late to do anything now. The massive machinery of matchmaking has been set in motion by my undiscourageable father, and the smooth engines of my proud homemaking mother's hospitality are already purring away. To throw my body into the works in an attempt to bring it all to a halt—well, I might as well try to bring down the New Jersey Bell Telephone Company by leaving our receiver off the hook. Only Dr. Kafka can save me now. But to my muttered invitation, he replies, with a formal bow that turns me scarlet—who has ever seen a person do such a thing outside of a movie house?—he replies that he would be *honored* to be my family's dinner guest. "My aunt," I rush to tell him, "will be there too." It appears that I have just said something mildly humerous; odd to see Dr. Kafka smile. Sighing, he says, "I will be delighted to meet her." Meet her? He's supposed to *marry* her. How do I warn him? And how do I warn Aunt Rhoda (a very great admirer of me and my marks) about his sour breath, his roomer's pallor, his Old World ways, so at odds with her up-to-dateness? My face feels as if it will ignite of its own—and spark the fire that will engulf the synagogue, Torah and all—when I see Dr. Kafka scrawl our address in his notebook, and beneath it, some words *in German*. "Good night, Dr. Kafka!" "Good night, and thank you, thank you." I turn to run, I go, but not fast enough: out on the street I hear Schlossman—that fiend!—announcing to my classmates who are punching one another under the lampost down from the synagogue steps (where a card game is also in progress, organized by the Bar Mitzvah boys): "Roth invited Kishka to his *house!* To *eat!*"

Does my father do a job on Kafka! Does he make a sales pitch for familial bliss! What it means to a man to have two fine boys and a wonderful wife! Can Dr. Kafka imagine what that's like? The thrill? The satisfaction? The pride? He tells our visitor of the network of relatives on his mother's side that are joined in a "family association" of over two hundred and fifty people located in seven states, including the state of Washington! Yes, relatives even in the Far West: here are their photographs, Dr. Kafka; this is a beautiful book we published entirely on our own for five dollars a copy, pictures of every member of the family, including infants, and a family history by "Uncle" Lichtblau, the eighty-five-year-old patriarch of the clan. This is our family newsletter that is published twice a year and distributed nationwide to all the relatives. This, in the frame, is the menu from the banquet of the family association, held last year in a ballroom of the "Y" in Newark, in honor of my father's mother on her seventy-fifth birthday. My mother, Dr. Kafka learns, has served *six consecutive years* as the secretary-treasurer of the family association. My father has served a two-year term as president, as have each of his three brothers. We now have fourteen boys in the family in uniform. Philip writes a letter on V-mail stationery to five of his cousins in the Army every single month. "Religiously," my mother puts in, smoothing my hair. "I firmly believe," says my father, "that the family is the cornerstone of everything." Dr. Kafka, who listened with close attention to my father's *spiel*, handling the various documents that have been passed to him with great delicacy and poring over them with a kind of rapt absorption that reminds me of myself over the watermarks of my stamps, now for the first time expresses himself on the subject of family; softly he says, "I agree," and inspects again the pages of our family book. "Alone," says my father, in conclusion, "alone, Dr. Kafka, is a stone." Dr. Kafka, setting the book gently upon my mother's gleaming coffee table, allows with a nod how that is so. My mother's fingers are now turning the curls behind my ears; not that I even know it at the time, or that she does. Being stroked is my life; stroking me, my father, and my brother is hers.

My brother goes off to a Boy Scout "council" meeting, but only after my father has him stand in his neckerchief before Dr. Kafka and describe to him the skills he has masterd to earn each of his badges. I am invited to bring my stamp album into the living room and show Dr. Kafka my set of triangular stamps from Zanzibar. "Zanzibar!" says my father rapturously, as though I, not even ten, have already been there and back. My father accompanies Dr. Kafka and myself into the "sun parlor," where my tropical fish swim in the aerated, heated, and hygienic paradise I have made for them with my weekly allowance and my Hanukah *gelt*. I am encouraged to tell Dr. Kafka what I know about the temperament of the angelfish, the function of the catfish, and the family life of the black molly. I know quite a bit. "All on his own he does that," my father says to Kafka. "He gives me a lecture on one of those fish, it's seventh heaven, Dr. Kafka." "I can imagine," Kafka replies.

Back in the living room my Aunt Rhoda suddenly launches into a rather recondite monologue on "scotch plaids," designed, it would appear, only for the edification of my mother. At least she looks fixedly at my mother while she delivers it. I have not yet seen her look directly at Dr. Kafka; she did not even turn his way at dinner when he asked how many employees there were at "The Big Bear." "How would I know?" she replies, and continues conversing with my mother, something about a grocer or a butcher who would take care of her "under the counter" if she could find him nylons for his wife. It never occurs to me that she will not look at Dr. Kafka because she is shy—nobody that dolled up could, in my estimation, be shy—I can only think that she is outraged. *It's his breath. It's his accent. It's his age.* I'm wrong—it turns out to be what Aunt Rhoda calls his "superiority complex." "Sitting there, sneering at us like that," says my aunt, somewhat superior now herself. "Sneering?" repeats my father, incredulous. "Sneering and laughing, yes!" says Aunt Rhoda. My mother shrugs: "*I* didn't think he was laughing." "Oh, don't worry, by himself there he was having a very good time—*at our expense*. I know the European-type man. Underneath they think they're all lords of the manor," Rhoda says. "You know something, Rhoda?" says my father, tilting his head and pointing a finger, "I think you fell in love." "With *him?* Are you *crazy?*" "He's too quiet for Rhoda," my mother says, "I think maybe he's a little bit of a wallflower. Rhoda is a lively person, she needs lively people around her." "Wallflower? He's not a wallflower! He's a gentleman, that's all. And he's lonely," my father says assertively, glaring at my mother for coming in over his head like this *against* Kafka. My Aunt Rhoda is forty years old—it is not exactly a shipment of brand-new goods that he is trying to move. "He's a gentleman, he's an educated man, and I'll tell you something, he'd give his eye teeth to have a nice home and a wife." "Well," says my Aunt Rhoda, "let him find one then, if he's so educated. Somebody who's his equal, who he doesn't have to look down his nose at with his big sad refugee eyes!" "Yep, she's in love," my father announces, squeezing Rhoda's knee in triumph. "With him?" she cries, jumping to her feet,

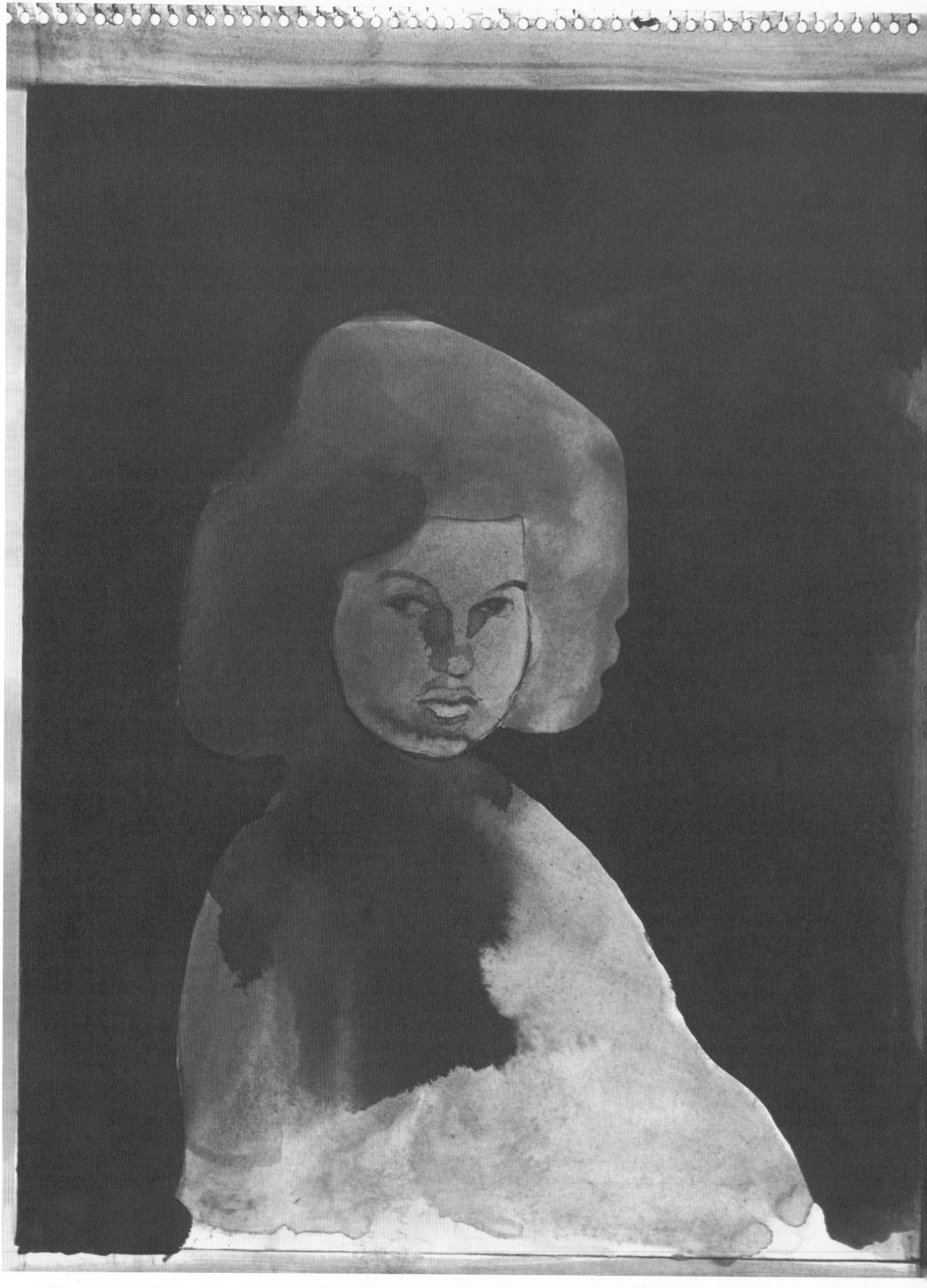

taffeta crackling around her like a bonfire. "With *Kafka?*" she snorts, "I wouldn't give an old man like him the time of day!"

Dr. Kafka calls and takes my Aunt Rhoda to a movie. I am astonished, both that he calls and that she goes; it seems there is more desperation in life than I have come across yet in my fish tank. Dr. Kafka takes my Aunt Rhoda to a play performed at the "Y." Dr. Kafka eats Sunday dinner with my grandmother and my Aunt Rhoda, and at the end of the afternoon, accepts with that formal bow of his the Mason jar of barley soup that my grandmother presses him to carry back to his room with him on the No. 8 bus. Apparently he was very taken with my grandmother's jungle of potted plants—and she, as a result, with him. Together they spoke in Yiddish about gardening. One Wednesday morning, only an hour after the store has opened for the day, Dr. Kafka shows up at the dry goods department of "The Big Bear"; he tells Aunt Rhoda that he just wanted to see where she worked. That night he writes in his diary, "With the customers she is forthright and cheery, and so managerial about 'taste' that when I hear her explain to a chubby young bride why green and blue do not 'go,' I am myself ready to believe that Nature is in error and R. is correct."

One night, at ten, Dr. Kafka and Aunt Rhoda come by unexpectedly, and a small impromptu party is held in the kitchen—coffee and cake, even a thimbleful of whiskey all around, to celebrate the resumption of Aunt Rhoda's career on the stage. I have only heard tell of my aunt's theatrical ambitions. My brother says that when I was small she used to come to entertain the two of us on Sundays with her puppets—she was at that time employed by the W.P.A. to travel around New Jersey and put on puppet shows in schools and even in churches; Aunt Rhoda did all the voices, male and female, and with the help of another young girl, manipulated the manikins on their strings. Simultaneously she had been a member of the "Newark Collective Theater," a troupe organized primarily to go around to strike groups to perform *Waiting for Lefty;* everybody in Newark (as I understood it) had had high hopes that Rhoda Pilchik would go on to Broadway—everybody except my grandmother. To me this period of history is as difficult to believe in as the era of the lake-dwellers that I am studying in school; of course, people say it was once so, so I believe them, but nonetheless it is hard to grant such stories the status of the real, given the life I see around me.

Yet my father, a very avid realist, is in the kitchen, *schnapps* glass in hand, toasting Aunt Rhoda's success. She has been awarded one of the starring roles in the Russian masterpiece, *The Three Sisters,* to be performed six weeks hence by the amateur group at the Newark "Y." Everything, announces Aunt Rhoda, everything she owes to Franz, and his encouragement. One conversation—"One!" she cries gaily—and Dr. Kafka had apparently talked my grandmother out of her life-

long belief that actors are not serious human beings. And what an actor *he* is, in his own right, says Aunt Rhoda. How he had opened her eyes to the meaning of things, by reading her the famous Chekhov play—yes, read it to her from the opening line to the final curtain, all the parts, and actually left her in tears. Here Aunt Rhoda says, "Listen, listen—this is the first line of the play—it's the key to everything. Listen—I just think about what it was like that night Pop passed away, how I thought and thought what would happen, what would we all do—and, and, listen—"

"We're listening," laughs my father.

Pause; she must have walked to the center of the kitchen linoleum. She says, sounding a little surprised, "'It's just a year ago today that father died.'"

"Shhh," warns my mother, "you'll give the little one nightmares."

I am not alone in finding my aunt "a changed person" during the ensuing weeks of rehearsal. My mother says this is just what she was like as a little girl. "Red cheeks, always those hot red cheeks—and everything exciting, even taking a bath." "She'll calm down, don't worry," says my father, "and then he'll pop the question." "Knock on wood," says my mother. "Come on," says my father, "he knows what side his bread is buttered on—he sets foot in this house, he sees what a family is all about, and believe me, he's licking his chops. Just look at him when he sits in that club chair. This is his dream come true." "Rhoda says that in Berlin, before Hitler, he had a young girlfriend, years and years it went on, and then she left him. For somebody else. She got tired of waiting." "Don't worry," says my father, "when the time comes I'll give him a little nudge. He ain't going to live forever, either, and he knows it."

Then one weekend, as a respite from the "strain" of nightly rehearsals—which Dr. Kafka regularly visits, watching in his hat and coat from a seat at the back of the auditorium until it is time to accompany Aunt Rhoda home—they take a trip to Atlantic City. Ever since he arrived on these shores Dr. Kafka has wanted to see the famous boardwalk and the horse that dives from the high board. But in Atlantic City something happens that I am not allowed to know about; any discussion of the subject conducted in my presence is in Yiddish. Dr. Kafka sends Aunt Rhoda four letters in three days. She comes to us for dinner and sits till midnight crying in our kitchen; she calls the "Y" on our phone to tell them (weeping) that her mother is still ill and she cannot come to rehearsal again—she may even have to drop out of the play — no, she can't, she can't, her mother is too ill, she herself is too upset! Good-bye! Then back to the kitchen table to cry; she wears no pink powder and no red lipstick, and her stiff brown hair. down, is thick and spiky

as a new broom.

My brother and I listen from our bedroom, through the door that silently he has pushed ajar.

"Have you ever?" says Aunt Rhoda, weeping. "Have you ever?"

"Poor soul," says my mother.

"*Who?*" I whisper to my brother. "Aunt Rhoda or—"

"Shhhh!" he says, "Shut *up!*"

In the kitchen my father grunts. "Hmm. Hmm." I hear him getting up and walking around and sitting down again—and then grunting. I am listening so hard that I can hear the letters being folded and unfolded, stuck back into their envelopes and then removed to be puzzled over one more time.

"Well?" demands Aunt Rhoda. "*Well?*"

"Well what?" answers my father.

"Well what do you want to say *now?*"

"He's *meshugeh*," admits my father. "Something is wrong with him all right."

"But," sobs Aunt Rhoda, "no one would believe me when *I* said it!"

"Rhody, Rhody," croons my mother in that voice I know from those times that I have had to have stitches taken, or when I awaken in tears, somehow on the floor beside my bed. "Rhody, don't be hysterical, darling. It's over, kitten, it's all over."

I reach across to my brother's "twin" bed and tug on the blanket. I don't think I've ever been so confused in my life, not even by death. The speed of things! Everything good undone in a moment! By what? "*What?*" I whisper. "*What is it?*"

My brother, the Boy Scout, smiles leeringly and with a fierce hiss that is no answer and enough answer, addresses my bewilderment: "Sex!"

Years later, a junior at college, I receive an envelope from home containing Dr. Kafka's obituary, clipped from the *Jewish News*, the tabloid of Jewish affairs that is mailed each week to the homes of the Jews of Essex County. It is summer, the semester is over, but I have stayed on at school, alone in my room in the town, trying to write short stories; I am fed by a young English professor and his wife in exchange for babysitting; I tell the sympathetic couple, who are also loaning me the money for my rent, why it is I can't go home. My tearful fights with my father are all I can talk about at their dinner table. "Keep him away from me!" I scream at my mother. "But, darling," she asks me, "what is going on? What is this all about?"—the very same question with which I used to plague my older brother, asked of me now out of the same bewilderment and innocence. "He *loves* you," she explains. But that, of all things, seems to me to be precisely what is blocking my way. Others are crushed by paternal criticism—I find myself oppressed by his high opinion of me! Can it possibly be true (and can I possibly admit) that I am coming to hate him for loving me so? praising me so? But that makes no sense—the ingratitude! the stupidity! the contrariness! Being loved is so obviously a blessing, *the* blessing, praise such a rare bequest; only listen late at night to my closest friends on the literary magazine and in the drama society—they tell horror stories of family life to rival *The Way of All Flesh,* they return shell-shocked from vacations, drift back to school as though from the wars. What they would give to be in my golden slippers! "What's going on?" my mother begs me to tell her; but how can I, when I can neither fully believe that this is happening to us, nor that I am the one who is making it happen. That they, who together cleared all obstructions from my path, should seem now to be my final obstruction! No wonder my rage must filter through a child's tears of shame, confusion, and loss. All that we have constructed together over the course of two century-long decades, and look how I must bring it down—in the name of this tyrannical need that I call my "independence"! Born, I am told, with the umbilical cord around my neck, it seems I will always come close to strangulation trying to deliver myself from my past into my future. . . . My mother, keeping the lines of communication open, sends a note to me at school: "We miss you"—and encloses the very brief obituary notice. Across the margin at the bottom of the clipping, she has written (in the same hand that she wrote notes to my teachers and signed my report cards, in the very same handwriting that once eased my way in the world), "Remember poor Kafka, Aunt Rhoda's beau?"

"Dr. Franz Kafka," the notice reads, "a Hebrew teacher at the Talmud Torah of the Schley Street Synagogue from 1939 to 1948, died on June 3 in the Deborah Tuberculosis Sanitorium in Browns Mills, New Jersey. Dr. Kafka had been a patient there since 1950. He was 70 years old. Dr. Kafka was born in Prague, Czechoslovakia, and was a refugee from the Nazis. He leaves no survivors."

He also leaves no books: no *Trial*, no *Castle*, no "Diaries." The dead man's papers are claimed by no one, and disappear—all except those four "*meshugeneh*" letters that are, to this day as far as I know, still somewhere in amongst the memorabilia accumulated in her dresser drawers by my spinster aunt, along with a collection of Broadway "Playbills," sales citations from "The Big Bear," and transatlantic steamship stickers.

Thus all trace of Dr. Kafka disappears. Destiny being destiny, how could it be otherwise? Does the Land Surveyor reach the Castle? Does K. escape the judgment of the Court, or Georg Bendemann the judgment of his father? " 'Well, clear this out now!' said the overseer, and they buried the hunger artist, straw and all." No, it simply is not in the cards for Kafka ever to become *the* Kafka—why, that would be stranger even than a man turning into an insect. No one would believe it, Kafka least of all.

ARTINTYPE-METRO

1

Typographers to The Push Pin Graphic
228 East 45 Street, New York, N.Y. (212) 972-9200

ASTORIA PRESS

2

Printers to The Push Pin Graphic
435 Hudson Street, New York, N.Y. (212) 255-6768

CA

3

The Magazine of Communication Arts
200 California Avenue, P.O. Box 10300, Palo Alto, California 94303
Subscription : $18 Yr., $20 Foreign

PUSH PIN FILMS

4

207 East 32nd Street, New York, (212) LE 2-9247
Contact Harold Friedman, Director's Circle, 765-9550
Los Angeles Representative : Perks & Jolivette, (213) 652-6065

PUSH PIN STUDIOS

5

207 East 32nd Street, New York, (212) LE 2-9247
In New York, Phyllis Flood Represents : Seymour Chwast, Milton Glaser,
Haruo Miyauchi, Christian Piper, George Stavrinos
Chicago Representative : Bill Rabin, (312) 944-6655
European Representative : Evelyne Menasce, Paris, Tel. : 38039-96

AUTOMOTIVE METAPHOR

NUMBER

60

1974

What if an artist could design his dream car? That was the premise of this issue with illustrations by Chwast, Miyauchi, and Piper. The art deco cover and endpapers fit Chwast's retro sensibility and the cars ran the gamut from crazy to absurd.

162

1940 Chevrolet Limousine.
The Chevrolet Limousine, a fine example of General Motors
assembly line know how, commands a high degree of owner loyalty.
Split skirt aluminum alloy pistons and a torque tube spiral
bevel transmission are standard on this 1940 model.

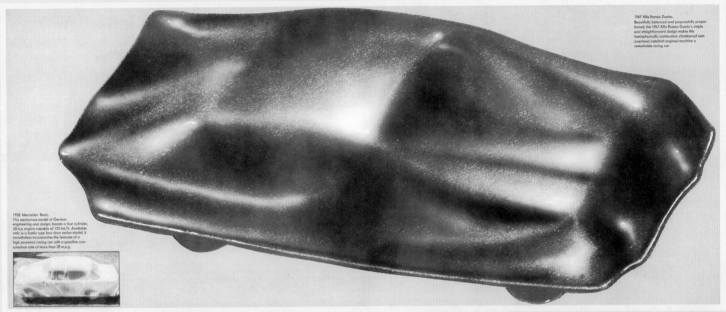

1967 Alfa Romeo Duetto.
Beautifully balanced and purposefully propor-
tioned, the 1967 Alfa Romeo Duetto's simple
and straightforward design makes this
hemispherically combustion-chambered twin
overhead camshaft engined machine a
remarkable racing car.

1958 Mercedes Benz.
This meritorious model of German
engineering and design, boasts a four cylinder,
50 h.p. engine capable of 125 km/h. Available
only in a family type four door sedan model, it
nonetheless incorporates the features of a
high powered racing car with a gasoline consumption rate of more than 28 m.p.g.

163

Model 810 Cord.
Low and long with racy rakish lines. The Model 810 Supercharged Sportsman's Convertible
Coupe boasts a rated power of 190 b.h.p. at 4200 r.p.m., and an obtainable speed from
standing start through gears of 70 m.p.h. in 19.6 seconds. The custom model has a 132 inch
wheelbase and a front suspension independent trailing arms with a semi-elliptical transverse
leaf spring. The transmission features 'Electro-Vacuum' finger tip control.

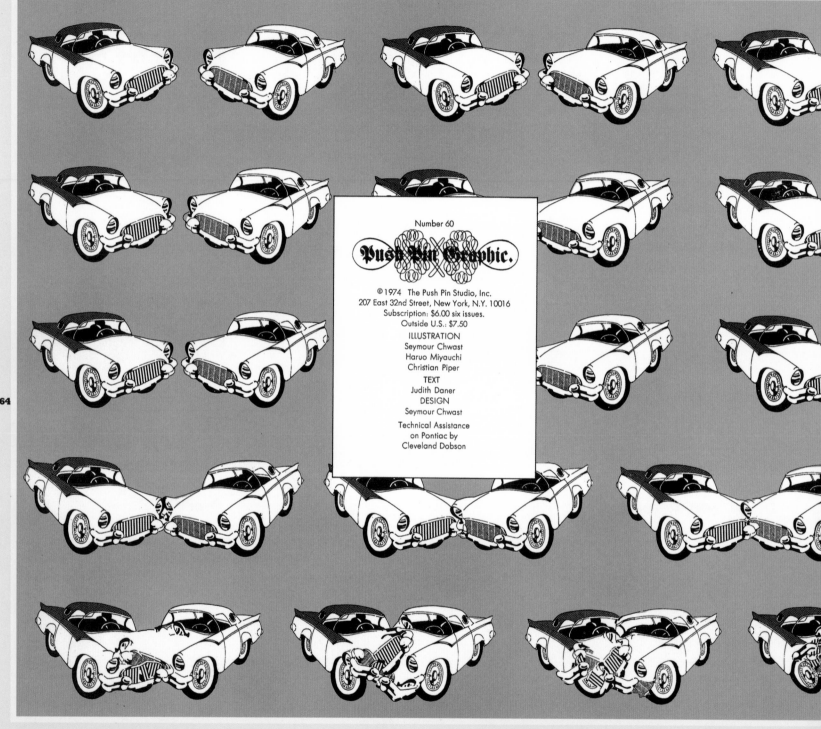

Number 60

Push Pin Graphic.

©1974 The Push Pin Studio, Inc.
207 East 32nd Street, New York, N.Y. 10016
Subscription: $6.00 six issues.
Outside U.S.: $7.50
ILLUSTRATION
Seymour Chwast
Haruo Miyauchi
Christian Piper
TEXT
Judith Daner
DESIGN
Seymour Chwast

Technical Assistance
on Pontiac by
Cleveland Dobson

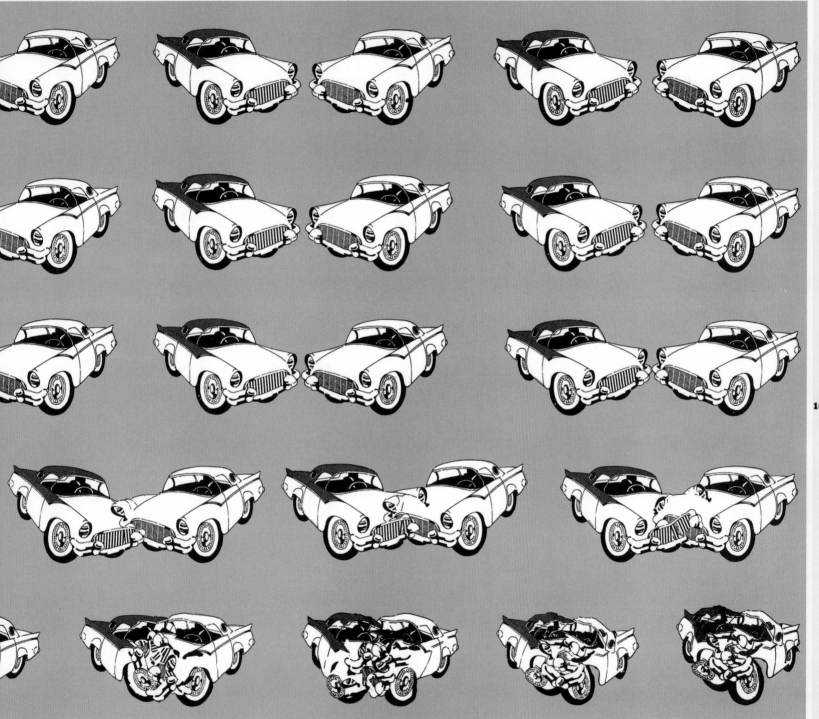

PUSH PIN GRAPHIC Number 61   ©1974 Push Pin Studios, Inc., 207 East 32 St., New York, 10016. Subscription: $6.00 six issues. Outside U.S.: $7.50.

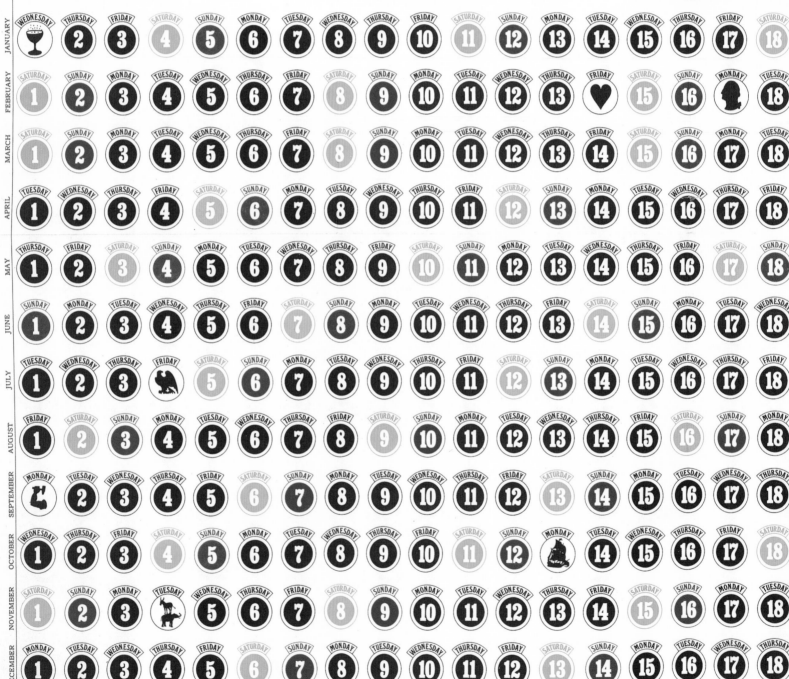

PUSH PIN STUDIOS, 207 E. 32 St:, New York, 10016. (212) LE 2-9247. Phyllis Flood Represents: Seymour Chwast, Doug Gervasi, Milton Glaser, Haruo Miyauchi, Christian Piper, George Stavrinos, John Van Hamersveld, Chica

A PRESS, 435 HUDSON ST., NEW YORK, (212) 255-6768.   TYPOGRAPHY: SECURITY TYPOGRAPHIC CORP., 304 E. 45 ST., NEW YORK, (212) LE 2-0620.

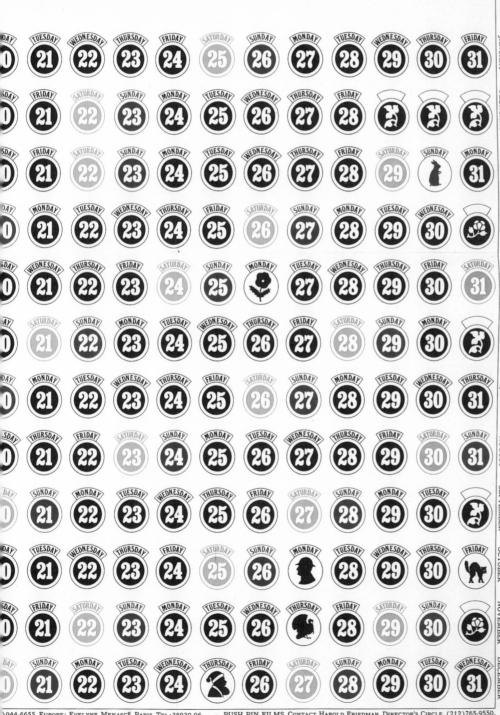

944-6655. EUROPE: EVELYNE MENASCÉ, PARIS, TEL: 38039-96.   PUSH PIN FILMS, CONTACT HAROLD FRIEDMAN, DIRECTOR'S CIRCLE, (212) 765-9550.

THE
YEAR
AT A GLANCE

NUMBER
61

1974

This entire issue was a calendar
showing Push Pin's interest in pattern.
This was the third calendar used in the
Graphic, yet the least functional.
The blocky layout of dates—à la bingo
card—contrasts with the bold
"high school" script for the masthead.

167

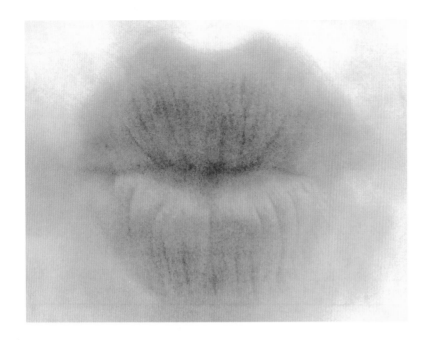

THE
MOUTH
NUMBER
62
1975

In "Uses of the Mouth" Nicholas J. Perella offered anthropological and psychological studies on the most interesting oral activity—the kiss. Chwast, Glaser, Piper, Miyauchi, George Stavrinos, and Joyce MacDonald contributed the mouth art. The front cover was by photographer Benno Friedman and the back by Arnold Rosenberg.

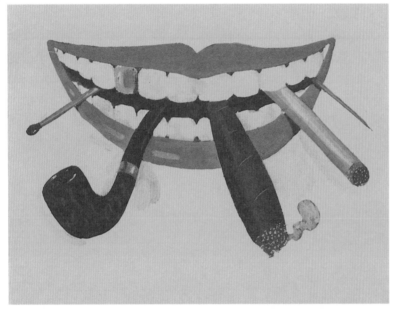

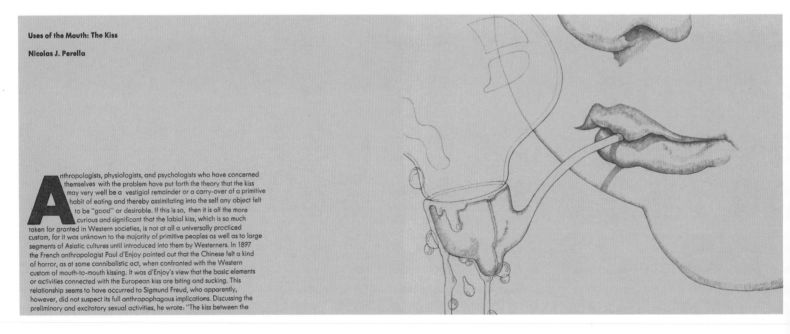

Uses of the Mouth: The Kiss

Nicolas J. Perella

Anthropologists, physiologists, and psychologists who have concerned themselves with the problem have put forth the theory that the kiss may very well be a vestigial remainder or a carry-over of a primitive habit of eating and thereby assimilating into the self any object felt to be "good" or desirable. If this is so, then it is all the more curious and significant that the labial kiss, which is so much taken for granted in Western societies, is not at all a universally practiced custom, for it was unknown to the majority of primitive peoples as well as to large segments of Asiatic cultures until introduced into them by Westerners. In 1897 the French anthropologist Paul d'Enjoy pointed out that the Chinese felt a kind of horror, as at some cannibalistic act, when confronted with the Western custom of mouth-to-mouth kissing. It was d'Enjoy's view that the basic elements or activities connected with the European kiss are biting and sucking. This relationship seems to have occurred to Sigmund Freud, who apparently, however, did not suspect its full anthropophagous implications. Discussing the preliminary and excitatory sexual activities, he wrote: "The kiss between the

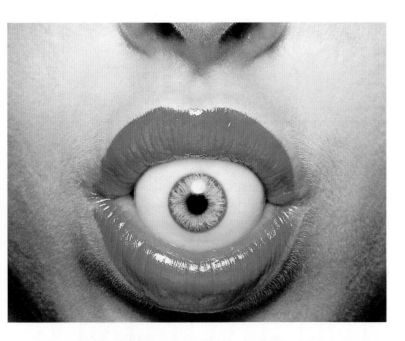

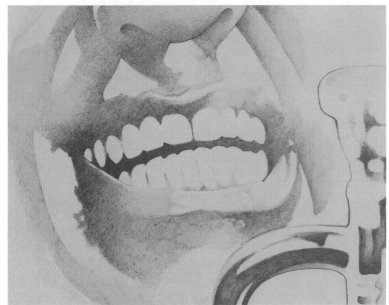

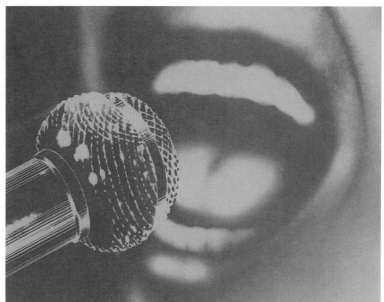

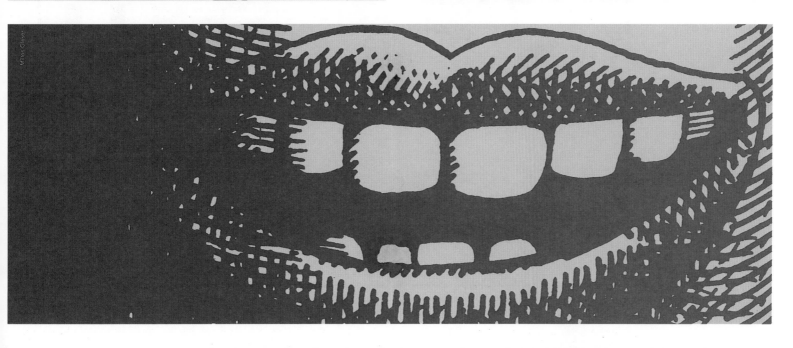

Milton Glaser

This issue celebrated the misunderstood chicken. Push Pin illustrators at the time, Stavrinos, MacDonald, David Croland, Fred Marshall, and Jeff Krassner, contributed to the foul debate, and Paula (aka Pollo) Scher wrote an essay that revealed everything everyone wanted to know (or not) about chickens. A rooster pattern covered an entire page and the icon was later used on the masthead of all subsequent *Graphics*.

NUMBER 63 · Push Pin Graphic · CHICKEN ISSUE

©1976 The Push Pin Studios, Inc.   207 East 32 Street   New York 10016   Subscription: $6.00 six issues   Outside U.S.: $7.50

CHICKEN!

A NOTE FROM THE EDITOR: WHY CHICKEN?

The general public for generations has had a misguided and somewhat demeaning attitude toward the importance of the chicken to the civilization of man.

The chicken has constantly been regarded as an unattractive, noisy, smelly bird that exists on a diet of low quality food; happily lays eggs, and is delicious broiled, boiled, fried, baked and poached. All this, of course, is true, but this tabloid serves to point out the long buried historic facts about the chicken and man, and why we are in continual debt to this magnificent bird.

THE CHICKEN IN HISTORY

BY POLLO SCHER

THE PREHISTORIC CHICKEN

To answer the age old question of which came first, the chicken or the egg, the chicken came first. Its predecessor was the giant logundo bird which is still known to North-Eastern parts of outer Mongolia. It is believed that the giant logundo bird mated with the now extinct cockasouras and the result was chicken. The first known chicken is believed to have been sighted in what is now Red China, seven miles east of present day Peking. Archeologists have constructed a model of this prehistoric chicken, which is presently on display at the Museum of Natural History in St. Paul, Minnesota. The construction shows the bird to be approximately 6 feet 5 inches in height (from crown to claw) and the estimated weight of the bird is 247 lbs. Unfortunately, the left wing section is an imaginary construction, as the original bones are thought to be destroyed in an earthquake. The estimated date of this original chicken is 2,542 B.C.

THE CHINESE CHICKEN

Our word "chicken" is derived from the Chinese "chi-ki-en" meaning large, ugly bird. It was later shortened to "chi-ken" which means ugly bird. According to Dr. Loa Su Sing, Chinese professor of archeology at Colum-

THE LATEST FROM PARIS BY DAVID CROLAND

MOTHERS

NUMBER

64

DECEMBER 1976

The "Mothers" issue launched the first standard (nine-by-twelve-inch, thirty-two-page) magazine format that continued until issue number 86. Chwast appointed himself editor and art director. Included were essays and pictures devoted to famous and infamous mothers: Friedman's photo of Jackson Pollock's, Miyauchi's painting of Giotto's, and others. "Trixie and Dixie" (Pamela Vassil and Lilly Filipow) introduced an advice column, and Scher wrote about the "Mother Mafia." With this issue ten thousand copies were distributed to subscribers. This issue was Glaser's last appearance in the *Graphic*.

174

JACKSON POLLACK'S MOTHER BY BENNO FRIEDMAN

Push Pin Graphic

Number 64   December 1976

♥ Mothers. ♥

EDWARD MUNCH'S MOTHER BY FRED MARSHALL.

THE MOTHER MAFIA

BY PAULA SCHER

The power of mothers to control and manipulate their offspring is age old and widely known. Therefore the Mother Mafia has existed since man began, but the classic organization, as we know it today began in Italy, France, England and the United States in the 1890's.

The Victorian era was the most repressive period that women had known. The role society gave them made manipulation difficult because they continually had to control their aggressions.

Emma Rice Thompson, born in Manchester, England in 1857, was a key founder of the British Mother Mafia. She was married to a London stockbroker, and after the birth of her third son found that family control was slipping away from her. An avid reader, Emma Rice Thompson greatly admired *Oedipus Rex* and *Hamlet*, and it is believed that these two classic pieces of literature inspired an entire movement.

Mrs. Thompson set up regular Thursday Tea Meetings with the wives of prominent lawyers, doctors, lords and of course stockbrokers. At these teas, she and the other women, most notably Lady Olivia Prickett mapped out a strategy for increased control and manipulation of families and ultimately the world.

THE INFAMOUS EMMA RICE THOMPSON 10 POINT CREDO FOR CONTROL AND MANIPULATION

1. It is our assumption that the process of birth entitles all mothers to total loyalty, obedience and homage from their offspring. It is essential that mothers continually remind their children of their great debt.
2. All children are inferior beings intellectually, socially, and culturally and will never, during an entire lifetime, assume the knowledge and position of their mothers.
3. All female children who become parents are still technically children themselves. They cannot assume the full title of "Mother" However, it is assumed that throughout their lives they will receive the education to assume this role when their mother dies.
4. The only important commandment "Honor thy mother and father" means "Honor Thy Mother."
5. All mothers are natural martyrs by pain of birth and lifelong sacrifice. To betray your mother is to betray Christ.
6. An offspring can produce no success that is great enough to please his mother or ease his debt.
7. Successful offspring must provide for their mothers to the greatest extent they can. Monetary success is of the utmost importance second only to the acquisition of power.
8. Children who fail are never to be forgiven. If the children are failures their mothers will be dropped immediately from this organization. Mothers who condone or make excuses for failure in their children are to be blacklisted.
9. Mothers are all sisters moving toward a common goal—money, power, and very good jewelry. Status in our organization corresponds directly to wealth and power.
10. Mothers may express pride to one another in the success of the offspring, but never to the offspring directly. Pride may be expressed only when it has been acknowledged that the offspring is basically ignorant and inferior.

THE MOMIA

Emma Rice Thompson's famous credo was published in 1892 and distributed throughout the world. In the summer of 1894 Mrs. Thompson and Lady Prickett made a lecture tour visiting New York, Philadelphia, Boston, Minneapolis and San Francisco. American women joined the organization in droves. The New York co-ordinator of the Mother Mafia was Frances McKinley Powers, a childhood friend of Sara Delano Roosevelt. Powers and Roose-

WHAT THE U.S. MOMIA CONTROLS

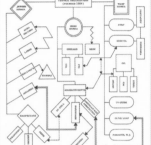

velt felt that the organization's credo, while strong in substance, was weak in technique. Powers proposed courses for mothers in guilt manipulation. However, Emma Rice Thompson felt that debt was a much stronger tool for manipulation and the guilt theory lacked finesse. The two women feuded over theory and ultimately the American organization broke away from its English counterpart with Frances McKinley Powers as its new leader. The organization was christened "THE MOMIA" or Mothers for Overbearing Manipulation of Infants and Adolescents. Powers and Roosevelt co-authored the Movement's universally acclaimed thesis, "Theories and Practices of Guilt Manipulation". The following are excerpts.

On Health:

"Health is the key to guilt manipulation. All children are sensitive to the fact that their births may have in some way physically impaired their mothers. It is often helpful to create an age old ailment that exists since the birth of each child such as a bad back, recurring headaches, tendency to faint, weak stomach, etc. Make the child know that he is responsible for these ailments. Manage to have attacks when the child is about to make a decision that does not concur with your beliefs or does something which is distasteful to you."

On Marriage:

"Marital arguments can be a helpful instrument in maintaining total guilt manipulation of your offspring. Make the child aware of the fact that he is responsible for all your marital difficulties and the cause of your unhappy life. It is often helpful to portray your husband as a brute and yourself as a helpless partner who can only succeed in protecting the child from the father's atrocities. It is also to your advantage to have your offspring assume that you live with your husband only because you want your child to have a normal home."

On Martyrdom:

"Martyrdom is the most essential of all the tools of guilt manipulation. True guilt can not be established without it. When serving meat,

LA MÈRE DE TOULOUSE LAUTREC

TOULOUSE-LAUTREC'S MOTHER BY JEFFREY KRASSNER

MOTHER MAFIA CO-FOUNDER
LADY OLIVIA PRICKETT

Push Pin Graphic

NUMBER 65   FEBRUARY 1977

THE COMPLETE HISTORY AND KNOWLEDGE OF THE WORLD
(CONDENSED)

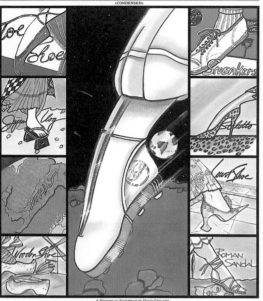

A HISTORY OF FOOTWEAR BY DAVID CROLAND

EVERYTHING YOU'VE WANTED TO KNOW

NUMBER

65

FEBRUARY 1977

The sum of shared knowledge in the entire world was crammed with aplomb into this issue. The cover was by Croland, Carmen Miranda by Michael Hostovich, and the New York Philharmonic by Miyauchi. Scher condensed all history and even the complete Shakespeare into a few pages. The issue also included a condensed 1977 calendar in six pages.

HORTICULTURE BY MICHAEL HOSTOVICH

176

BIOLOGY
CONDENSED COURSE NO. 4

(Continued from page 6)

their protoplasts and differentiate themselves from animal cells though both can develop tissue which is often called epidermis in more complex forms of life while the four basic types of animal tissue are epithelium, connective tissue, muscle and nerve and sometimes blood which is basically liquid plasma and bone which is a complex of calcium, carbonate and phosphate and if nutrition is proper will result in growth sometimes caused by mitosis which is a nuclear division with the formation of compacted chromosomes, spindle fibers, cell division and the disappearance of the nuclear membrane or metaphase when the chromosomes change position or finally, mutation which is a change in the normal structure of chromosomes or cells which can occur independently of organism reproduction which can be both sexual or non sexual though sexual is more interesting because cells and eggs get to be fertilized and the chromosomes and genes assemble themselves in all different ways and DNA molecules duplicate themselves by splitting down the middle and breaking their hydrogen bonds, while all that plants have is seed germination.

CINEMATOLOGY
CONDENSED COURSE NO. 5

FILMS

FUNNY GIRL: Ugly Jewish lady finds fame with Flo Ziegfeld. Ugly Jewish lady falls in love with handsome Jewish man, Nicky Arnstein who's a nogoodnik. He goes to jail, but the show must go on so she keeps singing. He gets out of jail, dumps her, show must go on so she keeps singing.

DARK VICTORY: Rich dilettante debutant Bette Davis makes a general nuisance of herself until she starts getting dizzy and sees double. She gets taken to a rich handsome young doctor who tells her she has a brain tumor and operates. Bette thinks she has recovered, falls in love with doctor and they decide to marry. Bette arrives at her young doctor's office, is alone and looks through her records only to find prognosis, negative. Plot thick-

ens. Bette gets drunk and carries on for weeks. Bette sobers up, decides what the hell might as well marry the doctor who she loves anyway. They marry, and live happily ever after until she dies three months later.

TAXI DRIVER: Loner takes job as taxi driver. Loner drives uptown, downtown, crosstown all around the town. Loner sees Cybil Shepheard and takes her to porno movie. Loner loses Cybil. Loner shaves head and buys guns. Shoots up city. Becomes hero and drives taxi.

THE SWIMMER: Burt Lancaster swims all over country. Arms get tired.

SABRINA: Audrey Hepburn and caretaker father work for wealthy family with two sons. Sabrina falls in love with younger son. Sabrina goes to school in Paris. Sabrina comes back still in love with younger son who is going to be married to another woman. The younger son decides he loves Sabrina and so does the older son who won't acknowledge it. The younger son realizes that the older son loves Sabrina. He bows out and the older son marries Sabrina.

CASABLANCA: Rick owns club in Casablanca. Friend Sam plays piano, but not allowed to play "As Time Goes By". Times goes by, and Ingrid Bergman goes to Casablanca with husband to escape from the Nazis and come to America. Ingrid sees Rick and they remember their love affair which is why Sam can't play "As Time Goes By". Rick helps Ingrid and husband escape to America. Times goes by, Peter Lorre gets shot, Sidney Greenstreet gets nothing and Claude Rains get Rick.

NOW VOYAGER: Bette Davis, ugly spinster lives in Boston with her mother. Bette has nervous breakdown, leaves institution, goes on trip and falls in love with married man who has a daughter and sends Bette camellias everyday. Bette goes home to Boston, tells mother off, mother dies. Married man's daughter has nervous breakdown and goes to same institution Bette was in. Bette meets daughter, Bette likes daughter. Husband stays married. Perfect relationship, Both smoke. "Why reach for the moon when they already have the stars…"

THE EGG AND I—Claudette Colbert marries Fred MacMurray. Both give up successful life in New York and buy an egg farm. Fred MacMurray meets spring chicken down the block. Claudette gets pregnant, gets jealous, leaves Fred moves back to New York. Has baby goes back to Fred who bought spring chicken's farm as present for Claudette.

LAST TANGO IN PARIS: After his wife dies, Marlon Brando meets Maria Schneider in an empty apartment and they make passionate love for a couple of hours, sometimes with butter, sometimes not, but they don't tell each other their names until Brando comes clean and Schneider shoots him dead.

AFRICAN QUEEN: Charlie Alnut runs a river boat in Africa and Rose Sayer is a preacher's sister. After Alnut's stomach rumbles, the Germans kill everybody but Alnut and Rose. So they take the African Queen down the river and build torpedoes to blow up the Germans, they fall in love, sin, get attacked by insects, blow up the German ship Louisa, escape, and swim to Kenya.

PILLOW TALK: Hard working interior decorator Doris Day, shares a party line with infamous playboy songwriter Rock Hudson. They quarrel over the telephone without meeting. Then Rock sees Doris and wants to seduce her but has to disguise himself as a bumbling Texan. Rock finally almost seduces Doris but she discovers that he is Rock Hudson and they: 1. quarrel 2. reconcile 3. get married.

LOVER COME BACK: Hard working advertising executive Doris Day, hates infamous playboy advertising executive Rock Hudson. They quarrel over the phone without meeting. Then Rock sees Doris and wants to seduce her but has to disguise

himself as a bumbling scientist. Rock finally almost seduces Doris when they accidentally get married but she discovers he is Rock Hudson and they: 1. get divorced 2. discover that Doris is pregnant 3. get married.

LANGUAGE
CONDENSED COURSE NO. 6

ENGLISH
In a constant effort to conserve space, we introduce the new condensed alphabet which makes reading and writing a simple task.
A B C D E F G H I J K L M O P
Vowels consist of A,E,I, and sometimes O.
I before E always.
In the combination P-FGH, the P is silent.
THIS IS HOW THE NEW SYSTEM WORKS:
Consider the sentence, "Now is the time for all good men to come to the aid of their country."
WITH THE NEW SYSTEM:
Oi fghe im fgho ajkl fghood me o bco o fghe ad a fghe bco. Wasn't that easy?

FRENCH
French is the simplest of all foreign languages because it is structured entirely around English. To prove this theory, we suggest you write your sentence in English first.
EXAMPLE:
Louie, hard of hearing, and Gary kill a mare.

A mare	a mer
kill	qu'il
hard of hearing	et
a man's name	Lui
nickname for gary	guère

Lui et Guère qu'il a mer.

GERMAN
German is basically a very easy language to learn. Here are some simple rules to follow in order to excelerate the learning process:
W always pronounced as V
TH always pronounced as Z
Add umlaut over first A to indicate feminine gender.
EXAMPLE:
Future Tense
Walter Wilhelm will want the weiner with wine.
Present Tense
Walter Wilhelm wants the weiner with wine.
Past Tense
Walter Wilhelm wanted the weiner with wine.
Feminine
Wälter Wilhelm wanted the weiner with wine.

SPANISH
Because of the tremendous latin population residing in metropolitan areas, we have formulated one basic sentence that will assist you in most street situations.
Purse your lips as if to whistle or kiss. Suck in and make a kiss noise that lasts about five seconds. Then quickly yell out, "Que linda."

'77 Calendar Condensed

MONDAY	MONDAY	TUESDAY	WEDNESDAY	THURSDAY	FRIDAY	SATURDAY	SUNDAY

NOV

      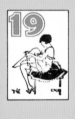 

1978

JAN

DEC

SATURDAY	SUNDAY	MONDAY	TUESDAY	WEDNESDAY	THURSDAY	FRIDAY	SATURDAY

1  **JAN** | **13**  | **14**  | **15**  | **16**  | **17**  | **18**  | **19**

8  | **20**  | **21**  | **22**  | **23** | **24**  | **25**  | **26**

15  | **27**  | **28**  | **1**  **MAR** | **2**  | **3**  | **4**  | **5**

22  | **6**  | **7**  | **8**  | **9**  | **10**  | **11**  | **12**

29  | **13**  | **14**  | **15**  | **16**  | **17**  | **18**  | **19**

12  | **27**  | **28**  | **29**  | **30**  | **31**  | **1** **APR** | **2**

SUNDAY	MONDAY	TUESDAY	WEDNESDAY	THURSDAY	FRIDAY
26 	**27**	**28** 	**29** 	**30** 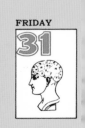	**31** 
2	**3**	**4** 	**5**	**6** 	**7** 
9 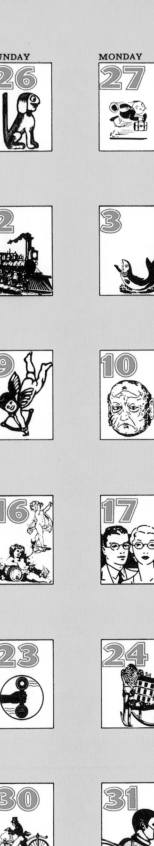	**10**	**11** 	**12** 	**13** 	**14** 
16	**17**	**18** 	**19** 	**20** 	**21** 
23	**24**	**25** 	**26** 	**27** 	**28** 
30 	**31** 	**1** 	**2** 	**3** 	**4** 

FEB

| **6**  | **7**  | **8**  | **9**  | **10**  | **11**  |

MONDAY	TUESDAY	WEDNESDAY	THURSDAY	FRIDAY	SATURDAY
5 	6 	7 	8 	9	10
12 	13 	14 	15 	16 	17
19 	20 	21 	22 	23 	24 
26 	27 	28 	29 	30 	31 
2 	3 	4 	5 	6 	7 
9 	10 	11 	12 	13 	14 
16 	17 	18 	19 	20 	21

SUNDAY	MONDAY	TUESDAY	WEDNESDAY	THURSDAY	FRIDAY
10 	**11** 	**12** 	**13** 	**14** 	**15** 
17 	**18** 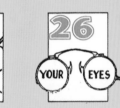	**19** 	**20** CIGARS 	**21** 	**22** 
24 	**25** 	**26** YOUR EYES 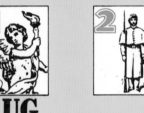	**27** 	**28** 	**29** 
31 	**1**  AUG	**2** 	**3**	**4** 	**5** 
7 	**8** 	**9** 	**10** 	**11**	**12** HARDWARE
14 	**15**	**16** 	**17** 	**18** 	**19** 
21 	**22** 	**23**	**24**	**25**	**26**

MONDAY	TUESDAY	WEDNESDAY	THURSDAY	FRIDAY	SATURDAY
23 	**24** 	**25** 	**26** 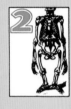	**27** 	**28** 
30 	**31** 	**1**  **JUN**	**2** 	**3** 	**4** 
6 	**7** 	**8** 	**9** 	**10** 	**11** 
13 	**14** 	**15** 	**16** 	**17** 	**18** 
20 	**21** 	**22** 	**23** 	**24** 	**25** 
27 	**28** 	**29**	**30** 	**1**  **JUL**	**2** 
4 	**5**	**6**	**7**	**8**	**9**

SUNDAY	MONDAY	TUESDAY	WEDNESDAY	THURSDAY	FRIDAY	SATURDAY	SUNDAY
3 	4 	5 	6 	7 	8 	9 	22 
10 	11 	12 	13 	14 	15 	16 	29 
17 	18 	19 	20 	21 	22 	23 	5 
24 	25 	26 	27 	28 	29 	30 	12 
1 	2 	3 	4 	5 	6 	7 	19 

MAY

8 	9 	10 	11 	12 	13 	14 	26 
15 	16 	17 	18 	19 	20 	21 	3 

SATURDAY	SUNDAY	MONDAY	TUESDAY	WEDNESDAY	THURSDAY	FRIDAY	SATURDAY

16   28   29   30   31   1   2   3

SEP

23   4   5   6   7   8   9   10

30 KEEP SMILING   11   12   13   14   15 STORE   16   17

 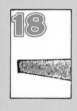      

6   18   19   20   21   22   23   24

13   25   26 CIGARS and POOL   27   28   29   30   1

OCT

20   2   3   4   5 Thank You   6   7   8

27   9   10   11   12   13   14   15

This issue surveyed the events during the twenty years of publishing the *Graphic* and announced a retrospective exhibition of work at the Mead Library of Ideas in New York. Push Pin associates, including Arnold Rosenberg, John Collier, Friedman, Stavrinos, and Chwast, created images representing events during the fifties, sixties, and seventies.

Push Pin Graphic

Number 66   April 1977

TWENTIETH ANNIVERSARY CELEBRATION!

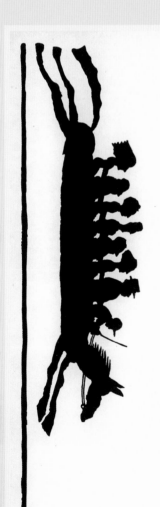

HINDSIGHTS

1973

"Racing can't survive if everybody's in the bookie parlors. They've got to get out to the track. I highly recommend it. It's quite a lot of fun."
Charles B. Delafield in a report to Governor Rockefeller

"The only way to attack crime in America is the way crime attacks our people—without pity."
Nixon in a message to Congress

1974

"There is not a sailor—and I was one for ten years—there is not a Frenchman who will not consider with sorrow the prospect of no longer seeing the Tricolor fluttering over the *France*, but we cannot ignore the pressing economic problems of the day."
Aymar Achille Fauld Transport Minister of France in announcing that the liner is being taken out of service

"I know very few boys—including my own son —who would object to being beaten out by a better girl. Besides, I have more daughters than sons."
Governor Byrne of New Jersey upholding the right of girls to participate in Little League baseball

"You learn from your defeats, and then go on, fight again, never quit, never quit. Always go on and fight for those things you believe in."
President Nixon at a Young Republicans rally

"I'm standing in the window so people can see me. What a thing to be doing in this day and age of gas shortages."
John Doerrbacker attendant at a Westbury Long Island Shell Service Station

1975

"No breakfast is worth $37.00."
Peggy Candito of Carteret, New Jersey traveling to Miami on a discounted "no frills" flight

1976

"Look over your city and weep, for your city is dying."
Episcopal Bishop Paul Moore Jr. in the Easter Sermon at the Cathedral of St. John the Divine

"We have no doubt, in these unhappy circumstances, that if Karen, were herself miraculously lucid for an interval and perceptive of her irreversable condition, she could effectively decide upon discontinuance of the life support apparatus, even if it meant the prospect of natural death."
The New Jersey Supreme Court in a ruling that Karen Ann Quinlan's parents could let her die if doctors saw no recovery hope

1977

"Let's do it!"
Gary Mark Gilmore, when asked by the warden if he had any last words ➤➤

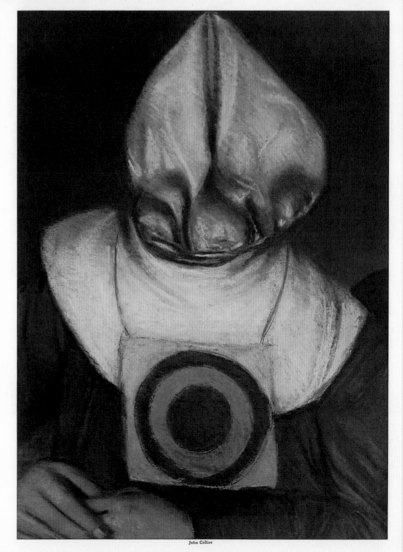

John Collier

New York City, 1957 by Benno Friedman

South Vi

179

Massapequa, Long Island, 1977 by George Stavrinos

DIGESTION

START

RULES

SELECT AND CUT OUT TOKEN PRINTED ON PAGE 13. HOLD PENCIL OR POINTED OBJECT 10 INCHES ABOVE SPACE CHART. CLOSE EYES. OPEN EYES. MOVE TOKEN APPROPRIATE NUMBER OF SPACES INDICATED IN BOX WHERE PENCIL LANDS. DO OVER IF IT LANDS ON LINE OR OUTSIDE BOX. FOLLOW DIRECTIONS CORRESPONDING TO NUMBER (BELOW). THE FIRST PLAYER TO PASS THROUGH THE DIGESTIVE SYSTEM TO THE WINNER'S CIRCLE OR BEYOND IS THE WINNER. START AT (1). IF YOU LAND ON (3) ON SPACE CHART, GET AN EXTRA TURN.

SPACE CHART

(2) SAFE
(3) SAFE
(4) CAUGHT IN WIND PIPE: LOSE ONE TURN
(5) CHOKED: GO BACK TO (1)
(6) HICCUP: LOSE ONE TURN
(7) BURP: GO BACK TO (1)
(8) HEARTBURN: LOSE 2 TURNS
(9) SAFE
(10) STOMACH GURGLE: GO AGAIN
(11) GAS PAIN: LOSE ONE TURN
(12) SAFE
(13) BREAK WIND: GO BACK TO (11)
(14) SAFE
(15) LIVER COMPLICATIONS: LOSE TWO TURNS
(16) INDIGESTION: GO BACK TO (1)
(17) SAFE
(18) VOMIT: OUT OF GAME
(19) ACIDITY: LOSE ONE TURN
(20) ACID DISSOLVED: GO AGAIN
(21) SAFE
(22) INTESTINAL CRAMP: LOSE 1 TURN
(23) SAFE
(24) ILEITIS: GO AGAIN AND MOVE BACKWARD ACCORDING TO NUMBER SELECTED
(25) SAFE
(26) TRAPPED GAS: GO BACK TO (13)
(27) SAFE
(28) DIARRHEA: GO BACK TO (1)
(29) SAFE
(30) SAFE
(31) NUTRIENTS ABSORBED INTO BLOOD: ADVANCE 7 SPACES
(32) SAFE
(33) SAFE
(34) SAFE
(35) INTESTINAL VIRUS: GO BACK TO (1)
(36) SAFE
(37) SAFE
(38) INTESTINES INFLAMED: LOSE 2 TURNS
(39) SAFE
(40) SAFE
(41) NERVES REACT: GO BACK TO (23)
(42) SAFE
(43) SAFE
(44) SAFE
(45) FOOD POISONING: GO BACK TO HOSPITAL. PLAYERS IN HOSPITAL MAY BE RELEASED BY SHOWING PROOF OF MEDICAL INSURANCE PRIOR TO NEXT TURN. IF NO INSURANCE, GO BACK TO (1).
(46) SAFE
(47) SAFE
(48) COLITIS: LOSE 2 TURNS
(49) APPENDICITIS: GO TO HOSPITAL
(50) SAFE
(51) INFLAMMATION OF LARGE INTESTINE: GO BACK TO (44)
(52) SAFE
(53) CONSTIPATION: LOSE 3 TURNS
(54) SAFE
(55) LAXATIVE REACTING: ADVANCE TO (65)
(56) SAFE
(57) SAFE
(58) GAS PRESSURE: ADVANCE TO (65)
(59) SAFE
(60) ENEMA APPLIED: ADVANCE TO (70) AND WIN
(61) SAFE
(62) SAFE
(63) ANNOYING RECTAL ITCH: LOSE 1 TURN
(64) SAFE
(65) SAFE
(66) SAFE
(67) HEMORRHOIDS: SELECT NUMBER ON SPACE CHART AND MOVE BACKWARD TWICE THE AMOUNT
(68) SAFE
(69) PILES: LOSE 2 TURNS
(70) WIN

HOSPITAL H

Paula Scher/Seymour Chwast

BODYSCRAP

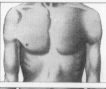

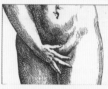

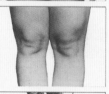

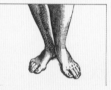
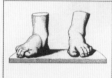

As summer approaches, it's time to get back in shape and restore all the natural oils to your body that the long cold winter has taken away. Here are some beauty tips for every important part of your body, guaranteed to make you a knock-out on Fire Island this summer.

Your Feet.
Here they come in neat little sandals or barefoot on the beach. There's no getting around it. In the summer, the entire world will be examining your feet. Oh, you can put a little toenail polish on and hope for the best. Or, you can waste a lot of money on an expensive pedicure, but there's no substitute for daily care. Start off with a simple foot bath. It's just a little dish washing liquid and warm water. Make some suds and soak. It softens your feet as you do dishes. Callouses will fly away in two weeks of nightly soaking. However if you're suffering from ugly corns, you can't beat Frea-Zone. Apply as directed and watch corns vanish in days.

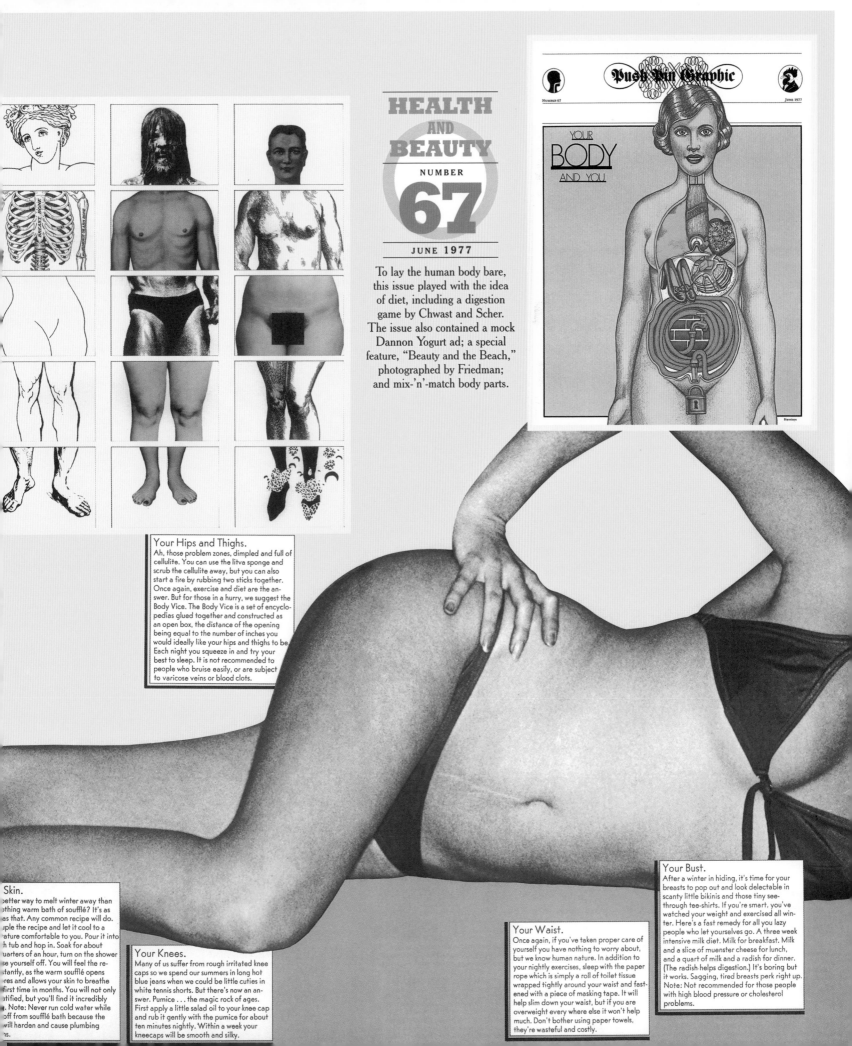

Push Pin Graphic

NUMBER 67   JUNE 1977

YOUR BODY AND YOU

HEALTH AND BEAUTY

NUMBER

67

JUNE 1977

To lay the human body bare, this issue played with the idea of diet, including a digestion game by Chwast and Scher. The issue also contained a mock Dannon Yogurt ad; a special feature, "Beauty and the Beach," photographed by Friedman; and mix-'n'-match body parts.

Your Hips and Thighs.
Ah, those problem zones, dimpled and full of cellulite. You can use the litva sponge and scrub the cellulite away, but you can also start a fire by rubbing two sticks together. Once again, exercise and diet are the answer. But for those in a hurry, we suggest the Body Vice. The Body Vice is a set of encyclopedias glued together and constructed as an open box, the distance of the opening being equal to the number of inches you would ideally like your hips and thighs to be. Each night you squeeze in and try your best to sleep. It is not recommended to people who bruise easily, or are subject to varicose veins or blood clots.

Skin.
etter way to melt winter away than othing warm bath of soufflé? It's as as that. Any common recipe will do. uple the recipe and let it cool to a rature comfortable to you. Pour it into h tub and hop in. Soak for about uarters of an hour, turn on the shower se yourself off. You will feel the re-tantly, as the warm soufflé opens res and allows your skin to breathe first time in months. You will not only atified, but you'll find it incredibly . Note: Never run cold water while off from soufflé bath because the will harden and cause plumbing s.

Your Knees.
Many of us suffer from rough irritated knee caps so we spend our summers in long hot blue jeans when we could be little cuties in white tennis shorts. But there's now an answer. Pumice . . . the magic rock of ages. First apply a little salad oil to your knee cap and rub it gently with the pumice for about ten minutes nightly. Within a week your kneecaps will be smooth and silky.

Your Waist.
Once again, if you've taken proper care of yourself you have nothing to worry about, but we know human nature. In addition to your nightly exercises, sleep with the paper rope which is simply a roll of toilet tissue wrapped tightly around your waist and fastened with a piece of masking tape. It will help slim down your waist, but if you are overweight every where else it won't help much. Don't bother using paper towels, they're wasteful and costly.

Your Bust.
After a winter in hiding, it's time for your breasts to pop out and look delectable in scanty little bikinis and those tiny see-through tee-shirts. If you're smart, you've watched your weight and exercised all winter. Here's a fast remedy for all you lazy people who let yourselves go. A three week intensive milk diet. Milk for breakfast. Milk and a slice of muenster cheese for lunch, and a quart of milk and a radish for dinner. (The radish helps digestion.) It's boring but it works. Sagging, tired breasts perk right up. Note: Not recommended for those people with high blood pressure or cholesterol problems.

NEW YORK AT NIGHT

NUMBER

68

AUGUST 1977

This issue covered the nighttime underworld of New York from a variety of vantage points. A series of thumbnail film stills followed a man as he wakes up in Staten Island in the middle of the night and goes to work by ferry and subway to his job in underground Manhattan. Other features included nightlife at a dance club (Stavrinos), a strip joint (Chwast), and an interview with an all-night cab driver.

Your Hair.
We have finally come up with a recipe for the ultimate conditioner. Two tablespoons peanut oil, one lemon, two egg whites beaten until stiff, one cup milk, one cup beer, a pinch of paprika. Pour the ingredients into an electric blender and press frappé. The mixture should be creamy, but not curdled. Apply the mixture to towel dry hair, wait thirty seconds, then rinse. The results will be amazing. Note: Vegetable oil may be used when peanut oil is unavailable.

Your Nose.
Your poor nose. Three months of frost bite and sniffles can really do it in. What your nose needs now is protection. It is not enough to merely use a skin moisturizer because it tends to rub off on the pillow while you are sleeping. What we recommend is the simple nose guard. It can be purchased in Lamstons, or Woolworths in the novelty section. The nose guard is a flesh colored piece of plastic in the shape of a large nose, that will easily cover your own. (One size fits all.) It usually comes attached to glasses with bushy black eyebrows. Each night, after you generously apply the moisturizer to your nose, put on the nose guard and sleep peacefully. Caution: Not recommended for those who suffer from asthma, or serious allergies.

Your Eyes.
The cold weather does more harm to your eyes than a death in the family. Loss in natural oils may result in premature crows feet, puffy lids and sometimes conjunctivitis. A simple remedy is a mayonnaise eyebath. For 14 consecutive nights, apply two tablespoons of mayonnaise to gauze strips. Lie in a vertical position, and apply the strips to your eyes, which should remain partially open. The gauze should remain over your eyes for at least 30 minutes per evening if the treatment is to produce fast results. After you remove the gauze, rinse your face with luke warm water, and pat your eyes gently. Caution: Contact lenses should always be removed before treatments.

Your Lips.
Chapped lips? So what else is new? Here's a real lip saver, and we're not kidding. Ready? Chicken Fat! It's the oldest and best cure for chapped lips. Any butcher can supply the fat. Buy seven pounds and freeze it, and it will last you the year. Each evening, before the eyebath, and after the nose guard, cut one and half tablespoons of the chicken fat. Boil a half cup of water with a little diced celery, (salt and pepper to taste). Add the schmaltz and bring to a boil. Then let the mixture cool until luke warm, and gently apply it to your lips, using your fingers.

Push Pin Graphic

Number 68   August 1977

New York at Night

184

STAVRINOS

INTERIOR DESIGN

NUMBER

69

OCTOBER 1977

Here is a parody of *House Beautiful* magazine, with features on exotic doorknobs by Emanuel Schongut and Miyauchi; a stain removal guide illustrated by Arnold Rosenberg; photography of a murder scene (blood and all); Richard Mantel's nineteenth-century-style collage of the Mormon Tabernacle Choir's living room; Chwast's "Maid's Revenge"; and a selection of wacky swimming pools.

Push Pin Graphic

NUMBER 69   OCTOBER 1977

House Nice

EDGAR ALLAN POE'S DOORKNOB BY JOHN COLLIER

POOL PUZZLE

Many people nowadays build pools appropriately shaped for the work they do. Match the correct professions to the illustrations. The correct answers are given below.

1. a. brain surgeon
   b. podiatrist
   c. cabinet maker
2. a. Mexican
   b. disc jockey
   c. soda jerk
3. a. violinist
   b. cellist
   c. guitarist
4. a. painter
   b. ballet dancer
   c. poet
5. a. actress
   b. astronomer
   c. actor
6. a. locksmith
   b. accountant
   c. scientist
7. a. ice skater
   b. draftsman
   c. dentist
8. a. secretary
   b. chef
   c. geriatric

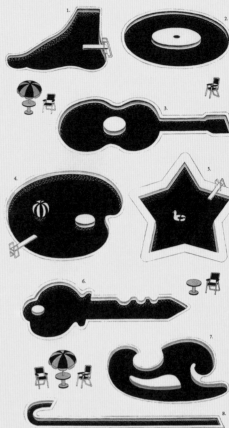

Answers: 1.b, 2.b, 3.c, 4.a, 5.a, 6.a, 7.b, 8.c

13

BETTER HOUSEKEEPING

BY PAULA SCHER

I MADE IT MYSELF

Many of us think we need a high income in order to make our HOUSE NICE. Nothing could be further from the truth. With a little ingenuity and patience you can turn your drab, ordinary, tacky home into a palace fit for Monty Hall. Here are some wonderful homemade decorating tips.

THE CORRUGATED SOFA

This is perfect for the guest room, den, playroom, or even your living room. Materials needed: 3 corrugated cardboard crates, 15" x 15", Elmer's glue, paint (optional). Instructions: lay the 3 crates side by side, upside down. Coat the right hand side of the first two boxes with Elmer's glue. Let stand for one minute then press all three boxes together until a sofa is formed. Allow one hour for glue to dry. Decorate with paint if you so desire, or cover with material or clear plastic.

THE CLASSIC NAPKIN HOLDER

We all know about this one, but classics are always worth repeating. Materials needed: 25 popsicle or fudgsicle sticks (cleaned), Elmer's glue, shellac, paint and seashells (optional). Instructions: lay first 10 sticks together side by side. Coat right edge of first 9 sticks with Elmer's glue. Wait thirty seconds then press together forming a flat surface. Repeat the process with another 10 popsicle sticks. Then do the same to the remaining 5 sticks. After the flat areas of the sticks have dried sufficiently, (about half an hour), glue the three panels together. The 5 sticks should form the base and the two sets of ten sticks should form the sides. Be sure to support the construction with your hands for five minutes while the glue is setting. Leave to dry one hour, then coat with shellac or paint. There is nothing lovelier than decorating the finished napkin holder with assorted collected shells.

THE CLAY TURTLE ASHTRAY

This popular ashtray gets its name from the fact that it is shaped like the back of a turtle. Materials needed: approximately ⅓ pound of pottery clay, firing kiln, colored glaze. Instructions: hold clay with both hands and form a round ball about the size of a baseball. Hold clay ball in left hand, take right fist and press into balls, surface forming a pocket. Lightly, with both thumbs smooth surface of pocket, and outside of entire ashtray. If desired, create three indentures in the rim of ashtray for holding cigarettes. Do this by pressing clay firmly with right index finger. Smooth again and leave to dry. Drying period is two days. Fire in pottery kiln. Coat with glaze of your choice. Fire again and voila!

PAPIER MACHE NAPKIN RINGS

Why spend a fortune on expensive napkin rings when you can whip some up at home without spending a dime. Materials needed: 3 cardboard tubes from paper towels or 6 cardboard tubes from toilet paper, ½ cup flour, 1 cup water, Sunday Times, paint, shellac. Instructions: saw through tubes every inch. Set rings aside. Make paste by mixing flour and water. Set aside. Tear newspaper strips approximately ½ inch wide and 4 inches long. Drench strips in paste and then start rolling around each ring. Paste about 20 to 30 strips on each ring and set aside to dry for 24 hours. When dry, paint with your favorite color and then shellac.

JUBILANT BATHROOM

Bathrooms have traditionally been boring affairs. Pastel tile with wallboard and a little formica thrown in are about as exciting as a bottle of antidiarreal. The ultimate goal of bathroom design should be to allow the personality of the homeowner to shine through while at the same time, establishing all the sanitary bathroom needs. We have created some bathroom decorating ideas for just that purpose. Below are several suggestions and one is just right for you.

BATH A LA ROMA

Rel flocked wallpaper with a simple gold fleur de lis design is a good beginning. The built in sink counter should be white formica with random gold speckles. An alternative for this could be a black counter with gold swirls. The bathroom floor should remain in style with the counter, perhaps a white linoleum with gold embellishments, or black and gold linoleum. Sticking to the gold motif we move on to the sink basin, tub and commode. Try to obtain these in solid gold. If that runs too expensive settle for gold painted. Now for the accessories. The shower curtain, red imitation velvet. The towels and washcloths, red, gold, and black. For the final touch, a crystal water glass with gold trim, found in any department store and, gold and black soaps.

THE AMERICAN BATH

Early American is the theme here. Start by papering your walls with a heritage print and then laying down avocado colored linoleum that has a traditional brick pattern. Next add avocado colored fixtures. The shower curtain should be black and white with an illustration depicting the signing of the Declaration of Independence. The sink counter and bathroom hamper you buy should be imitation wood contact paper. Don't forget matching avocado towels and a bathmat with an eagle that reads, "E PLURIBUS UNUM."

THE FOUNTAINBLEAU BATH

The motif here is turquoise and hot pink. All fixtures should be bright turquoise porcelain. The bottom half of the bathroom wall and floor should be tiled, alternating pink and turquoise tiles. Finish off with a black trim. For the remaining wall board, you have a choice. Paint it hot pink or turquoise. A clear plastic shower curtain with pink flamingos is recommended for it will enhance the colors in the room. Of course, don't forget matching soaps and towels. And for the finishing touch, corner shelves with pink flamingo garden sculpture.

WHAT'S GOING ON

UNDER YOUR BED

Okay. Let's have it. What have you got there? An old sock and a couple of dust balls? Maybe there's only a pair of ripped galoshes. The fact of the matter is the space under your bed particularly if you have a queen or king sized mattress is the most misused space in your home. Now, of course, many of us have practiced the age old method of throwing everything under the bed when company arrives unexpectedly, but there are really much more creative and practical uses for the space.

Consider this. If you had to hide something in a hurry where would be the most natural place be? *Under the bed*. Right?

Here are some unpleasant objects that belong under the bed. *continued on page 23*

continued on page 23

THE LINOLEUM BUYER'S GUIDE BY WILLIAM SLOAN

THE
BATTLE
IN THE
LIVING ROOM,
OR,
THE MAID'S
REVENGE.

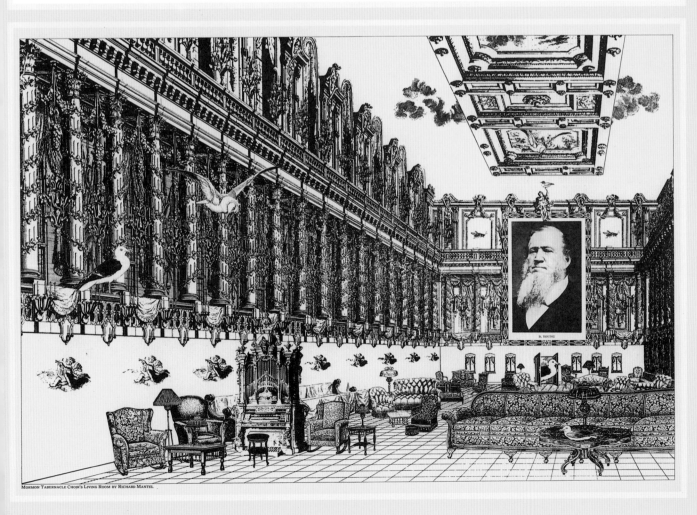

MORMON TABERNACLE CHOIR'S LIVING ROOM BY RICHARD MANTEL

FOOD & VIOLENCE

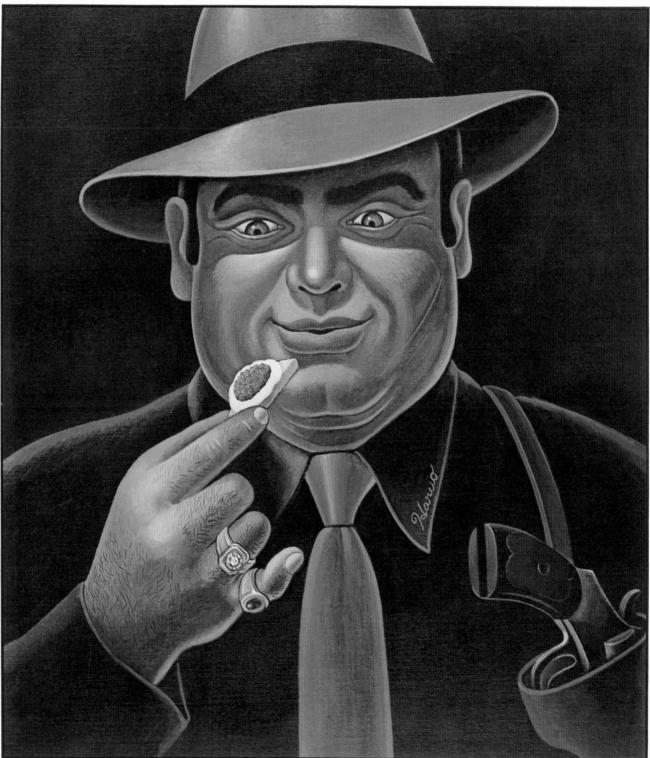

AL CAPONE EATING FRESH MALOSSOL MEDIUM GRAIN CHUM SALMON CAVIAR ON TOAST WITH SOUR CREAM.

IN-DIGESTION

NUMBER

70

DECEMBER 1977

Juxtaposing food and violence
may have been inspired by scenes in
The Godfather, but the appetizing
relationship was digested even further in
this issue. An excerpt from Upton
Sinclair's *The Jungle* chronicled brutal
and unsanitary meatpacking conditions.
Scher's "Gastric Aggression" explained
why gas-bloated Germany went to war,
and "What Are You Eating,"
a list of surprising food ingredients,
predated America's obsession
with these concerns.

LAMB TO THE SLAUGHTER

BY ROALD DAHL

MARY—
Can the police
guess what she's
cooked up?

Specially posed for
the Push Pin Graphic
by professional models

THE room was warm and clean, the curtains drawn, the two table lamps alight—hers and the one by the empty chair opposite. On the sideboard behind her, two tall glasses, soda water, whiskey. Fresh ice cubes in the Thermos bucket.

Mary Maloney was waiting for her husband to come home from work.

Now and again she would glance up at the clock, but without anxiety, merely to please herself with the thought that each minute gone by made it nearer the time when he would come. There was a slow smiling air about her, and about everything she did. The drop of the head as she bent over her sewing was curiously tranquil. Her skin—for this was her sixth month with child—had acquired a wonderful translucent quality, the mouth was soft, and the eyes, with their new placid look, seemed larger, darker than before.

When the clock said ten minutes to five, she began to listen, and a few moments later, punctually as always, she heard the tires on the gravel outside, and the car door slamming, the footsteps passing the window, the key turning in the lock. She laid aside her sewing, stood up, and went forward to kiss him as he came in.

"Hullo darling," she said.

"Hullo," he answered.

She took his coat and hung it in the closet. Then she walked over and made the drinks, a strongish one for him, a weak one for herself; and

HUBBY GETS JUST DESSERTS BEFORE DINNER

WHAT ARE YOU EATING?

The ingredients of some food products we bought from our local supermarket are listed here. Can you guess what these products are. Answers below.

INGREDIENTS: WATER, SUGAR, NON-FAT DRY MILK, FOOD STARCH-MODIFIED, PARTIALLY HYDROGENATED COTTONSEED AND SOYBEAN OIL, SODIUM ALGINATE (THICKENER), SALT, CARAGEENAN AND DEXTRIN (THICKENER), SODIUM STEAROYL-2-LACTYLATE (EMULSIFIER), ARTIFICIAL FLAVORS, ARTIFICIAL COLORS AND SODIUM HEXAMETA-PHOSPHATE (IMPROVES TEXTURE).

1.

INGREDIENTS: SUGAR, ANIMAL AND/OR VEGETABLE SHORTENING (CONTAINS ONE OR MORE OF THE FOLLOWING PARTIALLY HYDROGENATED FATS: SOYBEAN OIL, COTTONSEED OIL, BEEF TALLOW, PALM OIL, LARD), WATER, CORN SYRUP, WHEAT STARCH, MONO AND DIGLYCERIDES, NON-FAT MILK, SALT, POLYSORBATE 60, SUNKIST* PERMA-STABIL* NATURAL ORANGE FLAVOR, ARTIFICIAL COLORS, ARTIFICIAL AND NATURAL FLAVOR, CITRIC ACID, SOY LECITHIN, SODIUM ACID PYROPHOSPHATE, DEXTROSE, PECTIN, FRESHNESS PRESERVED BY POTASSIUM SORBATE, BHA AND BHT.

2.

INGREDIENTS: CORN SYRUP SOLIDS, VEGETABLE FAT, SODIUM CASEINATE, DI-POTASSIUM PHOSPHATE, MONOGLYCERIDES, SODIUM SILICO ALUMINATE, SODIUM TRIPOLYPHOSPHATE, BETA CAROTENE AND RIBOFLAVIN (ARTIFICIAL COLORS).

3.

INGREDIENTS: MODIFIED FOOD STARCH, CORNSTARCH, HYDROLYZED VEGETABLE PROTEIN, WHEY, MUSHROOMS, VEGETABLE SHORTENING, SUGAR, SALT, ARTIFICIAL FLAVOR, YEAST EXTRACT, CARAMEL COLOR, NONFAT DRY MILK, DEHYDRATED ONION, SPICES, DISODIUM INOSINATE, DISODIUM GUANYLATE.

4.

INGREDIENTS: SUGAR, GRAHAM CRACKER CRUMBS (ENRICHED WHEAT FLOUR), FLOUR, NIACIN, IRON, THIAMINE (VITAMIN B₁), RIBOFLAVIN (VITAMIN B₂), GRAHAM FLOUR, SUGAR, RYE FLOUR, HYDROGENATED VEGETABLE OIL (SOYBEAN AND COTTONSEED OIL), MOLASSES, CORN SYRUP, BAKING SODA, AMMONIUM BICARBONATE, SALT, NATURAL FLAVOR, HYDROGENATED COCONUT OIL, CORN SYRUP SOLIDS, DRIED MARGARINE (HYDROGENATED SOYBEAN OIL, SALT, NON-FAT MILK, LECITHIN, MONO- AND DIGLYCERIDES, ARTIFICIAL COLOR, ARTIFICIAL FLAVOR, SODIUM BENZOATE ADDED AS A PRESERVATIVE), MODIFIED TAPIOCA STARCH, DRIED BAKERS CHEESE, WHEY, DRIED CREAM CHEESE, CULTURED BUTTERMILK, SODIUM CASEINATE, LACTIC ACID, DRIED SOUR CREAM PRESERVED WITH BHA, MONO- AND DIGLYCERIDES, PROPYLENE GLYCOL MONOSTEARATE, DISODIUM PHOSPHATE, SILICON DIOXIDE, KARAYA GUM, CITRIC ACID, GLYCERYL MONOSTEARATE, NATURAL AND ARTIFICIAL FLAVOR, SALT, ADIPIC ACID, ARTIFICIAL COLOR, BHA AND BHT (PRESERVATIVES).

5.

MADE WITH ENRICHED FLOUR [BARLEY MALT, FERROUS SULFATE (IRON), NIACIN (A "B" VITAMIN), THIAMINE MONONITRATE (B₁), RIBOFLAVIN (B₂)], WATER, CORN SYRUP, PARTIALLY HYDROGENATED VEGETABLE SHORTENING (MAY CONTAIN SOYBEAN AND/OR COTTONSEED AND/OR PALM AND/OR PEANUT OIL), YEAST, SALT, SOY FLOUR, CALCIUM SULFATE, SODIUM STEAROYL-2-LACTYLATE, MONO- AND DIGLYCERIDES, WHEY, DICALCIUM PHOSPHATE, POTASSIUM BROMATE; CALCIUM PROPIONATE (TO RETARD SPOILAGE).

6.

INGREDIENTS: SUGAR, GRAHAM CRACKER CRUMBS [ENRICHED WHEAT FLOUR, GRAHAM FLOUR, SUGAR, RYE FLOUR, VEGETABLE SHORTENING (PARTIALLY HYDROGENATED SOYBEAN AND COTTONSEED OIL), MOLASSES, CORN SYRUP, LEAVENING, SALT, NATURAL FLAVOR], MODIFIED TAPIOCA STARCH, HYDROGENATED VEGETABLE SHORTENING, ENZYME MODIFIED SOY PROTEIN, NONFAT MILK, GELATIN, NATURAL AND ARTIFICIAL FLAVOR, CITRIC ACID, SALT, DISODIUM PHOSPHATE, ARTIFICIAL COLOR.

7.

190

ANSWERS
1. Comstock® Banana Cream Filling, Curtice Burns, Inc.
2. Betty Crocker® Ready To Spread Frosting, General Mills, Inc.
3. Cremora™ Non Dairy Creamer, Borden®, Inc.
4. Ehlers® Mushroom Gravy Mix, Brooke Bond Foods, ® Inc.
5. Pillsbury Cheese Cake with Sour Cream, The Pillsbury Company ®
6. Wonder Bread, ITT Continental Baking Co. Inc. ®
7. Pillsbury Lemon Chiffon Pie Mix, The Pillsbury Company ®

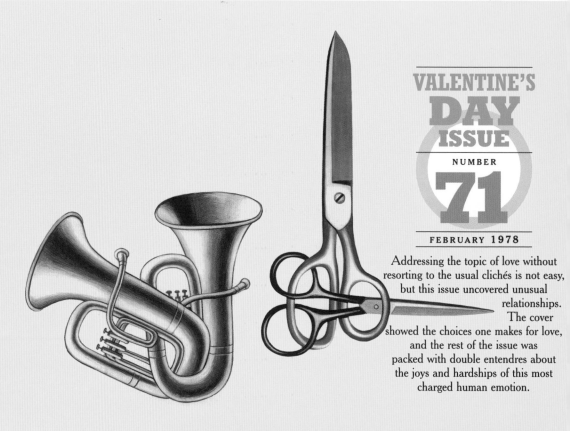

VALENTINE'S
DAY
ISSUE

NUMBER
71

FEBRUARY 1978

Addressing the topic of love without resorting to the usual clichés is not easy, but this issue uncovered unusual relationships. The cover showed the choices one makes for love, and the rest of the issue was packed with double entendres about the joys and hardships of this most charged human emotion.

WHAT IS THIS THING CALLED LOVE?

A Hot Dog for Your Jelly Roll

Leavin' Here Rotten Woman Blues
By Crippled California Willie
(as collected by Ken Robbins)

You don't want my peaches, baby
Don't shake up on my tree
You a low down woman
Give it away for free

Oooh-whee baby, movin' down the road
Oooh, babe, I didn't know it showed
But I just can't help to love that jelly roll

Got somethin' for ya mama
Gonna put you on ice
I got it wrapped in swaddlin'
For to keep it all nice

Oooh Baby, burnin' up that road
I'm burnin' all night long, mama
Can't help but love that jelly roll

Oh jelly
Love that jelly roll

Low down woman
Goin' straight to hell
Tell what you been doin'
By the way you smell

My old woman,
She got her head in the hall
Her feet's in the kitchen
She's too damn tall

Oooh babe, love that jelly roll
Oh, mama, walkin's most too slow.

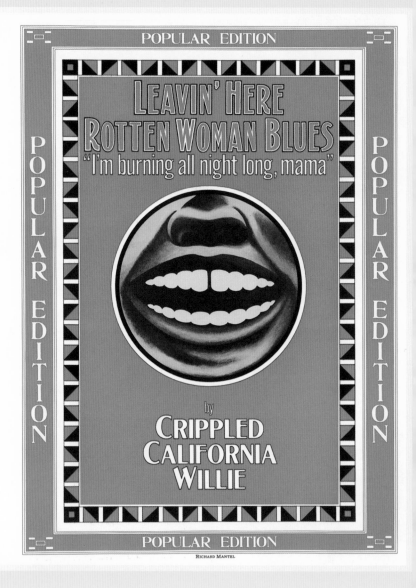

POPULAR EDITION

LEAVIN' HERE ROTTEN WOMAN BLUES
"I'm burning all night long, mama"

POPULAR EDITION

POPULAR EDITION

by
CRIPPLED
CALIFORNIA
WILLIE

POPULAR EDITION

RICHARD MANTEL

Push Pin Graphic

NUMBER 71   FEBRUARY 1978

WHAT IS THIS THING CALLED LOVE?

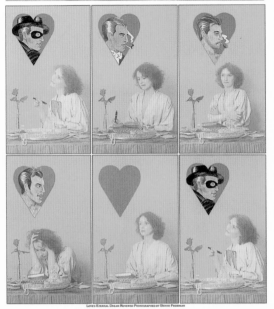

The Sound of Ringing Bells

A Telephone Call
By Dorothy Parker

Please, God, let him telephone me now. Dear God, let him call me now. I won't ask anything else of You, truly I won't. It isn't very much to ask. It would be so little to You, God, such a little, little thing. Only let him telephone now. Please, God. Please, please, please.

If I didn't think about it, maybe the telephone might ring. Sometimes it does that. If I could think of something else. If I could think of something else. Maybe if I counted five hundred by fives, it might ring by that time. I'll count slowly. I won't cheat. And if it rings when I get to three hundred, I won't stop; I won't answer it until I get to five hundred. Five, ten, fifteen, twenty, twenty-five, thirty, thirty-five, forty, forty-five, fifty....Oh, please ring. Please.

This is the last time I'll look at the clock. I will not look at it again. It's ten minutes past seven. He said he would telephone at five o'clock. "I'll call you at five, darling." I think that's where he said "darling." I'm almost sure he said it there. I know he called me "darling" twice, and the other time was when he said good-by. "Good-by, darling." He was busy, and he can't say much in the office, but he called me "darling" twice. He couldn't have minded my calling him up. I know you shouldn't keep telephoning them—I know they don't like that. When you do that, they know you are thinking about them and wanting them, and that makes them hate you. But I hadn't talked to him in three days—not in three days. And all I did was ask him how he was; it was just the way anybody might have called him up. He couldn't have minded that. He couldn't have thought I was bothering him. "No, of course you're not," he said. And he said he'd telephone me. He didn't have to say that. I didn't ask him to, truly I didn't. I'm sure I didn't. I don't think he would say he'd telephone me, and then just never do it. Please don't let him do that, God. Please don't.

"I'll call you at five, darling." "Good-by, darling." He was busy, and he was in a hurry, and there were people around him, but he

THE
GARDEN (!)
STATE

NUMBER
72

APRIL 1978

Chwast threw caution to the wind with this mock travel guide to the Garden State, New Jersey, long the butt of New Yorkers' jokes. The state was treated ironically on the cover by Mantel and as an oil slick by Miyauchi, but realistically in "Route 22 Typographica," a precursor to the nineties celebration of vernacular design. Collier's somber painting of bathers moodily reflected the seedy essence of the seaside.

SPRING TRAVEL ISSUE

Push Pin Graphic

Number 72   April 1978

EXPLORING NEW JERSEY

The Garden State by Richard Mantel

194

Atlantic City by John Collier

196

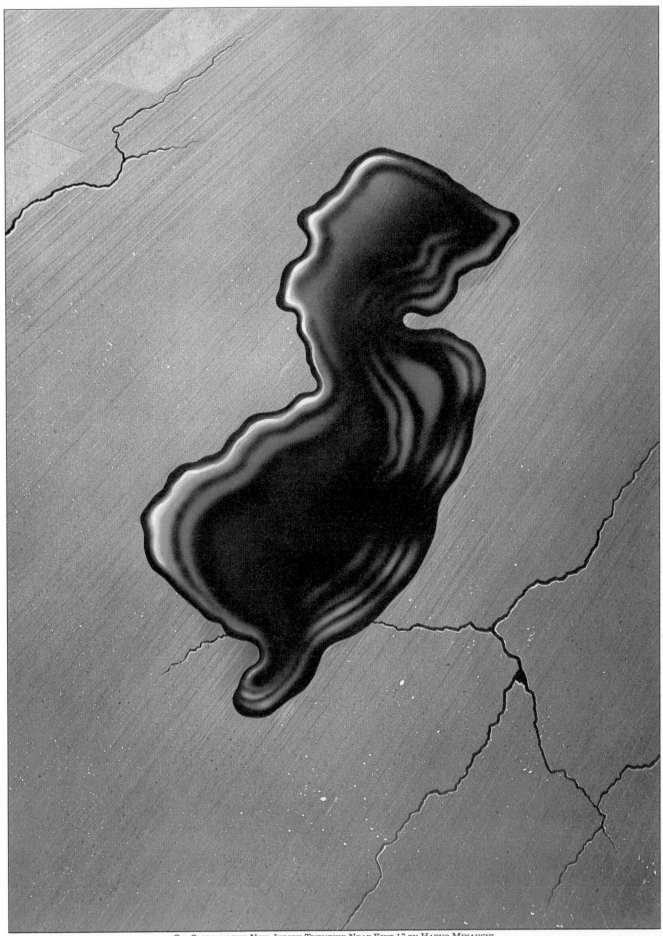

OIL SLICK ON THE NEW JERSEY TURNPIKE NEAR EXIT 17 BY HARUO MIYAUCHI

We asked some of our friends to contribute portraits of clowns. Herewith are their submissions for which we thank them all. Some of them admittedly exceeded the prescribed 7 minutes.

CLOWNS

NUMBER

73

JUNE 1978

Everyone loves a clown, so the saying goes, which is why so many friends and members of Push Pin responded to the "7 Minute Clowns" project. Also in this special issue were Miyauchi's painting of famous and infamous people as clowns and Chwast's parable "Bobo's Smile."

THE CLOWNS

NUMBER 73   JUNE 1978

JOHN COLLIER

198

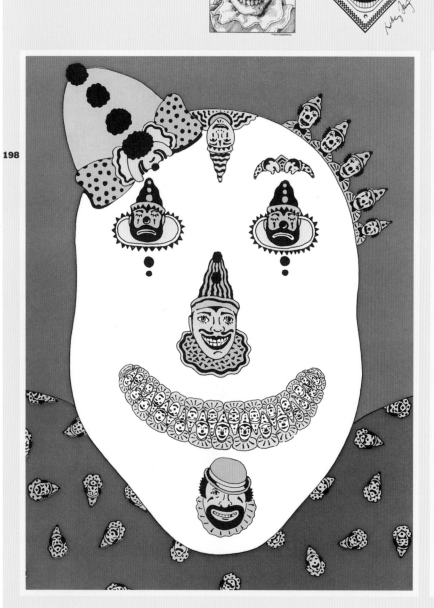

We asked some of our friends to contribute portraits of clowns. Herewith are their submissions for which we thank them all. Some of them admittedly exceeded the prescribed 7 minutes.

CLOWN COUTURE

Pierrot Jardin's sketches for the upcoming season promise a return of the "baggy jump suit" look. The three pom-poms down the front are cleverly repeated at the instep. Note the loose, floppy collar ruffle.

STANDING: KU KLUX KLOWN, IDI AMIN CLOWN, KAISER WILHELM CLOWN II, SPIRO T. CLOWN. SEATED: CLOWN VICTORIA

199

ADVENTURES IN SLEEP

NUMBER 74

AUGUST 1978

The challenge was how to make an exciting *Graphic* devoted, more or less, to putting the readers to sleep. Features included dream interpretations and how famous people sleep. Ken Robbins wrote a contemporary version of "Sleeping Beauty." But for insomniacs, Chwast selected a "boring story," which he set in 8-point type, while for really serious nonsleepers the text was repeated in 7-point and 6-point type.

BACK TO SLEEP ISSUE

Push Pin Graphic

NUMBER 74   AUGUST 1978

SEYMOUR CHWAST

200

SLEEPY HEADS

Three Sleeping Potions

BROMIDE OF POTASH	HYDRATE OF CHLORAL	BROMIDIA
10 grains	10 grains	1 drachm
SYRUP OF ORANGE	BROMIDE OF POTASH	SYRUP OF ORANGE
½ drachm	15 grains	½ drachm
WATER TO AN OUNCE	SYRUP OF ORANGE	WATER TO AN OUNCE
Two or three tablespoonfuls	½ drachm	Two tablespoonfuls
to be taken at bed-time.	WATER TO AN OUNCE	to be taken at bed-time.
	Two tablespoonfuls	
	to be taken at bed-time.	

MORE SLEEP KIT

Count the Dots

Frank Buck's Dream.

EMANUEL SCHONGUT

Karl Wallenda's Dream.

HARUO MIYAUCHI

COSTUME PARTY

Stanislaw Zagorski

Seymour Chwast

Emanuel Schongut

Costume Created and Modeled by Pat Oleszko

FASHION
NUMBER
75
OCTOBER 1978

All the Push Pin artists joined to produce a history of costumes, using collaged vintage engravings to inject an absurd historical dimension. Tom Wolfe reported on alternative youth in Los Angeles in "The Hair Boys." And performance artist Pat Oleszko's futurist clown costume was featured among the other "Costume Party" guests. Robbins, newly appointed managing editor, wrote "How Clothes Began."

IRON

CLAD

"In" this season is the industrial look, evoking the high technology ambiance of the really high rent discos. An ecological, technological wonder, it starts with you and your concern about putting the products of our industrialized society to truly human uses. It's the haute couture of today, the ready-to-wear of tomorrow, and it's guaranteed to put the wear back in hardware.

Photographed by Richard Pan

Reversible Mask

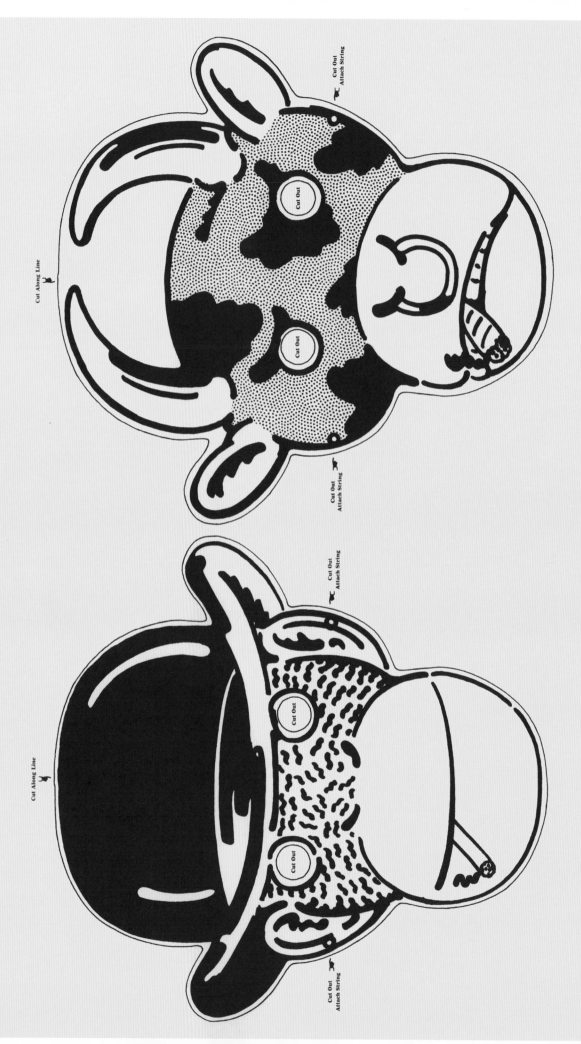

Cut Along Line

Cut Out
Attach String

Cut Out

Cut Out

Cut Out
Attach String

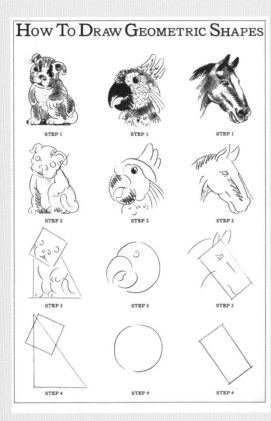

STEP 1   STEP 1   STEP 1

STEP 2   STEP 2   STEP 2

STEP 3   STEP 3   STEP 3

STEP 4   STEP 4   STEP 4

Push Pin Graphic

ANIMAL FOLLIES ISSUE

NUMBER 76

DECEMBER 1978

EMANUEL SCHONGUT

ANIMAL FOLLIES

NUMBER

76

DECEMBER 1978

"How to Draw Geometric Shapes," a send-up on the chestnut "Draw Me" matchbook ads, was one of the most ironic of the *Graphic*'s features and a fitting coda for an issue devoted to the animal kingdom. Featured was "Animal Almanac—Strange Facts, Odd Tidbits, and Weird Wonders" by Robbins. Also a composite animal/fish/bird by Miyauchi called the Barantaphantabull illustrated "Save Our Endangered Species" by Scher.

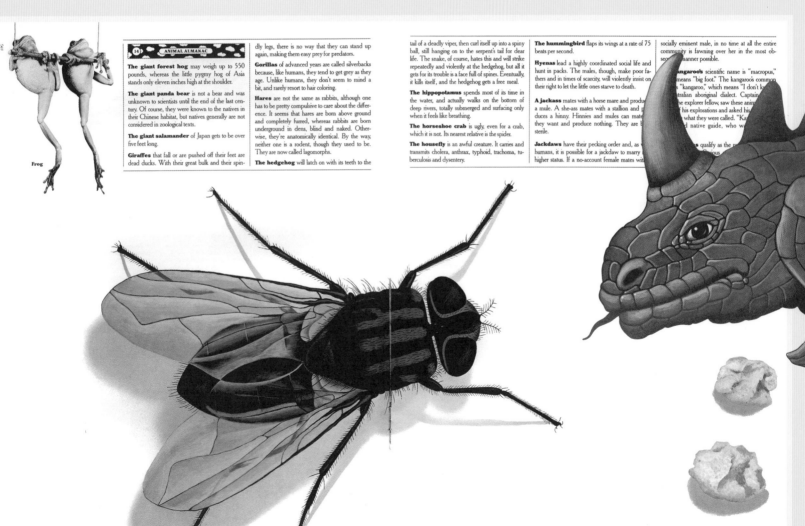

Frog

(14) ANIMAL ALMANAC

The giant forest hog may weigh up to 550 pounds, whereas the little pygmy hog of Asia stands only eleven inches high at the shoulder.

The giant panda bear is not a bear and was unknown to scientists until the end of the last century. Of course, they were known to the natives in their Chinese habitat, but natives generally are not considered in zoological texts.

The giant salamander of Japan gets to be over five feet long.

Giraffes that fall or are pushed off their feet are dead ducks. With their great bulk and their spin-dly legs, there is no way that they can stand up again, making them easy prey for predators.

Gorillas of advanced years are called silverbacks because, like humans, they tend to get grey as they age. Unlike humans, they don't seem to mind a bit, and rarely resort to hair coloring.

Hares are not the same as rabbits, although one has to be pretty compulsive to care about the difference. It seems that hares are born above ground and completely furred, whereas rabbits are born underground in dens, blind and naked. Otherwise, they're anatomically identical. By the way, neither one is a rodent, though they used to be. They are now called lagomorphs.

The hedgehog will latch on with its teeth to the tail of a deadly viper, then curl itself up into a spiny ball, still hanging on to the serpent's tail for dear life. The snake, of course, hates this and will strike repeatedly and violently at the hedgehog, but all it gets for its trouble is a face full of spines. Eventually, it kills itself, and the hedgehog gets a free meal.

The hippopotamus spends most of its time in the water, and actually walks on the bottom of deep rivers, totally submerged and surfacing only when it feels like breathing.

The horseshoe crab is ugly, even for a crab, which it is not. Its nearest relative is the spider.

The housefly is an awful creature. It carries and transmits cholera, anthrax, typhoid, trachoma, tuberculosis and dysentery.

The hummingbird flaps its wings at a rate of 75 beats per second.

Hyenas lead a highly coordinated social life and hunt in packs. The males, though, make poor fathers and in times of scarcity, will violently insist on their right to let the little ones starve to death.

A jackass mates with a horse mare and produces a mule. A she-ass mates with a stallion and produces a hinny. Hinnies and mules can mate all they want and produce nothing. They are sterile.

Jackdaws have their pecking order and, as with humans, it is possible for a jackdaw to marry higher status. If a no-account female mates with a socially eminent male, in no time at all the entire community is fawning over her in the most obsequious manner possible.

The **kangaroo's** scientific name is "macropus," which means "big foot." The kangaroo's common name is "kangaroo," which means "I don't know" in the Australian aboriginal dialect. Captain Cook, the explorer fellow, saw these animals on his explorations and asked his Australian native guide, who was unaware what they were called. "Ka..." said the native guide, who was...

Housefly by Richard Mantel

THE **LIFE** AND **DEATH** OF **MACHINES**

NUMBER

77

1979

Long before *The Matrix* proffered Earth's domination by machines, the *Graphic* offered its own cautionary tales. Elwood Smith (right) posed for a demonstration of building a cardboard motorcycle. Chwast executed a machine in the electric chair. Another pictorial essay looked back to when the shape of machines reflected their function. And in a song illustrated by Stanislaw Zagorski the mythic John Henry beat a machine with only his human strength.

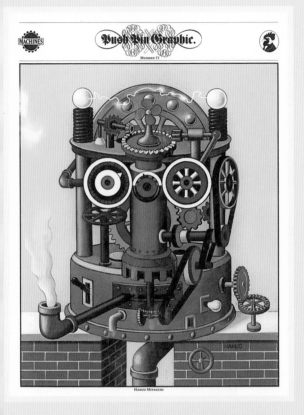

Push Pin Graphic.

Number 77

HASUO MIYAUCHI

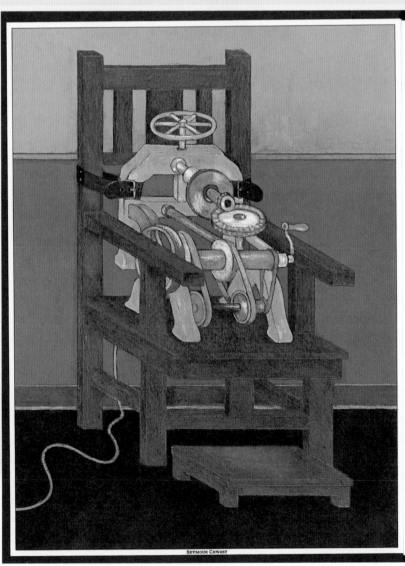

SEYMOUR CHWAST

The Death of the Machine

Webster's New World Dictionary defines magic as "...any mysterious, seemingly inexplicable or extraordinary power or influence." Since it has been precisely this quest for power and influence that has characterized Mankind's progress through history, it might be said that human epochs can be measured by the kind of magic that we practice. In our own age the key to power and influence has surely been the magic of the machine.

But of magic it is wise to know that there are two kinds. White magic is the kind that everyone understands on some level. In its feminine guise it is the work of the Muses and of Mother Nature; it is the magic of music and art and beauty, of fertility and organic growth; in its masculine guise it is the work of Prometheus and Hephaestus, the forging of elements, the magic of construction and artifice, of logic and mechanical causation. Black magic, on the other hand, has always been inaccessible to all but a few. It is the instantaneous, unfathomable, disjunctive, cool running, solid state, electronic mystery. In its feminine guise it is the work of witches, in its masculine guise, it stinks of electronic engineers.

Until recently we have imbued our machines with white magic, decorated and elaborated them with the designs and conceits of human whimsey, and we have *understood* them.

But the days of elegance and understanding and white magic are numbered. Black magic and the black box prevail. No one knows how machines work. They are meant to be disposable, or else to be sent away to be repaired by cyborgs who alone know their secrets. Gone is the friendly neighborhood shaman who made housecalls and repaired our televisions and *explained* what he did, while we looked on fascinated.

Everything today is "solid state," meaning, I suppose, impenetrable and dense; circuits boiled down, as it were, to solid kernels of resin and semi-conductors, so that design, that most human of choices, follows not function, not caprice, not even style, but limits itself to the box. Primal in its implications, the box has always, since Pandora, been a symbol for the containment of awful mysteries. That we encase our new machines in black boxes betokens an act of obeisance to the Sinister.

So it's the end of the machine age. No more pistons and levers, gaskets and tie rods, so sexual in their mechanicalness (because what is the human body, in one sense, but levers and pistons and sockets?). Goodbye to all that, and hello to the chemical, nay, molecular way with things, like computers and test tube babies.

On the following pages is our lament for the days of white magic. Take one last look. Shed one last tear.
—Ken Robbins

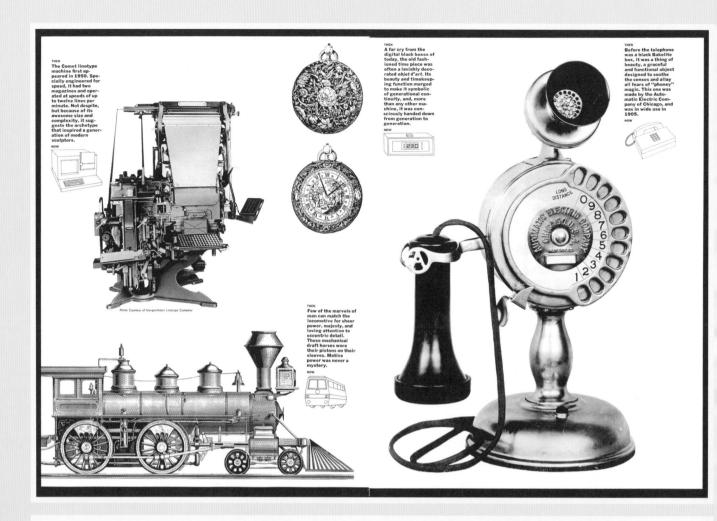

210

Pulling the Plug!
A Short Story by Paula Scher

I **bolt** up from a deep sleep. My face is warm with sunlight, my body is sweating under the blankets. I glance at the alarm clock. It is nine-thirty. There has been no alarm. I pull myself out of bed to examine the clock. It is set to **ring** at eight. The little chrome button is **pushed** toward "on". Why didn't it go off? I smack the top of the clock and it begins to **buzz**. I push the little chrome button to "off" and watch it snottily **POP** back to "on", all the while buzzing incessantly. It is also **shaking**. The whole top of my dresser begins to **vibrate** violently, and a glass ashtray, laden with cigarette butts crashes to the floor. I turn the chrome button to "off" again, but it deliberately **snaps** itself back to "on". "I'm sorry I hit you," I whimper, only half in jest, but the noise persists and it is **shattering** my nerves. The glowing numbers on the clock are now screaming "nine thirty-two". In desperation, I drop to the floor, and avoiding the shattered glass and ashes, I crawl under the dresser. I **SNATCH** the alarm clock plug from the socket with a vengeance, and at last all is quiet, I have won.

I survey the mess of broken glass, ashes, and cigarette butts still strewn all over the floor. I kneel and **pick** up the larger pieces of glass. Then, as I'm heading for the broom closet, I realize that I can clean up the whole mess faster with a vacuum cleaner. Fetching the vacuum cleaner from the hall closet, I gently untangle the cord, **PLUG** it into the hall socket, and gingerly turn it on. Up go the cigarette butts, up go the ashes. Then a rather large piece of glass **flies** into the vacuum. I hear it **rattling** and **crashing** inside the contraption, but I decide to ignore it. The machine begins to **roar** and **wheeze**.

All at once an enormous cloud of dust flies into my face in a deliberate attempt to asphyxiate me. I cough uncontrollably and drop the vacuum cleaner, which continues to **shimmy** on the floor in unguided spasms. It is now making obscene convulsive **HACKING** sounds. I clutch myself in terror and watch the monster give a final **gasp** and then vomit forth its insides all over the bedroom.

I am hopelessly covered with soot. I grope my way into the bathroom. It is cold and dank, so I plug in the electric heater, but the coils instantly become red hot and begin to **SMOKE**. I push the "off" button and step into the shower to wash off the soot. A burning smell permeates the bathroom. Smoky air combines with shower steam and my eyes tear and I begin to cough. Shoving my head out of the shower stall, I see that the heater coils are still **GLOWING** in a red-orange rage. They have become the devil's mouth, maliciously **grinning** at me. As the room becomes smokier still, I realize that I am about to be **suffocated** by a demon heater. I shut off the shower. The bathroom light is **flickering**, an omen, I think of my impending death. The heater has not shut off. The switch must be broken. I panic and **yank** the demon's plug from the socket with my wet and trembling fingers. In the next instant, my body is **wracked** with violent **spasms** from the ensuing shock. I am hurled against the shower stall and fall to the floor. While I lie in a helpless daze, the flickering light-bulb suddenly **shatters**, spraying glass all over the bathroom sink. Then all is quiet.

With great effort, I **heave** myself up from the bathroom floor where I had lain alternately sweating and shivering. My nerves are shot but I am alive! I know that danger is **LURKING** everywhere. Maybe not. It could all be totally coincidental. I must muster cour-age. I must have strength. I need sustenance. "I'll just make it to the kitchen." I **tiptoe** through the bedroom unperturbed by the fact that my newly cleaned feet are black with vacuum vomit. My body needs fuel. I pass the phonograph in the living room and spy my favorite Mozart record. Mozart and a piece of toast is all that man needs to survive. (Mozart and a piece of toast and a glass of orange juice; maybe a cup of coffee.) I feel my spirits lift. I put on Mozart. I **PLOP** two pieces of bread into the toaster and then empty a container of orange juice, and some water into the blender. I press **"mix"**. Having filled the electric coffee pot with cold water, I measure the coffee, **push** down the lid, and plug it into the socket. A piano concerto sings sweetly to me from the living room phonograph. The blender is **whirring** merrily. All seems well. Coffee mugs, I remember, are in the dishwasher. I open it and I am immediately confronted with a horde of greasy plates and **STICKY** coffee mugs. I pull out a mug and rinse it off under the faucet. Then I fill the soap compartment of the dishwasher, close the door, and turn the dial to "wash". I hear the machine **RATTLE** on, then make watery, swishy sounds. Soon it becomes a peaceful **hum**. But alas, now something is burning. The tiny kitchen fills with smoke. The toast! It didn't pop up. I can see it, **jammed** down at the bottom of the toaster, **charred** by red hot coils. I push the toaster button up. The toast barrels out of the toaster like a cannonball, **SMASHING** me in the face and **scorching** my left cheek. Now, the kitchen counter is **vibrating**, and the wall where my pots are hanging so violently that the pots unhook themselves and come **crashing** down on the floor. "My god, it's an earthquake! No it isn't, it's the blender! Turn the blender off. Turn it off!"

As I reach for the **"off"** button, the blender lid flies into the air, forced up by the pressure of angry orange juice lava, sticky devil's spit. I'm **burnt**, I'm tacky from orange juice, and I'm at the end of my rope. This is war. The machines are not simply malfunctioning. Oh no. This is a revolution. I accept this grim reality with defiance. It is a cruel **REVOLT**, completely premeditated and very carefully organized.

With vengeance, I **jam** two more pieces of bread into the toaster. I push them down hard and they fly back in my face totally shredded. Two more pieces of bread are **forced** down. Two more fly up, just as the glass cap **SHOOTS** off like a rocket from the top of the coffee pot, and boiling black venom is shot all over the room. First venom, then venom with coffee grounds. The **stream** of poison is endless, the coffee pot has become bottomless. There is no way I can save myself. I am about to be **boiled**. As I drop to the floor, to cower in peace, my bathrobe is caught on the dishwasher door. I **tug** at the robe, but the dishwasher refuses to let go. With all my strength I pull the robe away from the dishwasher, but it opens its door and a scorching whirlpool of murky water washes my already **mutilated** body into the living room. The last thing I remember is the record player repeating four notes of a Mozart concerto over and over again.

It's quiet here in the home. I have a lovely view from the window in my room and I can see a tree and a small duck pond. I had an apple for lunch. I am going for a little walk this afternoon, and then I may read until it gets dark. After sundown, I usually sing old Broadway musicals to myself until I fall asleep. Tomorrow I'll wake up to the early morning sun and the birds, and if it is cloudy, I'll get a little more **SLEEP**.

TOTAL DISASTERS

NUMBER

78

APRIL 1979

Years before real-life television drama became popular, the *Graphic* paid homage to the world's most disturbing disasters. The main text was Edgar Allan Poe's "The Masque of the Red Death." Robbins wrote about the attractive nature of disasters, and "Infelicities" was a series of surrealistic imaginary disasters dreamed up by the Push Pin artists.

Winds in excess of 130 miles per hour disrupted office routine for workers in Omaha's seventy-five story Petroleum Tower.

HARUO MIYAUCHI

FIRE

DROUGHT

EARTHQUAKE

BLIZZARD

HURRICANE

TORNADO

PLAGUE

FLOOD

GRAND ILLUSION ISSUE

Push Pin Graphic.

NUMBER 79

Seymour Chwast and Richard Mantel

214

Haruo Miyauchi
c/o Push Pin Studios
207 E. 32ND Street
New York, N.Y. 10016
U.S.A.

By nature, illustrators are illusionists, so this *Graphic* was a self-celebration. Smith illustrated life's mysteries in "Cherished Illusions." Chwast and Mantel collaborated on the realistic and impressionistic cover portrait. Miyauchi designed this double-page trompe l'oeil, art history's most timeworn illusionary method.

215

THE BEST OF US

NUMBER

80

SEP/OCT 1979

The heroic figure is a staple in art and literature, and this issue looked at the highs and lows of heroism. James Thurber's story "The Secret Life of Walter Mitty," a dream about becoming a hero, was the centerpiece. Smith's slapstick cover revealed the lighter side of heroism while the serious profiles of real and imagined heroes, from Robin Hood to Malcolm X, suggested its solemn side.

216

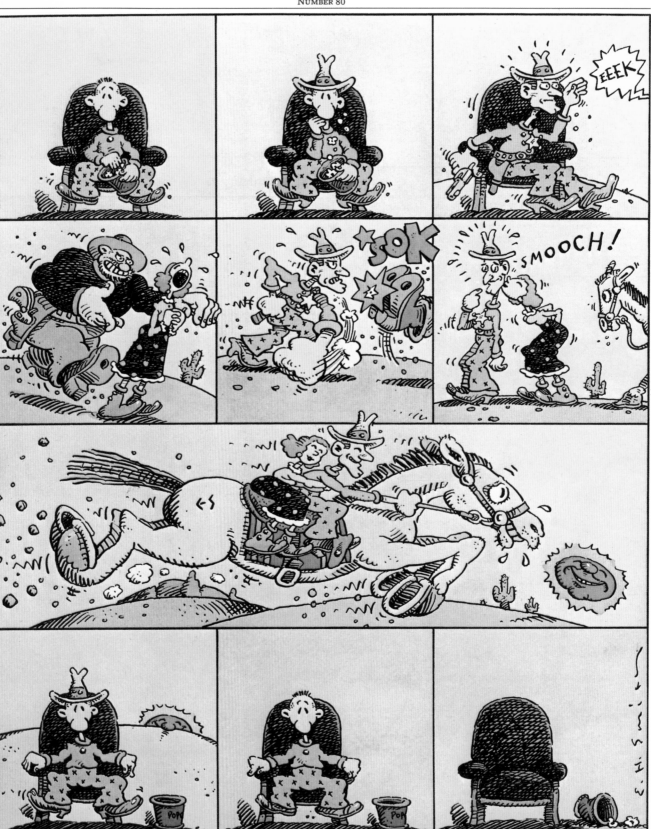

ELWOOD SMITH

STANISLAW ZAGORSKI

Malcolm X

But Malcolm kept snatching our lies away. He kept shouting the painful truth we whites and blacks did not want to hear from all the housetops. And he wouldn't stop for love nor money.

You can imagine what a howling, shocking nuisance this man was to both Negroes and whites. Once Malcolm fastened on you, you could not escape. He was one of the most fascinating and charming men I have ever met, and never hesitated to take his attractiveness and beat you to death with it. Yet his irritation, though painful to us, was most salutary. He would make you angry as hell, but he would also make you proud. It was impossible to remain defensive and apologetic about being a Negro in his presence. He wouldn't let you. And you always left his presence with the sneaky suspicion that maybe, after all, you were a man!

Excerpted from a statement by Ossie Davis from The Autobiography of Malcolm X by Malcolm X with the assistance of Alex Haley © 1964 by Alex Haley and Malcolm X. © 1965 by Alex Haley and Betty Shabazz. Reprinted by permission of Ossie Davis.

Rich people, for all the many hours they spend in therapy, have not yet learned how to avoid oppressing poor people. Historically speaking, poor people are a remarkably patient lot, but when abuses pile up over a period of time, they can get downright pushy. If, at such a time, there comes a person, not necessarily a warrior by nature, but a man of conviction and courage, who rouses the people to struggle for change, things may be a bit up in the air for a while, and heavy changes may be a possibility.

CHE GUEVARA
JOE HILL
EMMA GOLDMAN
SPARTACUS
MAHATMA GANDHI
MARTIN LUTHER KING
NAT TURNER
JOHN BROWN
CASTRO
SIMON BOLIVAR
GARIBALDI
LENIN
MOTHER JONES
MARCUS GARVEY
MAO TSE TUNG
LA PASIONARIA

13

Wilma Rudolph

HARUO MIYAUCHI

From the moment she first sped down the track of Rome's Olympic Stadium, there was no doubt that she was the fastest woman the world had ever seen. But that was only part of the appeal of the shy, 20-year-old Negro girl from Clarksville, Tenn. In a field of female endeavor in which the greatest stars have often been characterized by overdeveloped muscles and underdeveloped glands, Wilma ("Skeeter") Rudolph had long, lissome legs and a pert charm that caused an admiring Italian press to dub her "the Black Pearl." Last week Wilma Rudolph became the only track star, male or female of any country, to win three gold medals in the 1960 Olympics.

Running for gold-medal glory, Wilma Rudolph regularly got away to good starts with her arms pumping in classic style, then smoothly shifted gears to a flowing stride that made the rest of the pack seem to be churning on a treadmill. She tied the world record of 11.3 sec. in the 100 meters and won the final by three yds. She set an Olympic record of 23.2 sec. in the 200 meters and won the final by another three yds. Then, running with three of her Tigerbelle teammates from Tennessee State, Wilma anchored the winning 400-meter relay team and became the first American girl ever to win three gold medals in track.

The wonder was that Wilma Rudolph could run at all. The seventeenth in a family of nineteen children, Wilma had a series of crippling childhood diseases, did not walk until she was eight, and then had to wear a high-top, corrective shoe. By high school, Wilma had improved enough to become a four-year, allstate basketball player and to clean up in track. Now a junior at Tennessee State, Wilma is studying to be a teacher (average grade: B plus) has so little trouble winning races in the U.S. that she has sometimes slowed down in mid-sprint to shout encouragement to a teammate.

As her fame grew, Wilma got dozens of telegrams in a smattering of languages. She patiently signed autographs by the dozen as Italian fans threw their books down on the field. The home-town Clarksville *Leaf-Chronicle* ran a laudatory editorial ("an inspiration to the world in general"), and Tennessee's Governor Buford Ellington, who had run for office as an "old-fashioned segregationist," made plans to head the welcome-home party. When the Olympics were done, Coach Temple could find only one fault with the record of the world's fastest woman: "Wilma's never been tested since she came into her form. We don't know how fast she really can go."
© 1960, Time Inc. all rights reserved.

Personal achievement, self improvement, the desire for excellence, and the need to trash someone else's sense of self esteem—these are the basic motivations of the champion. *The Guiness Book of World Records* is full of them. We all like to think that we could be the best at *something*. Some of us succeed better than others. So it goes.

JIM THORPE
SAMSON
PAUL BUNYAN
JESSE OWENS
MUHAMMED ALI
JOE LEWIS
REGGIE JACKSON
MICKEY MANTLE
ROGER BANNISTER
BABE DIDRIKSON
FLORENCE CHADWICK
GERTRUDE EDERLE
JACKIE ROBINSON
SAM SNEAD

16   17

OUT OF THE BLUE
A CLOUDY ROMANCE

Seymour Chwast

ALL BLUE ISSUE

ALL BLUE ISSUE

NUMBER

81

NOV/DEC 1979

This issue devoted to the color blue included references to bluejay, blue sky, blue crab, blue collar, blue whale, blue blood, blue suede shoes, bluegrass, blue dahlia, Bluebeard, blue movie, blue sea, Blue Cross, blue pencil, blue serge suite, blue nose. Chwast's art described a romance between blue clouds, Friedman photographed four women in a "blue mood," and Barbara Sandler's Billie Holiday illustrated William Gass's "Dissertation on the Shades of Meaning in a Single Hue."

Stanislaw Zagorski

BLUEBEARD

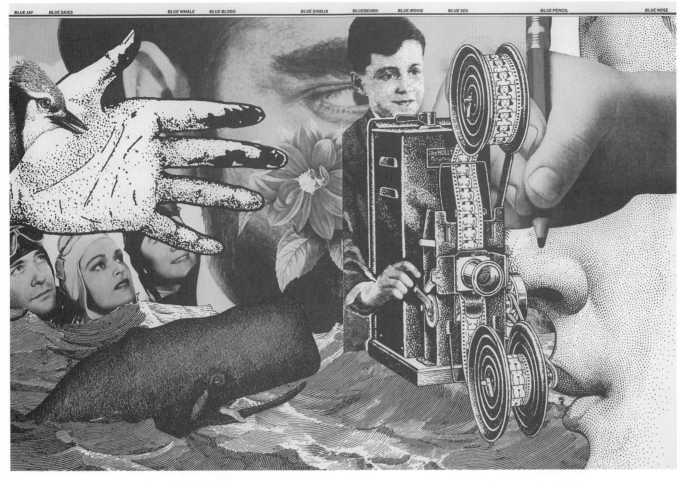

This cover by Mantel beckoned the reader to behold the Seven Deadly Sins. Inside, a series of mock posters cautioned against these all too common human pitfalls. A game of Snakes and Ladders took the winner to Heaven and the loser to Hell. This issue included text excerpts from Virgil's *Aeneid* and Dante's *Inferno*.

222

RICHARD MANTEL

NOT QUITE THE LAST JUDGEMENT

BY ELWOOD "HIERONYMUS" SMITH

Classical Hell

FROM THE AENEID
BY VIRGIL

Already they were approaching those farthest acres,
Those final fields where only the great war-heroes
Had their preserves. Here Tydeus ran to meet him,
Parthenopaeus famous in arms, and the pallid
Shade of Adrastus, here the Dardanids,
Fallen in battle and deeply mourned in the world,
And now as he saw them here in their long ranks
He grieved aloud—Glaucus, Thersilochus, Medon,
The three sons of Antenor, Polyphoetes
The priest of Ceres, and Idaeus still
Hand fast to his armor and his chariot.
These spirits thronged around him, left and right,

ENVY *Everybody's Enemy*
KEN ROBBINS

Nor was one look enough for them; they delighted
To linger with him step by step and discover
The reason for his coming. But when the Greeks,
Agamemnon's chiefs, and their massed followers
Saw the great hero in his glittering armor
Stride through the shades, they were convulsed with
  terror.
Some turned tail, as once towards their ships,
Some tried to raise a war-cry—but it died
Into a whimper, their mouths silently gawping.
And then he saw Deiphobus son of Priam,
His white body a mangled shambles; his face,
Both arms, his ears shorn from his head, his nostrils
Slit with a horrible wound—he scarcely knew him
As he cowered away to hide this ghastly vengeance.
But Aeneas addressed him in the voice he knew:
"Deiphobus, great warrior, born of the blood of
  Teucer,
Who was it craved to inflict so brutal a vengeance?
Who was allowed such a power over you?
On that last night the report of you I heard
Was that you sank down spent on a heap of bodies,
Worn out with slaughtering Greeks. Then I myself
Built on the Rhoetean shore an empty tomb,
And loudly called three times upon your spirit—

Your name and your arms are there to keep the place
In memory warm—but you yourself, my friend
I could not see nor lay your body to rest
In our native earth—the land I was forced to flee."
And the son of Priam answered, "You, my friend,
Left nothing undone—everything that was owed
To me or my shade, you have paid it in due order.
It was my own Destiny and the deadly
Wickedness of Helen that engulfed me
In this disaster—It is she that has left
These tokens of her love—you know yourself
How that last night was spent in false rejoicing:
One cannot but remember—with good reason—
When at one leap the Fateful Horse surmounted
The heights of our citadel, its womb heavy
With infantry full-armed, and she pretending
To lead a ritual dance ramped through the city
With a band of Trojan women in Bacchic frenzy
And, in their midst, held high a mighty firebrand
And from the top of the citadel summoned the
  Greeks.
But as for me, worn out with cares and sunk
In heavy sleep in our luckless bridal chamber
I lay and a sweet deep calm came over me
Most like the peace of death. But in the meanwhile
My splendid wife—she even had extracted
My trusty sword from under my own pillow—
Summoned Menelaus into the house and
Flung open the doors—hoping, I have no doubt,
That doing such a favor to her lover
Would soften his heart and erase the memory
Of all her evil misdeeds. But why should I
Drag out the story? Into the room they burst,
Ulysses with them instigator as ever
Of all things evil. O Gods, if the lips that pray
For retribution are pure, requite the Greeks
With equal barbarities!
          But tell me, Aeneas,
What chance has brought you living to this place?
Did you lose your bearing at sea? Or have you come
At the behest of heaven? Or what dire fortune
Has driven you to visit these sad sunless halls,
This place of confusion?"
          As they were thus engrossed,
The goddess of dawn in her rose-colored chariot
Had passed the zenith of her heavenly course,
And maybe in such talk they would have spent
The whole of their allotted time but the Sibyl
Upbraided her companion curtly and said:
"Night falls fast, Aeneas: yet we pass the time in
  weeping.
This is the spot where the road forks into two:
The right-hand path under the battlements
Of Mighty Pluto—there lies my own way to
  Elysium.
But the left-hand path leads evil men to Tartarus
And the exaction of due punishments."
Deiphobus answered: "Do not rage, great priestess,
I shall depart now and take my place again,
Back in the dark. But you Aeneas, go—
Our nation's glory—go on your way—go
And may Fate treat you better than I was treated."
Speaking these final words he turned and went.

From The Aeneid by Virgil, translated by Patric Dickinson. Copyright © 1961 by Patric Dickinson. Reprinted by arrangement with The New American Library Inc., N.Y., N.Y.

SEYMOUR CHWAST

Modern Hell

FROM DON JUAN IN HELL
BY BERNARD SHAW

THE OLD WOMAN. Excuse me; but I am so lonely; and this place is so awful.
DON JUAN. A new comer?
THE OLD WOMAN. Yes: I suppose I died this morning. I confessed; I had extreme unction; I was in bed with my family about me and my eyes fixed on the cross. Then it grew dark; and when the light came back it was this light by which I walk seeing nothing. I have wandered for hours in horrible loneliness.
DON JUAN [*sighing*] Ah! you have not yet lost the sense of time. One soon does, in eternity.
THE OLD WOMAN. Where are we?

WORKERS ARISE! END SLOTH!

DON JUAN. In Hell.
THE OLD WOMAN [*proudly*] Hell! I in Hell! How dare you?
DON JUAN [*unimpressed*] Why not, Señora?
THE OLD WOMAN. You do not know to whom you are speaking. I am a lady, and a faithful daughter of the Church.
DON JUAN. I do not doubt it.
THE OLD WOMAN. But how then can I be in Hell? Purgatory, perhaps: I have not been perfect: who has? But Hell! oh, you are lying.
DON JUAN. Hell, Señora, I assure you; Hell at its best: that is, its most solitary—though perhaps you would prefer company.
THE OLD WOMAN. But I have sincerely repented; I have confessed.
DON JUAN. How much?
THE OLD WOMAN. More sins than I really committed. I loved confession.
DON JUAN. Ah, that is perhaps as bad as confessing too little. At all events, Señora, whether by oversight or intention, you are certainly damned, like myself; and there is nothing for it now but to make the best of it.
THE OLD WOMAN [*indignantly*] Oh! and I might have been so much wickeder! All my good deeds wasted! It is unjust.

DON JUAN. No: you were fully and clearly warned. For your bad deeds, vicarious atonement, mercy without justice. For your good deeds, justice without mercy. We have many good people here.
THE OLD WOMAN. Were you a good man?
DON JUAN. I was a murderer.
THE OLD WOMAN. A murderer! Oh, how dare they send me to herd with murderers! I was not as bad as that: I was a good woman. There is some mistake: where can I have it set right?
DON JUAN. I do not know whether mistakes can be corrected here. Probably they will not admit a mistake even if they have made one.
THE OLD WOMAN. But whom can I ask?
DON JUAN. I should ask the Devil, Señora: he understands the ways of this place, which is more than I ever could.
THE OLD WOMAN. The Devil! I speak to the Devil!
DON JUAN. In Hell, Señora, the Devil is the leader of the best society.
THE OLD WOMAN. I tell you, wretch, I know I am not in Hell.
DON JUAN. How do you know?
THE OLD WOMAN. Because I feel no pain.
DON JUAN. Oh, then there is no mistake: you are intentionally damned.
THE OLD WOMAN. Why do you say that?
DON JUAN. Because Hell, Señora, is a place for the wicked. The wicked are quite comfortable in it: it was made for them. You tell me you feel no pain. I conclude you are one of those for whom Hell exists.
THE OLD WOMAN. Do you feel no pain?
DON JUAN. I am not one of the wicked, Señora; therefore it bores me, bores me beyond description, beyond belief.
THE OLD WOMAN. Not one of the wicked! You said you were a murderer.
DON JUAN. Only a duel. I ran my sword through an old man who was trying to run his through me.
THE OLD WOMAN. If you were a gentleman, that was not a murder.
DON JUAN. The old man called it murder, because he was, he said, defending his daughter's honor. By this he meant that because I foolishly fell in love with her and told her so, she screamed; and he tried to assassinate me after calling me insulting names.
THE OLD WOMAN. You were like all men. Libertines and murderers, all, all, all!
DON JUAN. And yet we meet here, dear lady.
THE OLD WOMAN. Listen to me. My father was slain by just such a wretch as you, in just such a duel, for just such a cause. I screamed: it was my duty. My father drew on my assailant: his honor demanded it. He fell: that was the reward of honor. I am here: in Hell, you tell me; that is the reward of duty. Is there justice in Heaven?
DON JUAN. No; but there is justice in Hell: Heaven is far above such idle human personalities. You will be welcome in Hell, Señora. Hell is the home of honor, duty, justice, and the rest of the seven deadly virtues. All the wickedness on earth is done in their name: where else but in Hell should they have their reward? Have I not told you that the truly damned are those who are happy in Hell?

Reprint permission given by The Society of Authors on behalf of the estate of Bernard Shaw.

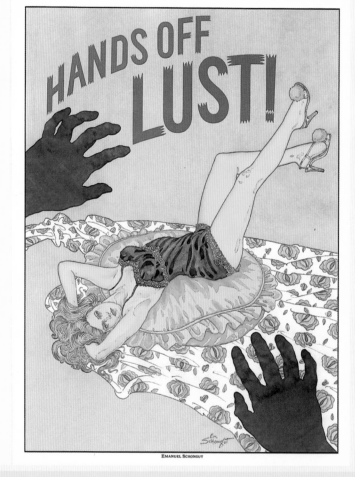

EMANUEL SCHONGUT

BARBARA SANDLER

PRIDE HURTS

STOP ANGER
KEEP YOUR SHIRT ON

SIN AND
SORROW

For some it is a literal pit of flames, complete with the shrieking of tortured souls and the stench of brimstone. For some it is a shuddering cold sweat, a hint of nausea, and a weakness of the knees at the brink of a howling mental abyss. For others it is a single germ of unsynchronous protoplasm, the seed of guilt and disunity, the cancer cell that corrupts. For still others it is simply the place of dead souls, waiting for eternity without passion or hope, a place of catatonic regression, of silent cries and darkness visible.

Dante thought of it as the place where the Guelfs got even with the Ghibilines (or was it the other way around?). General Sherman thought it was war. Samuel Johnson thought it was paved with good intentions, William Congreve thought it was a woman scorned, and we know several people who think it's Long Beach, California.

We call it hell, after the Norse goddess, Hel, named "The Hider," or else we say Hades, the Inferno, Avernus, Tartarus, or Perdition. Call it anything you like, but ignore the graphic warnings proffered by the posters herein at your own peril.
                                        —Ken Robbins

225

TWO BY TWO

NUMBER
83

1980

Drawn before smoking was considered a public nuisance, Chwast's cover symbolized the quintessential couples relationship. A portfolio of famous duos included James and Dolley Madison by Chwast, Prince Rainier and Princess Grace by Zagorski, and Leda and the Swan by Schongut. "Coitus Topographicus," a map combined with a page from a sex manual, rendered by Liz Gutowski, added a touch of whimsy to the proceedings.

LEDA AND THE SWAN

Emanuel Schongut

JAMES AND DOLLY MADISON

Seymour Chwast

PRINCE RAINIER AND PRINCESS GRACE

Stanislaw Zagorski

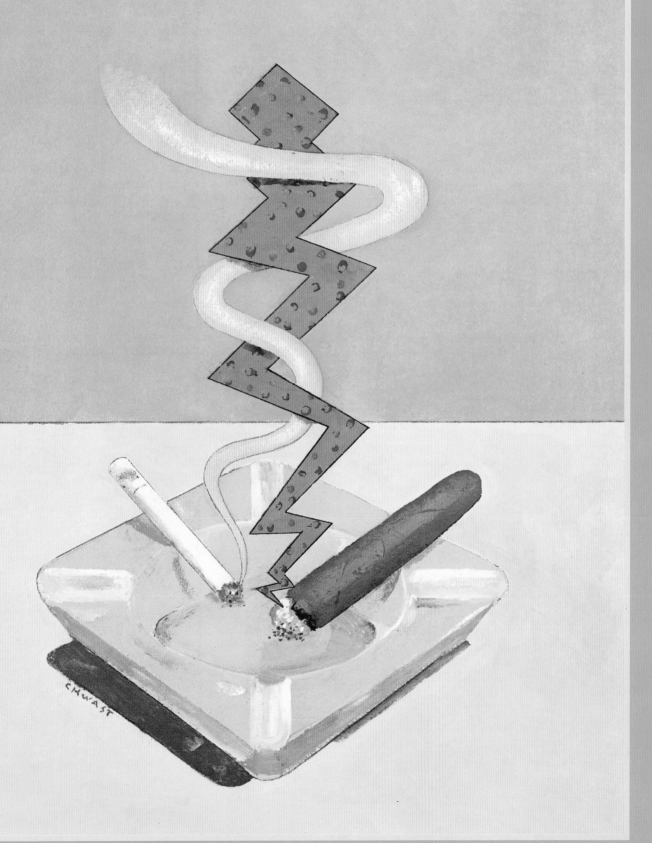

227

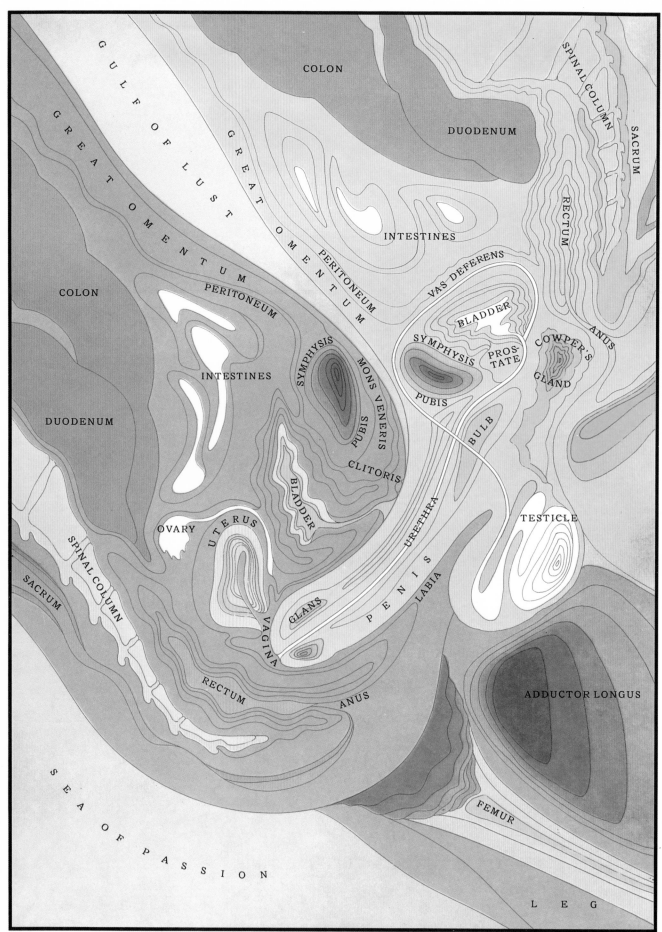

COITUS TOPOGRAPHICUS ILLUSTRATED BY LIZ GUTOWSKI

NOT QUITE HUMAN

NUMBER

84

MAY/JUNE 1980

In the centerpiece of this issue, Jorge Luis Borges described imaginary people in literature and mythology (illustrated by Mantel). Smith confounded biology with his humanimal creatures. Chwast contributed his Arcimboldo-inspired pasta chart. And his novelty typeface, Blimp, was transformed and renamed "Bestial Bold" in honor of this timeless theme.

RICHARD MANTEL

ABC DEFGH IJKLMNOP QRSTUVWXYZ&

FRESH AIR FIENDS

❖ ❋ THE BEAST IN YOU ❋ ❖

YOUR CHARACTER REVEALED!
Zoomorphic Anthropology, the study of physical and behavioral similarities between humans and animals, is no longer the exclusive domain of white-haired academic types. A growing number of self-styled "morph watchers" are roaming the shopping centers of the nation on weekends and holidays with cameras and sketchbooks in hand. In fact, the staid and venerable Institute for Zoomorphic Anthropology, which officially recognizes over 14,000 distinct morphotypes with zootropic tendencies, has been caught short by an unprecedented demand for copies of their quarterly bulletin, *The Mermaid*. The comparative sketches reproduced here should give the uninitiated some idea of the complexity of the subject. They are from a seminal work by Otho Schweinkopf entitled *Das Humannerpipplekind Vott ist Chust Lyk Animalembeastervolken*, Zweitag Verlag, 1923, Trans. Lula-Mae Pfefferschnozzel. —Ken Robbins

THE YAK TYPE.

THE KING OF THE JUNGLE TYPE.

THE SMOKED FISH TYPE.

THE HORNED OWL TYPE.

THE RACCOON TYPE.

THE MULISH TYPE.

LISTA DI PASTA

1 Farfallini
2 Farfalle
3 Spaghettini
4 Rotelle
5 Vermicelli
6 Yolanda
7 Lasagne
8 Maruzze
9 Tufoli
10 Mostaccioli
11 Concone
12 Ruffled Lasagne
13 Mezzani
14 Boccone
15 Fettuccine
16 Cavatelli
17 Ravioli
18 Manicotti
19 Rotini
20 Egg Pastina
21 Egg Oats
22 Egg Noodle Flake
23 Rigatoni
24 Ziti
25 Spaghetti
26 Tortellini
27 Anelli
28 Fusilli
29 Cappelletti
30 Egg Noodle

SEYMOUR CHWAST

GOOD
LUCK
BAD
LUCK

NUMBER

85

1980

This issue covered luck in all its permutations. The text, illustrated by Smith, described the odds for and against everything. There was a gambler's gallery of Damon Runyon characters, and graduation photos from the twenties through the seventies (with the typical "good luck" greeting) showed attitudinal shifts. Imaginary neon signs for nongambling Las Vegas institutions predated the mainstreaming of the city.

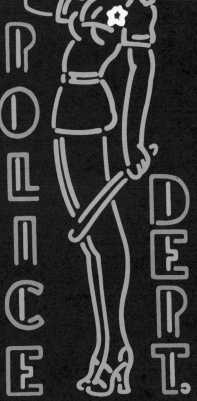

C R A P S

When or where "Craps" began is a mystery, but gambling with dice is almost as old as the human race. Prehistoric man gambled with a six-sided sheep ankle bone, called astragalus, that qualifies as the first die. So dice were, literally, "bones" at their beginning. And they have been rattling out with money wagered on them from the beginning of money's existence.

There are three forms of craps played today. "Private Craps" is played between two or more people who bet among themselves. In "Open Craps," one person banks the game, and some bets can be made only against the bank. "Bank Craps" is the Casino crap game, and it's the most popular game in the house.

To the player who's done all his crap-shooting with friends on a living room or home game-room floor, the first sight of a Bank Craps table is often awesome and intimidating. Craps has always been a simple, informal game, and this looks complicated and different.

It isn't. There may be a good many players in this game, and the layout is necessary to keep an accurate record of every bet that's down. It has nothing to do with the mechanics of the game and is necessary only because neither the players nor the dealers could possibly keep every bet straight if it weren't there.

BETTING PROCEDURE

Since more bets are made on the Pass Line than anywhere else, as a rule, let's consider Pass Line bets first.

Pass Line. Betting even money that the shooter will win is a Pass. The bet must be made before his first throw, or after he's won or lost. When the shooter rolls the dice, he is "coming out." You win a Pass Line bet, at even money, when the shooter's come-out roll of the dice is 7 or 11. When the come-out roll is a 4, 5, 6, 8, 9 or 10, that number is the shooter's point, and you win if he repeats it before he rolls a 7.

You lose a Pass Line bet when the shooter's comeout roll is craps—2, 3 or 12. You also lose when the shooter's point number is not repeated before he rolls a 7.

Pass Line, Taking Odds. When a Point number is determined by the shooter's come-out, anyone who has a bet on the Pass Line may make an additional bet that the number will be rolled before a 7. Usually, the amount of this Odds bet can't be any larger than the Line bet, except that the player is permitted to bet even units. Odds bets are paid at the correct odds:

Points 4 or 10—Odd paid, 2 to 1.
Points 5 or 9—Odds paid, 3 to 2.
Points 6 or 8—Odds paid, 6 to 5.

With a Pass Line bet of only $1, the bettor is usually permitted to make a $2 bet on five or 9. With 6 or 8, the player cannot take odds unless he has $3 on the line, in which case he can make an Odds bet of $5.

Don't Pass Line. This is the opposite of a Pass Line bet, an even-money bet that the shooter loses, and must be made before the come-out roll. You win a Don't Pass Line bet when the come-out roll is a 2 or 3 Craps (but not 12). A throw of 12 is a stand-off or "push." You also win when the shooter fails to repeat his point before rolling a 7.

You lose Don't Pass Line bets when the shooter comes out with a 7 or 11, or when he makes his point before throwing a 7.

Comparatively few players bet the Don't Pass Line, although the disadvantage to bettors is practically the same. The Pass Line disadvantage is 1.414 percent and the Don't Pass Line disadvantage is 1.402 percent.

Don't Pass Line, Laying Odds. Similar to Pass Line odds bets, except that the player lays the odds, within the limits of the original Don't Pass bet. The Odds bets are paid at the correct odds:

Point 4 or 10—Paid 1 to 2.
Points 5 or 9—Paid 2 to 3.
Points 6 or 8—Paid 5 to 6.

Odds bets on both the Pass Line and Don't Pass line should be made whenever possible, since the casino has no percentage in its favor.

Come Bets. Another area of the layout is designated simply, "Come." It is the same as a Pass Line bet, except that it is made after the first roll, when the shooter has a point. When you place a "Come" bet, the next roll of the dice is the come-out roll as far as your bet is concerned. You win if the roll turns up a 7 or 11, and you lose if 2, 3 or 12 come up. Rolls of 4, 5, 6, 8, 9 or 10 become the Point number for your come bet, and the dealer moves your chips or money to the correspondingly numbered box on the layout.

Odds bets can be made with Come bets, and should be, if possible.

Don't Come Bets. These are the same as Don't Pass Line bets, except that they're made after the shooter has a point. Here again, odds bets are permissible and should be placed, if you want to take advantage of the most favorable odds.

Place Bets. A Place bet is a wager that a Point number of your choice will come up before a 7. It doesn't require playing the Pass Line or Come and can be made with the dealer at any time. Place bets on 6 and 8 are the fifth and sixth best bets at casino crap tables. Place bets on these two numbers pay off 7 to 6, so it is necessary to bet a minimum of $6. At a $5 table, the minimum place bet on 6 or 8 would be $30.

The house percentage of these two numbers is 1.5 percent.

Pass Line and Come bets, with full odds taken on Point Numbers in both instances, are the best bets in Bank Craps, along with Don't Pass and Don't Come bets with full odds against the Point numbers. The only other bets that the experts consider good are Place bets on the 6 and 8.

A beginning player should probably confine himself to Pass Line and Come bets, taking the odds on Point numbers, until he acquires familiarity with the game and methods of play. Many experienced players will tell you never to have more than these bets in action simultaneously. Most of them will tell you to stay away from "Field" and Big 6 and Big 8 bets, which they regard as poor risks. Taking the Point Odds on Line and Come bets, however, they regard as sound, since this action reduces the house percentage to less than one percent.

Reprinted from Gambler's Digest © DBI Books, Inc.

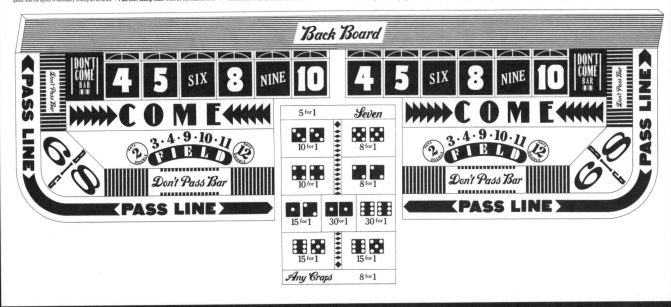

Personal styles at Cooper Union have changed drastically since the Twenties, but the graduates, fearful or confident by varying degrees, still wish themselves and each other "good luck" in the same old way.

The final issue of the *Graphic* looked at crime, criminals, and justice. The series "Find the Murder Weapon" asked readers to solve comic crimes. In nineteenth-century magazine style, Mantel illustrated a crime story by Edgar Allan Poe. And in addition to showing various designs for police badges, "The Crimeoleum Floor Covering Guide" featured a dead victim among the floor patterns.

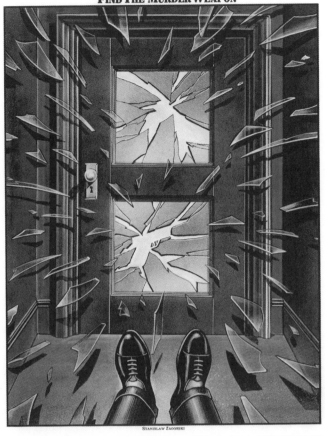

STANISLAW ZAGORSKI

DRATS!

ELWOOD H. SMITH

JOHN DILLINGER IS BROUGHT TO JUSTICE

Arch Criminal Is Shot …

and rolled over

and stamped out

and scraped

and cut up

and knocked out

and folded and spindled

and messed up

and bleached out

and incinerated

and slashed

and stomped on

and rubbed out

and underexposed

and torn to pieces

and smoked out

and crossed out

and boiled.

THE PUSH PIN APPENDIX

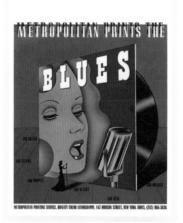

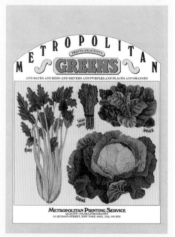

238

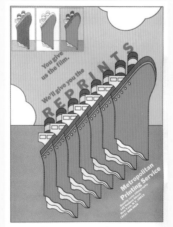

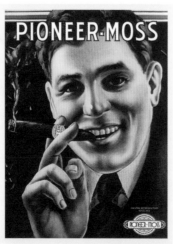

PUSH PIN COMMERCE

STARTING with issue number 64, Chwast designed all the advertisements for suppliers on these pages in exchange for services to help production of the *Graphic*. Chwast wrote and art directed these ads. The illustrators included himself, Haruo Miyauchi and Richard Mantel. Henry Wolf photographed the two on the bottom row right.

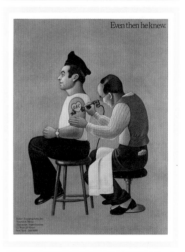

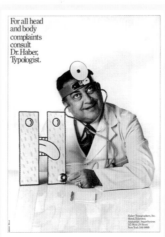

DESIGN
RESOURCES

WITH ISSUE number 65 Chwast started a "scrap file" feature in the *Graphic* that included "inspiring, inventive stuff, that excited us," he says. Some of the resources were keyed to specific issues, such as Victorian wanted bills for the "Crime" issue, while others, like masks and nineteenth-century fantastic illustration from Great Britian, were selected for their sheer beauty. Chwast sometimes reprinted existing texts or commissioned experts to place the artifacts in context, but often the objects spoke eloquently for themselves.

DESIGN RESOURCES

A SELECTION FROM TENDER BUTTONS, 143 EAST 62 STREET, NYC 10021. PHOTOGRAPHED BY RICHARD PAN

SHIRT BUTTONS

BUTTONS

Diana Epstein

From Buttons by Diana Epstein. Copyright © 1968. Used with permission of publisher, Holder and Co.

DESIGN RESOURCES

Car Grilles

DESIGN RESOURCES

Small Infernos: a sampling of matchbook advertising art from the 1940 catalogue of the Match Corporation of America.

These striking images drew instant attention and repeated their sales messages every time the consumer lit a cigarette.

A PUSH PIN MISCELLANY

BY STEVEN HELLER

ANIMATION

During the peak of the Vietnam War (1968) Milton Glaser and Lee Savage produced the acerbic short *Mickey Mouse in Vietnam*, a minute-long pencil-drawn animation in which the legendary Disney character catches a bullet in the head for his country. Glaser has not made another animated film since. Seymour Chwast, on the other hand, frequently worked with R. O. Blechman's Ink Tank studio in New York on various animated TV commercials and features. Among the most widely aired were an homage to Dick Tracy for Yoplait Yogurt, a promo for the PBS *Masterpiece Theatre* production of *Nicholas Nickleby*, and a spot for Hewlett-Packard (the first time a Beatles song, "It's Getting Better All the Time," was used in a commercial). Chwast later contributed a short to the 1977 animated PBS feature *Simple Gifts*, an adaptation of a chapter from *Orlando* by Virginia Woolf that takes place during the coldest winter England had known. Everything is frozen, including the Thames, where people come from miles around to a festival and ball. Orlando spots a Russian princess there and takes her for a sleigh ride. The two decide to run away together, but the next day she does not come to the appointed place. Instead, as the ice on the Thames melts, Orlando sees the princess leaving on her ship back home. In the early seventies Chwast also created the storyboards for a three-minute history of America produced by Harold Friedman, with oversized heads of historic characters, and commercials for Schweppes.

ART DECO

Art deco (or art moderne, as it was first known) was a resolutely commercial and decidedly elegant design style launched in Paris after World War I. It spread to virtually every industrialized nation in Europe, Asia, and South and North America and symbolized Jazz Age splendor and machine age exuberance. Art deco's defining decorative traits included stylized sunbursts, Aztec stair steps, airbrushed shadows, and all manner of modernistic rectilinear ornament applied to everything from building facades and

cosmetic packages to fashion and type. Its heyday was the interlude between World War I and the Great Depression, when markets flourished and floundered, after which austerity emerged as the mother of stylistic invention. Early in the 1950s Chwast bought a copy of Saul Steinberg's comic masterpiece *All in Line*, which "changed my life" because it sparked an interest in both Victoriana and art deco. Steinberg, who loved the futuristic ornament, often drew exaggerated decolike buildings in his ironic tableaux, including the Empire State and Chrysler Buildings. Chwast paid homage to the passé in a different way, through what he dubbed "Roxy Style," a pastiche of art moderne wedded to his contemporary style, the most vivid example of which is the cover of the *Push Pin Graphic* "The Meaning of Dreams" (issue 49, page 120). Glaser also adopted a variant of art deco, while other Push Pin members, notably Barry Zaid, built entire illustration styles on a moderne foundation.

ARTONE

In 1963 Push Pin Studios was commissioned to repackage the Artone Studio india ink carton by Louis Strick, the new owner of the art supply company and a Wall Street businessman. Both Chwast and Glaser produced sketches independently of the other. "We'd talk about it, do our own ideas, and then talk about it again," Chwast recalls, referring to his best sketch showing a large A. Although not directly copied from an existing alphabet, it echoed the fluid art nouveau/Jugendstil lettering he admired in vintage issues of *Jugend* (page 244). Chwast favored an unencumbered box with only three rows of nine smaller A's on the box top. Chwast also says that using the A by itself was not a radical idea since making a simple, distinctive trademark was a proven way of establishing the identity for a product. He

241

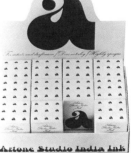

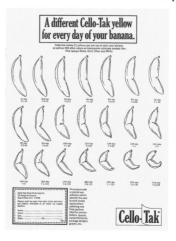

used an existing script for the secondary typeface but realized that having a complete alphabet and a set of numerals would be useful for future advertising and promotional purposes. He completed the design of the Artone Studio india ink package in 1964, and the *A* became the basis of his custom display typeface, Artone, released that same year by Photolettering Inc.

AUDIENCE

Elegant hardcover magazines free of advertisements, including such titles as *Panorama, Eros, American Heritage,* and *Art in America,* sold exclusively through subscription, had a respectable following during the sixties and early seventies. A devoted targeted audience was willing to pay higher annual rates to receive smartly produced periodicals—they were hybrids that fell somewhere between a book and a magazine. For two years, in 1970 and 1971, Chwast and Glaser were design directors of one of the last of this unique breed: *Audience,* a hardcover bimonthly published by Tim Hill, who was financially backed by an Avon cosmetics heir to create a literary and cultural magazine, something like the *New Yorker.* Ed Sorel designed a promotion piece to attract readers. Push Pin member Vincent Ceci was art director and Geoffrey Ward was editor. In addition to Push Pin's artists, a wide variety of illustrators and photographers were commissioned. Each lavish issue contained a special insert on butcher paper that focused on some aspect of popular culture. Despite the excellent printing and reproduction standards, however, someone specified the paper with the grain running the wrong way and for the entire run the magazine was bound with unsightly buckling. By the time the problem was solved, the investor had pulled the plug.

THE BOOK OF BATTLES

In 1954 Chwast self-published a limited-edition book titled *The Book of Battles,* an antiwar polemic inspired by his cousin Dachine Rainer, a poet and copublisher of the anarchist review *Retort,* who had introduced him to anarchist writers including Randolf Bourne (known for his pronouncement, "War is the health of the state"). She wrote the introduction. *The Book of Battles* featured an assortment of antiwar quotations illustrated entirely with comic linocuts, a medium Chwast had employed since his Cooper Union days because, he notes, "it offered gritty immediacy." Chwast also set the metal type by hand and printed and hand-colored seventy copies, one page at a time on a small handpress. He called his small imprint the 6 x 9 Press because that was the total image area on the actual press. *The Book of Battles* was his only production under this imprint.

CELLO-TAK

One graphic arts tool or material is quintessential to the Push Pin style: Cello-Tak, a dry-mount adhesive film used to create perfectly flat color. Glaser used primary Cello-Tak colors during his so-called psychedelic period, and Chwast continued to use the material until the advent of the computer. Chwast and Glaser would draw the black outlines and then specify on tissue overlays the respective colors. Designated members of the studio's production staff were expert at cutting the malleable material to the proper fit, and unused portions consumed drawing tables throughout the studio.

CHILDREN'S BOOKS

Chwast's first illustrated children's book, *Sara's Granny & the Groodle* (1967), launched a vocation as illustrator and designer. The first book that he wrote and illustrated was *Tall City, Wide Country* (1983) and in total he produced thirty-five children's books, mostly aimed at preschoolers and young readers. Glaser's first illustrated book, *The Smallest Elephant in the World* by Alvin Tresselt (1959), did not lead to as prodigious an oeuvre as Chwast's. It was followed by *If Apples Had Teeth* by Shirley Glaser (1960), *Cats and Bats and Things with Wings* by Conrad Aiken (1965), and *Fish in the Sky* by George Mendoza (1971). Because Glaser was not as well known as a children's book illustrator, the press erroneously dubbed *The Alphazeds* by Shirley Glaser (2003) as Glaser's children's book "debut."

THE DYLAN POSTER

On July 29, 1966, while speeding down the back roads in Woodstock, New York, on his motorcycle, Bob Dylan was thrown over the handlebars and seriously injured. Rumors about his death circulated; however, some believed the accident was a ruse to cover up a drug overdose. Whatever the truth, Dylan's music was silenced and after six months without any new material, Columbia Records panicked and unilaterally issued a greatest-hits album that included a free poster. Columbia art director John Berg commissioned the poster from Glaser, who had a history of mining of visual artifacts and archetypes from diverse and unexpected sources. For the poster, Glaser blended Persian miniatures, vibrating psychedelic colors, and a silhouette self-portrait by Marcel Duchamp (originally a profile torn from a single piece of colored paper and placed on a black background). In his only sketch, Glaser drew a harmonica in front of Dylan's mouth, but when Berg saw it he told Glaser to "simplify, simplify." Eliminating the harmonica focused more attention on Dylan's profile. The result was a dark

TOP
CHILDREN'S BOOKS
If Apples Had Teeth,
Milton Glaser, 1960.
Tall City, Wide Country,
Seymour Chwast, 1983.
CELLO-TAK
Advertisement, 1977.

ABOVE
AUDIENCE
Cover: Photographer unknown, 1972.

THE BOOK OF BATTLES
Seymour Chwast, 1954.

End Bad Breath.

243

profile of Dylan with rainbow-colored hair. The only word on the poster, "Dylan," was set in Glaser's own Baby Teeth typeface (page 249). Six million posters were printed.

END BAD BREATH

The Vietnam War polarized the American people like no other conflict since the Civil War. The nightly news barrage of video from battlefields impressed a horrific image on America's consciousness and inspired a prodigious number of protest posters. Chwast's 1968 "End Bad Breath," a comic woodcut portrait of an open-mouthed Uncle Sam with bombers dropping their load on Vietnam, suggested that this nation was engaged in keeping the peace by prolonging an unjust war. Chwast remembers being furious that President Lyndon Baines Johnson ordered American B-52s to bomb Hanoi to pound the North Vietnamese leader, Ho Chi Minh, into submission. Like others in the burgeoning antiwar movement, he believed that U.S. intervention was having disastrous effects on both nations. A poster would never equal the destructive power of napalm used to defoliate the Vietnamese countryside, but it could have a curative effect. Short of acts of civil disobedience, which were frequent during the late 1960s, Chwast's poster was the best way to express his own growing frustration. But he admits that the poster was by no means an innovation. "This was the kind of illustration method that was being done in those days. Little people on shoulders, things in mouths. So I didn't break any new ground." Chwast chose the woodcut medium because of its raw expressive quality, and the poster had an impact, Chwast adds, "If only as an icon for those of us who had already made up our minds about the war. But it certainly didn't change any minds."

FOLK ART

Chwast and Glaser introduced folk art to Push Pin Studios in the form of woodcarvings and ceramics they had brought back from trips to Mexico in the late 1950s. But it was Paul Davis who transformed the tropes of folk art, flat perspectives, and simplified forms, which in the early sixties was not yet celebrated as popular art, into his personal style. Raised in Tulsa, Oklahoma, he was already familiar with American Indian art and regional painting, but he was ultimately inspired by a book of eighteenth-century German shooting targets used in matches and decorated with various ornamental figures. From this Davis produced a solo *Push Pin Graphic* (number 32, page 82), devoted to his own interpretations; it was the first time his new style was published. Prior to this Davis had been working in a cross-hatched comic style, but he always wanted his work to become more painterly and so continued to experiment by painting wooden faux merchant signs in the nineteenth-century manner. After that issue of the *Graphic* was published, he started getting assignments in this style, the first from Irwin Glusker, art director of *Horizon*, who referred to Davis's work as "magic realism," though they were much cruder than that kind of fantasy painting. Glaser noted that Davis's work resembled René Magritte's surrealist canvases, and suggested further study. Davis had never heard of Magritte, but after viewing his work, started making his own paintings look more complex and less deliberately untutored.

FRANKFURTER ALLGEMEINE MAGAZIN

In the early 1980s Willy Flekhaus, the art director of the illustrious German teen magazine *TWEN*, became the art director of *Frankfurter Allgemeine Magazin*, the supplement to the *Frankfurter Allgemeine Zeitung (FAZ)* newspaper. He commissioned Chwast to produce and illustrate visual essays and stories. Flekhaus and his successor, Hans-Georg Pospischil, were voracious consumers of Chwast's ironic features, including "Museums That Look Like Their Collections," "People Who Look Like Their Dogs," "Motorcycles in World History," "Unusual Events in Bath Tubs," "Famous Artists' Cars," and "A Day in the Life of a Pharaoh." These were, in fact, conceptually similar to *Push Pin Graphic* ideas and served as Chwast's primary outlet for such things once the *Graphic* ceased publishing. Chwast usually conceived of the story and then the magazine assigned authors to illustrate the images, as it were, with words. "I never read the texts because I can't speak German," he notes.

GRAND UNION

In the mid-1970s Glaser and Clay Felker were losing control of *New York* magazine because of a stock acquisition by Rupert Murdoch and sought an alternative buyer who shared their editorial philosophy. Although a successful match never materialized, they joined forces with Sir James Goldsmith, who owned a huge British publishing business and a large food business. After Glaser left *New York* (see *New York* Magazine, page 246), Goldsmith commissioned him to redesign his French newsweekly, *L'Express*, and eventually had him design the entire graphic, packaging, and signage scheme for his American supermarket chain, Grand Union. "I didn't know a thing about supermarket design but I learned quickly," says Glaser, whose fundamental design idea was unconventional by supermarket standards. Building on the structure of a magazine, Glaser felt that the store (or *magazin*) could be made more interesting if customers were informed through increased information and better pathways that were inspired more from editorial paradigms than merchandising ones. The aisles were widened and nutritional information, posted on panels and signs, increased the intensity of the shopping experience. Goldsmith despised what Glaser called "industrial filth" (packaged foods that should be fresh) and encouraged a total transformation of Grand Union into a well-designed experience that raised the standard of design for the general public. "It had to have great clarity," recalls Glaser. The project lasted almost eighteen years, and Glaser added twenty-five designers to his staff who worked exclusively on Grand Union. "It made me realize I didn't want to run a big studio," he recalls.

HAPPY BIRTHDAY, BACH

Chwast is a storyteller in word and picture and says his most satisfying work is the almost three hundred illustrations for *Happy Birthday, Bach* (Dolphin/Doubleday, 1985), which he conceived but Peter Schickele (aka PDQ Bach) wrote. "It was probably my most creative period," Chwast notes. "And having to do three hundred likenesses of Bach, tapping into the periods of the past three hundred years since his birth, came very easily for me." The book, a mock-serious tribute to Bach on the occasion of his three hundredth birthday, reveals Chwast's appreciation of classical music. "Bach is pretty good," he says, "but I like Mozart, too."

JUGEND

Jugend was a Munich-based weekly satire and art magazine published from 1896 to 1926 and during its first decade was the principal outlet for Jugendstil, the German variant of art nouveau. Chwast and Glaser acquired a set of bound volumes of the magazine that were a resource for much of Push Pin's early style. They were smitten with *Jugend*'s fanciful cover illustrations (above, right) and routinely changing logotypes. Jugendstil dismantled entrenched artistic conventions, replacing realism with abstraction and rococo with curvilinear ornament. *Jugend* revealed a French influence (some of its artists emulated Henri de Toulouse-Lautrec) but retained hard-edged German graphic traits, including an abundance of Black Letter type. Page layout was often dictated by the complexity of the illustration, causing untold headaches for the printer, whose job was to rag the type to conform to the curvilinear designs. Type and art were totally integrated, and this was Push Pin's hallmark.

I♥NY

During the sixties and early seventies New York City was a sinkhole. Crime and garbage were ubiquitous, and tourists were reluctant to spend their vacations in the city for fear of being mugged or worse. So in 1974 the New York State commissioner of commerce hired Charles Rosen of the advertising agency Wells Rich Green to create commercials designed to change perceptions. Introduced by the resounding musical refrain "I Love New York," the series of celebrity-filled TV spots successfully invested renewed civic pride in New Yorkers and triggered an influx of tourists. But the story does not end there. In 1974 Bill Doyle, assistant commissioner of commerce, approached Glaser to design a logo for the campaign. Originally, Glaser believed the campaign would last for a couple of months. So he solved the design problem accordingly: "I did a simple type solution with two lozenges," he recalls, and the commission's board of governors approved it. But a few days later Glaser had an epiphany while sitting in a taxicab and sketched out "I ♥ NY." At first, Doyle was reluctant to reconvene the six-member board, but Glaser prevailed and the members loved it. The "I ♥ NY campaign" sparked a "psychic shift," says Glaser. "It didn't occur to anyone that this was an abominable way to live. And the commercials forced people to say they were not going to be abused anymore." The "I ♥ NY" logo became the symbol of the resurrection. For the first ten years the logo was available copyright free to anyone who wanted to use it; then the state registered it, which has not thwarted countless infringements and imitations.

I♥NY

INFLUENCE (ON OTHERS)

Push Pin Studios exerted influence on designers and illustrators working throughout the sixties and seventies. In addition to those who copied the originators, Victor Moscoso, progenitor of the American psychedelic style, cited Push Pin as directly influencing his original vibrant and vibrating color palette as well his penchant for Victorian and art nouveau references. After the studio's golden years, various younger designers took their cues from Push Pin's eclecticism. Paula Scher, Woody Pirtle, Charles Spencer Anderson, the Duffy Group, Michael Vanderbyl, and Michael Mabry all used many similar methods from historical reference and pastiche to expressionism and constructivism, most importantly wedding typography and illustration (word and picture) into a unified whole.

LIFE MAGAZINE

By the mid-sixties *Life* magazine was feeling intense competition from TV for advertising revenues and thus was trying to encourage younger readers who, *Life* reasoned, would attract new advertisers. The December 1, 1967, cover was designed to rattle readers' cages. Replacing its typical full-page photograph was a smaller vintage photograph of a Native American inset into a wildly stylized, colorful contemporary drawing of an Indian that unfolded into an unprecedented gatefold. The cover, illustrated by Glaser in a psychedelic style, was the first to show a counterculture graphic approach on a mainstream periodical, let alone the publishing institution that was *Life*. Art director Bernard Quint believed that the cover was an effective and appropriate way to billboard the lead story, "Return of the Red

Man," which addressed renewed historical and cultural interest in Native Americans, and that Glaser's style was the telegraphing agent. Glaser recalled that the cover slipped right through the usual editorial handlers with very little interference. The style itself—cartoony black-and-white outlines filled in with intense primary color—was driven more by production shortcuts than aesthetic concerns and was for years one of Push Pin's fundamental ways of working. "George Leavitt had the fastest hands," Glaser says. "He could fill in the color in no time."

THE LOUVRE EXHIBITION

The exhibition of Push Pin Studios in Paris at the Palais du Louvre's Musée des Arts Décoratif from March 18 to May 18, 1970, was the most prestigious of all its many shows, yet also curiously the most frustrating. "We arrived a few days before the opening," recalls Chwast, "and nothing was hanging on the walls. The French workers did not know what to do, there was no plan, so during the next few days we hung the entire show." The result, however, prompted European reviewers to exclaim how amazed they were that Push Pin produced such expressionistic work in a capitalist society where business routinely clamps down on such things. Nonetheless, Push Pin had earned a reputation in Europe during the sixties for its unorthodox output. As for the attendees, Push Pin chartered a plane for more than one hundred present and former members and friends of the studio. That same year *Communication Arts* magazine published *The Push Pin Style* catalog, and later the show toured London, Milan, Rio de Janeiro, Lausanne, Tokyo, and Amsterdam, where it was exhibited in store windows along a prescribed route.

245

MASTER CLASSES

Glaser has been teaching for more than forty years at the School of Visual Arts in New York. "My attempt has always been to grapple with how you teach design," he says, and especially the distinction between doing work that was personal and doing work in which one's personality didn't enter into the equation—"to find when to introduce the personality and when to suppress that when it became intrusive." Glaser's intensive Summer Master Class began more than twenty years ago as an experiment he had proposed to SVA's founder, Silas Rhodes. "I was fascinated that Berlitz could teach French in three weeks, and wondered what about design could be learned under intensive conditions," Glaser says.

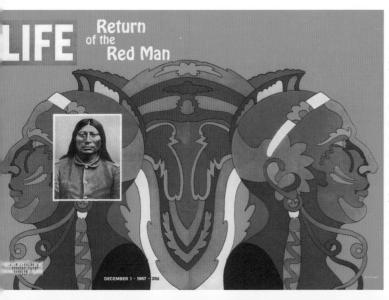

TOP LEFT
INFLUENCE
Charles Mingus Changes,
Paula Scher, 1973.

ABOVE
LOUVRE EXHIBITION
Poster, Milton Glaser, 1970.
Poster for a retrospective exhibit
in Tokyo, Seymour Chwast and
Milton Glaser, 1984.

LEFT
LIFE MAGAZINE
Cover, Milton Glaser, 1967.

He believes that there is a huge loss of learning in extended classes: "Twenty percent of what students learn is retained, but otherwise the rest leaks out because they must take so many other classes." Instead, students who take the Master Class for eight hours a day are placed in a sequential and continuous environment and the concentrated nature of the class forces a dramatic shift in perception. Glaser's goal is to challenge the assumptions the students (most of whom are professionals) have made about their practice. And because students who come to the class commonly feel stuck, they are looking for alternatives. Glaser continues to teach his Master Class and a class for MFA students in the School of Visual Arts graduate design program.

METAL SCULPTURE

Chwast had long experimented with different materials, and in 1990 he discovered the wonders of sheet metal. Designer Ivan Chermayeff had presented to him a gift of a small cutout metal sculpture that he had made. "And that's what inspired me," says Chwast about painting on metal. He was also inspired by Mexican ex-votos, usually made from tin cans, and produced a few of his own. But mostly Chwast's metal sculptures are figurative and usually deal with themes addressed in his two-dimensional work. He maintains a strong affinity for everyday objects in the manner of pop art—among them, shoes, radios, and clothing. His first exhibition at the Lustrare Gallery in New York in 1991 included what he called work in 2½ dimensions, insofar as the sculpture hung on walls and stood on tables. A piece called *Evolution* was an ordinary painter's ladder with a legged fish climbing the stairs; he also hung a *Suit on Hanger*. Chwast prefers metal to canvas because "it can be bent without breaking—it can be formed—and has a life of its own, while the only thing good about canvas is that you can roll it up easier." Among his themes are giant plates of exotic food, 130 busts of characters from all over, laughing businessmen, and dying toy soldiers on battlefields. His work has been frequently exhibited in one-person shows, including those at the Giraffics Gallery in East Hampton, New York, in 1994 and the GGG Gallery in Tokyo in 1995.

MONOGRAPHS

The first important graphic design monograph of the second half of the twentieth century (Paul Rand's *Thoughts on Design* was published in the first half, in 1947) is Glaser's *Graphic Design* (Viking Press, 1973). Not only did it spawn a whole book genre, it documented the era in which as cofounder of Push Pin Studios he created significant

posters, book jackets, and magazine design. After the book's publication, Glaser left Push Pin to launch Milton Glaser Inc. Although his posters were collected in *The Milton Glaser Poster Book* (Harmony, 1977), it was not until almost twenty-five years later that he published *Art Is Work: Graphic Design, Interiors, Objects, and Illustrations* (Overlook Press, 2000), a chronicle of his major post–Push Pin accomplishments. By comparison, Chwast's first monograph was curiously late in coming. *The Left-Handed Designer* (Harry N. Abrams, 1985) documents the continuum of his Push Pin accomplishments from the early days through Glaser's departure.

NEW YORK MAGAZINE

Originally a supplement of the now-defunct *New York Herald Tribune*, *New York* magazine premiered as a stand-alone in 1968. It garnered an immediate following for its unique blend of features, news, columns, criticism, and service aimed at a growing number of baby-boom, middle-class New Yorkers. The cofounders, editor Clay Felker and design director Glaser, headquartered in the Push Pin Studios building on East Thirty-first Street (until 1974), understood the need for a weekly guide that helped city dwellers navigate and appreciate food, fashion, and culture. Felker's editorial scheme and Glaser's design format became the model for "city magazines" elsewhere. *New York*'s typography was not radical but decidedly contemporary, and highly readable. Conceptual illustration and photography were generously used throughout every issue with many covers and interior illustrations created by Push Pin's artists and others. The unique title and job of "design director" allowed Glaser to oversee the editorial and visual character of the entire magazine, while the art director, Walter Bernard, addressed the day-to-day operations. All the illustrated front-of-the-book columns became prime real estate for many young and veteran illustrators—and the magazine was a destination for all portfolios. *New York* included comic strips by Edward Sorel and Robert Grossman, photo features by Carl Fisher, and a series of behind-the-scenes paintings about the Watergate scandal by Julian Allen. Glaser also cowrote "The Underground Gourmet" with Jerome Snyder, the first-of-its-kind weekly critique of affordable dining in New York. Glaser's involvement ended in 1976 with the sale of the magazine to Rupert Murdoch (at which point sixty staff members also voluntarily quit).

246

ABOVE
METAL SCULPTURE
Renee's Slip, Seymour Chwast, 1994.
Catching the 5:23, Seymour Chwast, 1992.
MONOGRAPHS
Seymour Chwast, *The Left Handed Designer*, 1985.
Milton Glaser, *Graphic Design*, 1973.
Milton Glaser, *Art Is Work*, 2000.

RIGHT
NEW YORK MAGAZINE
Milton Glaser, 1973.

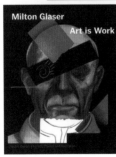

THE NOSE

After the *Push Pin Graphic* folded in 1981, Chwast produced and designed thematic magazines for paper companies (Mohawk's *Design and Style* series, 1986–1991) and printers (Ivy Hill's *P Chronicles*, 1990), but he always sought another studio publication. "I wanted to be a player again," admits Chwast. But even more he sought an outlet to express social, political, and cultural ideas through text and image. The result was the *Nose*, an occasional that premiered in 1997 and dealt with a specific theme, including a history of the world as told by children, hate words, food we love, capital punishment, and fear. Originally the *Nose* was to be a consortium with designers James Victore and Steven Brower, but after the first two issues Chwast became sole proprietor.

PAPERBACKS

Paperback cover design falls into two categories—mass and trade. The former demands hard-sell graphics that leave little room for designer nuances, while the latter can be (but is not always) more subtly artful. Push Pin Studios members produced scores of trade paperback covers for such publishers as Vintage Books; Simon & Schuster; Holt, Rinehart and Winston; Harper and Row; Farrar, Straus and Giroux; New American Library; and Doubleday. Glaser's Signet Classic Shakespeare series is doubtless the most classic of his entire oeuvre. He illustrated the cover for every one of the Bard's plays with a meticulously rendered pen-and-ink and watercolor drawing that was iconic of the drama. In total these drawings unified the series. Yet the most modern of Glaser's early covers, noted for its simplicity and poignancy, is the faceless portrait for Charles Norman's biography of e e cummings. Instead of facial features, the lowercase e's become the eyes and cummings becomes the mouth in this memorable yet simple image. Chwast used the paperback cover as a laboratory for testing out various styles, including the surreal line drawing of the bow of a vessel turned into a skull on B. Traven's *The Death Ship*, the machine-engraving collage face on Arthur O. Lewis's *Of Men and Machines*, the expressionist woodcut on Albert Camus's

The Plague, and the pictorial initials on Rexford G. Tugwell's *FDR: Architect of an Era*. Quite a few of Push Pin's paperback covers were commissioned by the publishing industry art director Harris Lewine, who saw to it that some of the members' most radical ideas were published without interference.

PMS 345

During the seventies pastel colors were in vogue. Light green, blue, pink, and creamy yellow were as common as basic black. Chwast used his favorite green, PMS 345, for various posters and illustrations. It has been called "Chwast Green" or "Toothpaste Green," and as a primary in the Push Pin palette it is not to be confused with Chwast's least favorite, chartreuse.

PUSHPINOFF

In 1978 Push Pin Studios mailed out a surprise Christmas gift to its clients and friends: a tin of Pushpinoff Caviar mints, designed by Chwast with a "fancy" label to resemble the actual Russian delicacy. "It was a hit," recalls Chwast, who with Phyllis Flood, Push Pin's business manager, created a commercial line of gourmet candies and snacks aimed at boutiques and department stores. Other products were given elegant faux names, such as Nite Spots, Almond Pearls, Strawberry Savories, Love Drops, After Coffee Coffee, Black Russian, Sesame Sweets, Berry Nice, Raspberry Snow, Cocoa Almandine, and Ming Mint Almonds. Novelty products were beginning to appeal to the economically flush baby-boomer market. Similar products existed at the time, but Pushpinoff was definitely in the vanguard.

PUSH PIN PRODUCTS

Push Pin had an entrepreneurial streak dating back to the *Monthly Graphic*, but the studio was also commissioned to produce commercial products for others, including illustrated shower curtains and towels for Bloomingdale's. Glaser designed a set of plastic children's blocks for *Art in America* (a very complicated grid with tens of thousands of combinations) that was later produced by George Beylarian and sold to museum shops; Chwast designed clocks with illustrated faces, as well as pens and glassware.

PANTONE®
345 C

247

TOP
THE NOSE
Number 6, Seymour Chwast, 2001.
PUSHPINOFF
Packages by Seymour Chwast, 1978–82.
PMS 345
Color swatch.

LEFT
PAPERBACKS
Covers by Milton Glaser, 1964.

PUSH PIN PRESS & PUSH PIN EDITIONS

In the late seventies, under the rubric Push Pin Press, Chwast designed various trade books on popular culture produced by J. C. Suares and written by Bill Maloney. Included were the highly successful *The Illustrated Cat* (and follow-up, *The Literary Dog*), which sparked a craze for cat books, *The Illustrated Flower*, *The CB Bible*, and *The Great American T-Shirt*. During the early eighties, under the banner Push Pin Editions, Chwast and Steven Heller produced books on art, design, and lifestyle, including *The Art of New York, New York Observed, Graphic Style: From Victorian to Post-Modern, The Graphic Design Source Book*, and *Not Tonight, I Have a Haddock: 100 Ways to Say No to a Man.*

PUSH PIN MEMBERS

John Alcorn
Samuel N. Antupit
Vincent Ceci
Seymour Chwast
Paul Davis
Loring Eutemy
Milton Glaser
Norman Green
Hedda Johnson
Jerry Joynor
Roger Law
Herb Leavitt
Tim Lewis
Peter Max
Richard Mantel
James McMullan
Jason McWhorter
Haruo Miyauchi
Christian Piper
Reynold Ruffins
Cosmos Sarchiapone
Isadore Seltzer
Jerry Smokler
Edward Sorel
Barry Zaid

PUSH PIN REPS

From almost the beginning, Push Pin Studios employed representatives to sell the studio's wares. While the *Push Pin Graphic* made an incalculable impact on the design and illustration fields, developing new clients was not a skill that studio members had in abundance—after all, they were artists. The following reps identified the clients, developed the new business, and helped promote the studio during its critical periods.

Warren Miller (1955–1957)   Barbara Fried (1967–1969)
Rosalie Janpol (1957–1960)   Phyllis Flood (1969–1994)
Jane Lander (1960–1967)   Ilse LeBrecht (1974–1993)

RESTAURANTS

In the early 1970s Glaser was itching to work in three-dimensional space, so it was fortuitous that restaurateur Joe Baum, of New York's Windows on the World, commissioned him to develop the graphics for a complex of restaurants in the World Trade Center. What began as logos, menus, and ancillary graphics evolved into signage, lamps, rugs, and uniforms. "Joe had a nose for people he wanted to work with," said Glaser about the relationship that launched a new facet of his career. For Glaser it was a perfect fit because "I wanted to see how many of the elements I could work with, apart from the usual graphic design responsibilities." For Baum's landmark Rainbow Room atop Rockefeller Center, Glaser went even further, creating everything from dishware to advertising. For Baum's Aurora restaurant Glaser developed the architectural and interior plans with architects Tim Higgins and Phil George. Another restaurant client, Shelley Fireman, commissioned Glaser to design Trattoria del Arte, which he based on a classic Italian art theme involving enlarged plaster casts, a fake skylight, and paintings that related to the huge casts leaning against the wall for that antiquarian aura. Glaser's involvement with restaurants opened new areas of practice, yet even before this he had an interest in food. In the sixties he coauthored "The Underground Gourmet" with Jerome Snyder for *New York* magazine, the first magazine column devoted to exploring cheap restaurants, and also started Beard, Glaser, Wolf, a company that sold professional food preparation equipment to nonprofessional people.

SAM'S BAR

Another of Chwast's graphic stories is *Sam's Bar* (Doubleday, 1987). Written by Donald Barthelme, it is also a total narrative and pictorial story. It captures in woodcut illustrations one night in a bar somewhere in America, people talking to each other and talking to themselves as the reader goes from one end of the bar to the other.

248

TOMATO RECORDS

In the sixties Kevin Eggers founded Poppy Records, which became Utopia, then Atlantic Deluxe, and ultimately Tomato. He was, however, much more consistent with the design of his products because Glaser has designed all the posters and album covers (and continues to do so) since day one. The most iconic of the posters show the surreal poppy flower growing in a stone block, and the tomato in an armchair. Also among the most iconic album covers is the one of Louis Armstrong. Tomato is very catholic in its music choices, including blues, classical, jazz, and folk—from Bach to Brubeck. "The dominant idea was to reflect the quality of each album," says Glaser. "But there is a coherent look." He adds that after more than three decades, "having a long-term client makes for an interesting process."

TONALITY

Glaser never had a favorite color, even to this day. "Most graphic design is not about color," he explains. "Most designers use primaries in full intensity." But if one comes from illustration instead of graphic design training, as he does, one is more interested in questions of tonality. "I was interested in diminishing color intensity, in fact, contrasting low-intensity with high-intensity color." Glaser admits that his color sense is still in the process of development. "I always try to get more into tonality and nuance, which is much more playful."

TYPEFACES

During the sixties and seventies Chwast and Glaser designed various display typefaces (by hand) that were distributed through Photolettering Inc. in New York. Some of their ideas were influenced by vintage type found in Push Pin's type catalog library, while others were created from scratch. Glaser's Futura Stencil and Baby Fat were inspired by Italian futurist type of the 1920s; Chwast's Artone was rooted in an art nouveau aesthetic. Some faces, like Chwast's Filmsense, were originally used as a client's logo—Buffalo was commissioned by Mergenthaler—and others were just diversions and formal exercises that complemented each designer's drawing styles. Chwast and Glaser also enjoyed giving their typefaces sarcastic names (which prefigured the comic naming trend of the nineties). Glaser's faces included Art Decko, Houdini, Eightway (with George Leavitt), and Baby Teeth. Chwast's included Myopic and Blimp.

AABBCCDDEEFFGGHHIIJJKKLLMMNN
OOPPQQRRSSTTUUVVWWXXYYZZ

ABCDEFGHIJ
KLMNOPQR
STUVWXYZ
1234567890

Artone
BLIMP
Filmsense
MYOPIC

250

MORE TYPEFACES
FROM THE TOP
Rainbow!, Milton Glaser, 1987.
Baby Teeth, Milton Glaser, 1966.
Artone, Seymour Chwast, 1964.
Blimp, Seymour Chwast, 1970.
Filmsense, Seymour Chwast, 1970.
Myopic, Seymour Chwast, 1971.

ABOVE RIGHT
VICTORIANA
Page from *Phillips Old-Fashioned
Type Book*, 1945.
Morgan Press Type Book, 1972.

RIGHT
YELLOW SUBMARINE
Time cover, Milton Glaser, 1969.

VICTORIANA

Although the Victorian graphic style got its name from the reign of Queen Victoria (1837–1901), the distinct period of manifestation took root throughout the industrialized world from the 1870s to the turn of the century and represented an overwrought fussiness throughout graphics, architecture, and industrial design. The most identifiable typographic traits included bold grotesque faces (so named because they lacked "humanist" serifs) and bulky slab serif wood types. Hard-edged decoration in the form of scrolls and flourishes replaced the previous sinuous rococo and baroque ornamentation. By the 1890s art nouveau began to surpass the Victorian style in mass popularity, and the latter was totally expunged from public view with the advent of twentieth-century modernism. Yet by the 1950s the passé conceit was enjoying a mini-revival. Chwast recalls being inspired by a sampling of Victorian typefaces in the *Phillips' Old-Fashioned Type Book* and engraved ads in old magazines that revealed the eccentricity common to Victorian design. This was ultimately incorporated into the Push Pin style.

YELLOW SUBMARINE

Before selecting the artist for the 1968 animated feature film *Yellow Submarine* (starring the Beatles), producer Al Brodax approached Glaser to design the characters and backgrounds of the legendary film. Glaser recalls turning the offer down "because it was an awful lot of work." Apparently, Brodax then contacted Peter Max, who had briefly worked for Push Pin in the early sixties. Ultimately, Heinz Edelman, a gifted German illustrator, was selected for the job. At the time there was considerable speculation on whether Edelman's *Yellow Submarine* style, clearly rooted in an ambient psychedelic aesthetic, was influenced by Glaser's work as it then appeared on covers of *Time* magazine and his first posters for WNEW-FM, a progressive rock radio station in New York. "How it informed his work is not clear," states Glaser. "Maybe it was possible there was something in the air that attracted both of us to the same thing." Edelman is not someone who would deliberately take things, but, as Glaser notes, "in an appropriate way borrowing influences are common in the graphic design profession." Nonetheless, some professionals believed Edelman's interpretation was a curious combination of what Chwast and Glaser were doing at the time, but even if it were, Glaser says, "It was perfectly okay as long as people didn't actually think we were taking ideas from the film." Ironically, Edelman once complained to Chwast that people often think that Peter Max did *Yellow Submarine*.

THE FINE PRINT

NUMBER **1**
MARCH 1957
14¼" x 22", printed on one side

ILLUSTRATOR
SEYMOUR CHWAST

NUMBER **2**
MARCH 1957
14¼" x 22", printed on one side

ILLUSTRATOR
REYNOLD RUFFINS

NUMBER **3**
APRIL 1957
14¼" x 22", printed on one side

DESIGNER & ILLUSTRATOR
MILTON GLASER

NUMBER **4**
APRIL 1957
15¼" x 22", printed on one side

DESIGNER & ILLUSTRATOR
JOHN ALCORN

NUMBER **5**
JUNE 1957
10¾" x 13¾", 4pp.

DESIGNER & ILLUSTRATOR
SEYMOUR CHWAST

NUMBER **6**
JULY 1957
10¾" x 14", 4pp.

DESIGNERS & ILLUSTRATORS
SEYMOUR CHWAST
REYNOLD RUFFINS

NUMBER **7**
AUGUST 1957
11" x 14", 4pp.

DESIGNER & ILLUSTRATOR
MILTON GLASER

NUMBER **8**
SEPTEMBER 1957
11" x 14", 4pp.

DESIGNER & ILLUSTRATOR
JOHN ALCORN

NUMBER **9**
OCTOBER 1957
10¾" x 14", 4pp.

DESIGNER & ILLUSTRATOR
SEYMOUR CHWAST

NUMBER **10**
NOVEMBER 1957
10¾" x 14", 8pp.

DESIGNERS
SEYMOUR CHWAST
MILTON GLASER

ILLUSTRATORS
JOHN ALCORN
SEYMOUR CHWAST
MILTON GLASER
REYNOLD RUFFINS

NUMBER **11**
DECEMBER 1957
10¾" x 14", 8pp.

DESIGNER & ILLUSTRATOR
MILTON GLASER

NUMBER **12**
JANUARY 1958
10¾" x 14¼", 8pp.

DESIGNER & ILLUSTRATOR
SEYMOUR CHWAST

NUMBER **13**
JANUARY 1958
10⅝" x 14", 4pp.

DESIGNER & ILLUSTRATOR
MILTON GLASER

NUMBER **14**
MARCH 1958
10⅝" x 14", 4pp.

DESIGNER & ILLUSTRATOR
REYNOLD RUFFINS

NUMBER **15**
APRIL 1958
10½" x 14", 4pp.

DESIGNER
MILTON GLASER

ILLUSTRATORS
MILTON GLASER
REYNOLD RUFFINS

NUMBER **16**
MAY 1958
10½" x 13⅝", 8pp.

DESIGNERS
JOHN ALCORN
SEYMOUR CHWAST

ILLUSTRATORS
JOHN ALCORN
SEYMOUR CHWAST
REYNOLD RUFFINS

NUMBER **17**
1958
10⅝" x 13⅞", 4pp.

DESIGNERS & ILLUSTRATORS
JOHN ALCORN
SEYMOUR CHWAST

NUMBER **18**
1959
10¾" x 14", 8pp.

DESIGNERS
SEYMOUR CHWAST
MILTON GLASER

ILLUSTRATORS
SEYMOUR CHWAST
MILTON GLASER
REYNOLD RUFFINS

NUMBER **19**
1959
10¾" x 14", 8pp.

DESIGNER & ILLUSTRATOR
MILTON GLASER

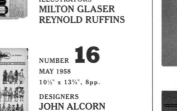

NUMBER **20**
1959
10¾" x 14", 8pp.

DESIGNERS
SEYMOUR CHWAST
MILTON GLASER

ILLUSTRATORS
SEYMOUR CHWAST
MILTON GLASER
REYNOLD RUFFINS

251

NUMBER **21**
1959
10½" x 13¾", 8pp.

DESIGNERS & ILLUSTRATORS
SEYMOUR CHWAST
MILTON GLASER
REYNOLD RUFFINS

NUMBER **22**
1959
10½" x 13¾", 8pp.

DESIGNERS & ILLUSTRATORS
SEYMOUR CHWAST
MILTON GLASER
REYNOLD RUFFINS

NUMBER **23**
1959
4⅝" x 10½", 20pp.

DESIGNER
MILTON GLASER

ILLUSTRATORS
SEYMOUR CHWAST
MILTON GLASER
REYNOLD RUFFINS

NUMBER **24**
1959
10¾" x 27½", 4pp.

DESIGNERS
SEYMOUR CHWAST
MILTON GLASER

ILLUSTRATORS
SEYMOUR CHWAST
MILTON GLASER
REYNOLD RUFFINS

NUMBER **25**
1960
10½" x 14", 8pp.

DESIGNER & ILLUSTRATOR
SEYMOUR CHWAST

252

NUMBER **26**
1960
10¾" x 13¾", 8pp.

DESIGNERS
SEYMOUR CHWAST
MILTON GLASER

ILLUSTRATORS
VARIOUS SCHOOL-
CHILDREN

NUMBER **27**
1960
10¾" x 14", 8pp.

DESIGNERS
SEYMOUR CHWAST
REYNOLD RUFFINS

ILLUSTRATORS
PAUL DAVIS
ISADORE SELTZER

NUMBER **28**
1960
10½" x 13¾", 8pp.

DESIGNER & ILLUSTRATOR
MILTON GLASER

NUMBER **29**
1960
10¾" x 14", 8pp.

DESIGNERS & ILLUSTRATORS
SEYMOUR CHWAST
MILTON GLASER

NUMBER **30**
1960
8¾" x 11", 12pp. (plus wrapper)

DESIGNERS
SEYMOUR CHWAST
MILTON GLASER

ILLUSTRATORS
SEYMOUR CHWAST
PAUL DAVIS
MILTON GLASER
ISADORE SELTZER

NUMBER **31**
1961
8½" x 11", 12pp.

DESIGNER & ILLUSTRATOR
SEYMOUR CHWAST

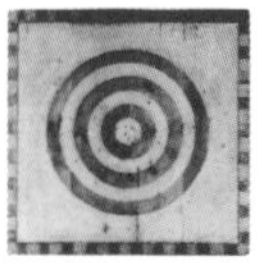

NUMBER **32**
1961
7⅛" x 7¼", 16pp.

DESIGNER & ILLUSTRATOR
PAUL DAVIS

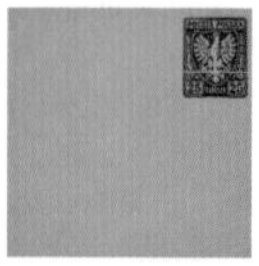

NUMBER **33**
1961
7¼" x 7⅛", 24pp.

DESIGNER
MILTON GLASER

NUMBER **34**
1961
7¼" x 7⅛", 24pp.

DESIGNER
SEYMOUR CHWAST

ILLUSTRATOR
ISADORE SELTZER

NUMBER **35**
1961
8¾" x 10⅞", 12pp. (plus wrapper)

DESIGNER
MILTON GLASER

ILLUSTRATORS
SEYMOUR CHWAST
PAUL DAVIS
MILTON GLASER

EDITOR
MYRNA MUSHKIN

NUMBER **36**
1962
7¼" x 7⅛", 24pp.

DESIGNER & ILLUSTRATOR
SEYMOUR CHWAST

NUMBER **37**
MAY 1962
10¾" x 14⅛", 12pp.

DESIGNERS
SEYMOUR CHWAST
MILTON GLASER

ILLUSTRATORS
SEYMOUR CHWAST
PAUL DAVIS
MILTON GLASER
ISADORE SELTZER

NUMBER **38**
1962
10¾" x 14⅛", XXpp.

DESIGNER & ILLUSTRATOR
MILTON GLASER

NUMBER **39**
1962
9" x 11", 12pp. (plus wrapper)

DESIGNERS
SEYMOUR CHWAST
MILTON GLASER

ILLUSTRATORS
SEYMOUR CHWAST
PAUL DAVIS
MILTON GLASER

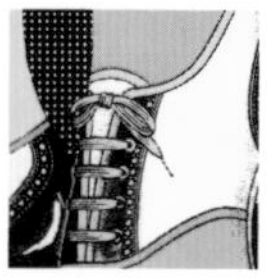

NUMBER **40**
1962
18" x 24", 4pp.

DESIGNERS & ILLUSTRATORS
SEYMOUR CHWAST
MILTON GLASER

NUMBER **41**
1963
8½" x 11", 16pp.

DESIGNERS
SEYMOUR CHWAST
MILTON GLASER

NUMBER **42**
1963
8½" x 11", 20pp.

DESIGNER
SEYMOUR CHWAST

PHOTOGRAPHER
ALLEN VOGEL

NUMBER **43**
1963
8½" x 11", 12pp.

DESIGNERS
SEYMOUR CHWAST
MILTON GLASER

ILLUSTRATOR
ISADORE SELTZER

NUMBER **44**
1964
7⅛" x 7⅛", 44pp.

DESIGNER
MILTON GLASER

ILLUSTRATORS
SEYMOUR CHWAST
MILTON GLASER
ISADORE SELTZER

NUMBER **45**
1964
12" x 20", 8pp.

DESIGNER & ILLUSTRATOR
SEYMOUR CHWAST

COPY EDITOR
MYRNA MUSHKIN

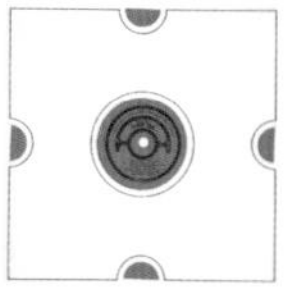

NUMBER **46**
1964
18" x 24", 1p.

DESIGNER & ILLUSTRATOR
MILTON GLASER

NUMBER **47**
1964
8⅛" x 10⅝", 24pp.

DESIGNERS
SEYMOUR CHWAST
MILTON GLASER

ILLUSTRATORS
SEYMOUR CHWAST
MILTON GLASER
JAMES McMULLAN

NUMBER **48**
1965
9¼" x 9", 24pp.

DESIGNER & ILLUSTRATOR
SEYMOUR CHWAST

PHOTOGRAPHER
ALAN VOGEL

NUMBER **49**
1965
5" x 7½", 68pp.

DESIGNERS
SEYMOUR CHWAST
MILTON GLASER

ILLUSTRATORS
SEYMOUR CHWAST
MILTON GLASER
JAMES McMULLAN

COPY EDITOR
MYRNA MUSHKIN

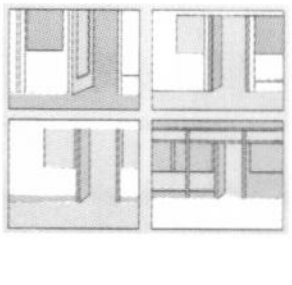

NUMBER **50**
1966
11" x 8½", 16pp.

DESIGNER & ILLUSTRATOR
JAMES McMULLAN

COPY EDITOR
MYRNA MUSHKIN

NUMBER 51
1967
8½" x 11", 20pp.

DESIGNER & ILLUSTRATOR
MILTON GLASER

NUMBER 52
1967
18" x 28", 6pp.

DESIGNERS & ILLUSTRATORS
SEYMOUR CHWAST
MILTON GLASER
JAMES McMULLAN

NUMBER 53
1967
10¾" x 7½", 16pp.

DESIGNER & ILLUSTRATOR
SEYMOUR CHWAST

NUMBER 54
1967
8½" x 8¾", 20pp.

DESIGNER & ILLUSTRATOR
SEYMOUR CHWAST

NUMBER 55
1969
8" x 8", 20pp.

DESIGNER & ILLUSTRATOR
MILTON GLASER

NUMBER 56
1971
10¾" x 14", 12pp.

DESIGNERS
SEYMOUR CHWAST
MILTON GLASER

ILLUSTRATORS
SEYMOUR CHWAST
MILTON GLASER
HEDDA JOHNSON
BARRY ZAID

COPY EDITOR
BARBARA SAMET

NUMBER 57
1972
8½" x 10⅝", 16pp.

DESIGNER & ILLUSTRATOR
SEYMOUR CHWAST

NUMBER 58
1973
9⅜" x 14¼", 16pp.

DESIGNER
SEYMOUR CHWAST

ILLUSTRATORS
SEYMOUR CHWAST
HARUO MIYAUCHI
CHRISTIAN PIPER

NUMBER 59
1974
9" x 12", 16pp.

DESIGNER & ILLUSTRATOR
MILTON GLASER

NUMBER 60
1974
12" x 10", 20pp.

DESIGNER
SEYMOUR CHWAST

ILLUSTRATORS
SEYMOUR CHWAST
HARUO MIYAUCHI
CHRISTIAN PIPER

WRITER
JUDITH DANER

TECHNICAL ASSISTANCE BY
CLEVELAND DOBSON

NUMBER 61
1974
24" x 36", printed on one side

DESIGNER
SEYMOUR CHWAST

NUMBER 62
1975
7" x 5½", 24pp.

DESIGNER
SEYMOUR CHWAST

ILLUSTRATORS
SEYMOUR CHWAST
MILTON GLASER
JOYCE MACDONALD
HARUO MIYAUCHI
CHRISTIAN PIPER
GEORGE STAVRINOS

PHOTOGRAPHERS
BENNO FRIEDMAN
ARNOLD ROSENBERG

COPY EDITOR
PHYLLIS LEVINE

NUMBER 63
1976
10½" x 14", 16pp.

DESIGNER
SEYMOUR CHWAST

ILLUSTRATORS
DAVID CROLAND
JEFF KRASSNER
JOYCE MACDONALD
FRED MARSHALL
GEORGE STAVRINOS

NUMBER 64
DECEMBER 1976
9" x 12", 32pp.

EDITOR/ART DIRECTOR
SEYMOUR CHWAST

PRODUCTION CHAIRPERSON
PAMELA VASSIL

PRODUCTION ASSISTANT
CLEVELAND DOBSON

EDITORIAL MANAGER
LILLY FILIPOW

CONTRIBUTING EDITOR
PAULA SCHER

ILLUSTRATORS
SEYMOUR CHWAST
DAVID CROLAND
MILTON GLASER
MICHAEL HOSTOVICH
JEFFREY KRASSNER
FRED MARSHALL
HARUO MIYAUCHI

PHOTOGRAPHER
BENNO FRIEDMAN

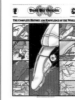

NUMBER 65
FEBRUARY 1977
9" x 12", 32pp.

EDITOR/ART DIRECTOR
SEYMOUR CHWAST

PRODUCTION CHAIRPERSON
PAMELA VASSIL

PRODUCTION ASSISTANTS
CLEVELAND DOBSON
WILLIAM SLOAN

EDITORIAL MANAGER
LILLY FILIPOW

CONTRIBUTING EDITOR
PAULA SCHER

ILLUSTRATORS
SEYMOUR CHWAST
DAVID CROLAND
MICHAEL HOSTOVICH
HARUO MIYAUCHI
GEORGE STAVRINOS

NUMBER 66
APRIL 1977
9" x 12", 32pp.

EDITOR/ART DIRECTOR
SEYMOUR CHWAST

ART & PRODUCTION
CHAIRPERSON
PAMELA VASSIL

PRODUCTION ASSISTANTS
CLEVELAND DOBSON
JEFFREY KRASSNER
WILLIAM SLOAN

EDITORIAL MANAGER
LILLY FILIPOW

CONTRIBUTING EDITOR
PAULA SCHER

ILLUSTRATORS
SEYMOUR CHWAST
JOHN COLLIER
DAVID CROLAND
MICHAEL HOSTOVICH
JEFFREY KRASSNER
FRED MARSHALL
HARUO MIYAUCHI
GEORGE STAVRINOS

PHOTOGRAPHER
BENNO FRIEDMAN
ARNOLD ROSENBERG

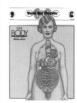

NUMBER 67
JUNE 1977
9" x 12", 32pp.

EDITOR/ART DIRECTOR
SEYMOUR CHWAST

ART & PRODUCTION
CHAIRPERSON
PAMELA VASSIL

PRODUCTION ASSISTANTS
CLEVELAND DOBSON
BILL KOBASZ
WILLIAM SLOAN

EDITORIAL MANAGER
LILLY FILIPOW

CONTRIBUTING EDITOR
PAULA SCHER

ILLUSTRATORS
JOHN COLLIER
MICHAEL HOSTOVICH
HARUO MIYAUCHI
EMANUEL SCHONGUT
GEORGE STAVRINOS

PHOTOGRAPHER
BENNO FRIEDMAN

253

NUMBER 68
AUGUST 1977
9" x 12", 32pp.

EDITOR/ART DIRECTOR
SEYMOUR CHWAST

ART & PRODUCTION
CHAIRPERSON
PAMELA VASSIL

EDITORIAL MANAGER
LILLY FILIPOW

CONTRIBUTING EDITOR
PAULA SCHER

PRODUCTION ASSISTANTS
CLEVELAND DOBSON
BILL KOBASZ
WILLIAM SLOAN

ILLUSTRATORS
SEYMOUR CHWAST
JOHN COLLIER
DAVID CROLAND
RICHARD MANTEL
HARUO MIYAUCHI
EMANUEL SCHONGUT
GEORGE STAVRINOS

PHOTOGRAPHER
BENNO FRIEDMAN

NUMBER **69**
OCTOBER 1977
9" x 12", 32pp.

EDITOR/ART DIRECTOR
SEYMOUR CHWAST

DESIGNER
RICHARD MANTEL

PRODUCTION MANAGER
JO ANN BERG

EDITORIAL MANAGER
LILLY FILIPOW

CONTRIBUTING EDITOR
PAULA SCHER

PRODUCTION ASSISTANTS
**CLEVELAND DOBSON
BILL KOBASZ
WILLIAM SLOAN**

ILLUSTRATORS
**SEYMOUR CHWAST
JOHN COLLIER
DAVID CROLAND
MILTON GLASER
RICHARD MANTEL
HARUO MIYAUCHI
EMANUEL SCHONGUT**

PHOTOGRAPHER
ARNOLD ROSENBERG

NUMBER **70**
DECEMBER 1977
9" x 12", 32pp.

EDITOR/ART DIRECTOR
SEYMOUR CHWAST

DESIGNER
RICHARD MANTEL

PRODUCTION MANAGER
JO ANN BERG

EDITORIAL MANAGER
LILLY FILIPOW

CONTRIBUTING EDITOR
PAULA SCHER

PRODUCTION ASSISTANTS
**CLEVELAND DOBSON
BILL KOBASZ
WILLIAM SLOAN**

ILLUSTRATORS
**BERNARD BONHOMME
SEYMOUR CHWAST
JOHN COLLIER
RICHARD MANTEL
HARUO MIYAUCHI
EMANUEL SCHONGUT**

PHOTOGRAPHER
BENNO FRIEDMAN

NUMBER **71**
FEBRUARY 1978
9" x 12", 32pp.

EDITOR/ART DIRECTOR
SEYMOUR CHWAST

DESIGNER
RICHARD MANTEL

PRODUCTION MANAGER
JO ANN BERG

EDITORIAL MANAGER
BARBARA MILAN

CONTRIBUTING EDITOR
PAULA SCHER

GUEST EDITOR
MARIA ROBBINS

PRODUCTION ASSISTANTS
**CLEVELAND DOBSON
BILL KOBASZ
WILLIAM SLOAN**

ILLUSTRATORS
**SEYMOUR CHWAST
JOHN COLLIER
RICHARD MANTEL
HARUO MIYAUCHI
EMANUEL SCHONGUT**

PHOTOGRAPHER
BENNO FRIEDMAN

NUMBER **72**
APRIL 1978
9" x 12", 32pp.

EDITOR/ART DIRECTOR
SEYMOUR CHWAST

DESIGNER
RICHARD MANTEL

PRODUCTION MANAGER
JO ANN BERG

EDITORIAL MANAGER
BARBARA MILAN

CONTRIBUTING EDITOR
PAULA SCHER

GUEST EDITOR &
PHOTOGRAPHER
KEN ROBBINS

PRODUCTION ASSISTANTS
**CHRISTOPHER
  AUSTOPCHUK
CLEVELAND DOBSON
BILL KOBASZ
MELISSA WATSON**

ILLUSTRATORS
**SEYMOUR CHWAST
JOHN COLLIER
RICHARD MANTEL
HARUO MIYAUCHI
EMANUEL SCHONGUT**

NUMBER **73**
JUNE 1978
9" x 12", 32pp.

EDITOR/ART DIRECTOR
SEYMOUR CHWAST

DESIGNER
RICHARD MANTEL

PRODUCTION MANAGER
JO ANN BERG

EDITORIAL MANAGER
BARBARA MILAN

GUEST EDITOR
KEN ROBBINS

PRODUCTION ASSISTANTS
**CHRISTOPHER
  AUSTOPCHUK
CLEVELAND DOBSON
BILL KOBASZ
MELISSA WATSON**

ILLUSTRATORS
**BERNARD BONHOMME
SEYMOUR CHWAST
RICHARD MANTEL
HARUO MIYAUCHI
EMANUEL SCHONGUT**

PHOTOGRAPHER
BENNO FRIEDMAN

NUMBER **74**
AUGUST 1978
9" x 12", 32pp.

EDITOR/ART DIRECTOR
SEYMOUR CHWAST

DESIGNER
RICHARD MANTEL

PRODUCTION MANAGER
JO ANN BERG

EDITORIAL MANAGER
BARBARA MILAN

GUEST EDITOR
KEN ROBBINS

PRODUCTION ASSISTANTS
**CHRISTOPHER
  AUSTOPCHUK
CLEVELAND DOBSON
LIZ GUTOWSKI
BILL KOBASZ**

ILLUSTRATORS
**BERNARD BONHOMME
SEYMOUR CHWAST
JOHN COLLIER
MILTON GLASER
RICHARD MANTEL
HARUO MIYAUCHI
EMANUEL SCHONGUT**

PHOTOGRAPHER
BENNO FRIEDMAN

NUMBER **75**
OCTOBER 1978
9" x 12", 32pp.

EDITOR/ART DIRECTOR
SEYMOUR CHWAST

DESIGNER
RICHARD MANTEL

PRODUCTION MANAGER
TERRY BERKOWITZ

MANAGING EDITOR
KEN ROBBINS

PRODUCTION ASSISTANTS
**CHRISTOPHER
  AUSTOPCHUK
CLEVELAND DOBSON
BILL KOBASZ
MELISSA WATSON**

ILLUSTRATORS
**BERNARD BONHOMME
SEYMOUR CHWAST
RICHARD MANTEL
HARUO MIYAUCHI
EMANUEL SCHONGUT
STANISLAW ZAGORSKI**

PHOTOGRAPHER
BENNO FRIEDMAN

NUMBER **76**
DECEMBER 1978
9" x 12", 32pp.

EDITOR/ART DIRECTOR
SEYMOUR CHWAST

DESIGNER
RICHARD MANTEL

MANAGING EDITOR
KEN ROBBINS

PRODUCTION MANAGER
TERRY BERKOWITZ

PRODUCTION ASSISTANTS
**CHRISTOPHER
  AUSTOPCHUK
CLEVELAND DOBSON
LIZ GUTOWSKI
BILL KOBASZ**

ILLUSTRATORS
**SEYMOUR CHWAST
RICHARD MANTEL
HARUO MIYAUCHI
EMANUEL SCHONGUT
STANISLAW ZAGORSKI**

PHOTOGRAPHER
BENNO FRIEDMAN

NUMBER **77**
1979
9" x 12", 32pp.

EDITOR/ART DIRECTOR
SEYMOUR CHWAST

DESIGNER
RICHARD MANTEL

MANAGING EDITOR
KEN ROBBINS

PRODUCTION MANAGER
TERRY BERKOWITZ

PRODUCTION ASSISTANTS
**CHRISTOPHER
  AUSTOPCHUK
CLEVELAND DOBSON
LIZ GUTOWSKI
BILL KOBASZ**

STAFF PHOTOGRAPHER
RICHARD PAN

ILLUSTRATORS
**SEYMOUR CHWAST
RICHARD MANTEL
HARUO MIYAUCHI
EMANUEL SCHONGUT
STANISLAW ZAGORSKI**

NUMBER **78**
APRIL 1979
9" x 12", 32pp.

EDITOR/ART DIRECTOR
SEYMOUR CHWAST

DESIGNER
RICHARD MANTEL

MANAGING EDITOR
KEN ROBBINS

PRODUCTION MANAGER
TERRY BERKOWITZ

PRODUCTION ASSISTANTS
**CLEVELAND DOBSON
LIZ GUTOWSKI
BILL KOBASZ**

ILLUSTRATORS
**SEYMOUR CHWAST
RICHARD MANTEL
HARUO MIYAUCHI
BARBARA SANDLER
EMANUEL SCHONGUT
ELWOOD SMITH
STANISLAW ZAGORSKI**

NUMBER 79
JULY/AUGUST 1979
9" x 12", 32pp.

EDITOR/ART DIRECTOR
SEYMOUR CHWAST

DESIGNER
RICHARD MANTEL

MANAGING EDITOR &
PHOTOGRAPHER
KEN ROBBINS

PRODUCTION MANAGER
TERRY BERKOWITZ

PRODUCTION ASSISTANTS
**CLEVELAND DOBSON
LIZ GUTOWSKI
BILL KOBASZ**

STAFF PHOTOGRAPHER
RICHARD PAN

ILLUSTRATORS
**SEYMOUR CHWAST
RICHARD MANTEL
HARUO MIYAUCHI
EMANUEL SCHONGUT
ELWOOD SMITH
STANISLAW ZAGORSKI**

NUMBER 80
SEPTEMBER/OCTOBER 1979
9" x 12", 32pp.

EDITOR/ART DIRECTOR
SEYMOUR CHWAST

DESIGNER
RICHARD MANTEL

EDITOR
KEN ROBBINS

PRODUCTION MANAGER
TERRY BERKOWITZ

PRODUCTION ASSISTANTS
**CLEVELAND DOBSON
LIZ GUTOWSKI
BILL KOBASZ
ARLENE LAPPEN**

ILLUSTRATORS
**SEYMOUR CHWAST
RICHARD MANTEL
HARUO MIYAUCHI
BARBARA SANDLER
EMANUEL SCHONGUT
ELWOOD SMITH
STANISLAW ZAGORSKI**

NUMBER 81
NOVEMBER/DECEMBER 1979
9" x 12", 32pp.

EDITOR/ART DIRECTOR
SEYMOUR CHWAST

DESIGNER
RICHARD MANTEL

EDITOR
KEN ROBBINS

PRODUCTION MANAGER
TERRY BERKOWITZ

PRODUCTION ASSISTANTS
**CLEVELAND DOBSON
LIZ GUTOWSKI
BILL KOBASZ
ARLENE LAPPEN**

ILLUSTRATORS
**SEYMOUR CHWAST
BARBARA SANDLER
ELWOOD H. SMITH
STANISLAW ZAGORSKI**

PHOTOGRAPHER
BENNO FRIEDMAN

NUMBER 82
1980
9" x 12", 32pp.

EDITOR/ART DIRECTOR
SEYMOUR CHWAST

DESIGNER
RICHARD MANTEL

EDITOR
KEN ROBBINS

PRODUCTION MANAGER
TERRY BERKOWITZ

PRODUCTION ASSISTANTS
**CLEVELAND DOBSON
LIZ GUTOWSKI
BILL KOBASZ
CHRISTIAN RIFAI
GARY ZAMCHICK**

ILLUSTRATORS
**SEYMOUR CHWAST
RICHARD MANTEL
KEN ROBBINS
BARBARA SANDLER
EMANUEL SCHONGUT
ELWOOD H. SMITH
STANISLAW ZAGORSKI**

NUMBER 83
1980
9" x 12", 32pp.

EDITOR/ART DIRECTOR
SEYMOUR CHWAST

DESIGNER
RICHARD MANTEL

EDITOR
KEN ROBBINS

GUEST EDITOR
BARBARA CHWAST

PRODUCTION MANAGER
TERRY BERKOWITZ

PRODUCTION ASSISTANTS
**CLEVELAND DOBSON
LIZ GUTOWSKI
BILL KOBASZ
CHRISTIAN RIFAI**

ILLUSTRATORS
**SEYMOUR CHWAST
RICHARD MANTEL
BARBARA SANDLER
EMANUEL SCHONGUT
ELWOOD H. SMITH
STANISLAW ZAGORSKI**

NUMBER 84
MAY/JUNE 1980
9" x 12", 32pp.

EDITOR/ART DIRECTOR
SEYMOUR CHWAST

DESIGNER
RICHARD MANTEL

EDITOR
KEN ROBBINS

PRODUCTION MANAGER
TERRY BERKOWITZ

PRODUCTION ASSISTANTS
**HEINER BUCK
CLEVELAND DOBSON
BILL KOBASZ
CHRISTIAN RIFAI**

ILLUSTRATORS
**SEYMOUR CHWAST
RICHARD MANTEL
STEVEN MAX SINGER
ELWOOD H. SMITH
STANISLAW ZAGORSKI**

PHOTOGRAPHER
SARAH MOON

NUMBER 85
1980
9" x 12", 32pp.

EDITOR/ART DIRECTOR
SEYMOUR CHWAST

DESIGNER
RICHARD MANTEL

EDITOR
KEN ROBBINS

PRODUCTION MANAGER
TERRY BERKOWITZ

PRODUCTION ASSISTANTS
**HEINER BUCK
CLEVELAND DOBSON
MIRIAM HAAS
BILL KOBASZ
CHRISTIAN RIFAI
PETER ROSS
JUAN TENORIO**

ILLUSTRATORS
**SEYMOUR CHWAST
EMANUEL SCHONGUT
ELWOOD H. SMITH**

NUMBER 86
1980
9" x 12", 32pp.

EDITOR/ART DIRECTOR
SEYMOUR CHWAST

DESIGNER
RICHARD MANTEL

EDITOR
KEN ROBBINS

PRODUCTION MANAGER
TERRY BERKOWITZ

PRODUCTION ASSISTANTS
**CLEVELAND DOBSON
MIRIAM HAAS
CHRISTIAN RIFAI
PETER ROSS
JUAN TENORIO**

ILLUSTRATORS
**SEYMOUR CHWAST
RICHARD MANTEL
JOHN OLEARY
ELWOOD H. SMITH
STANISLAW ZAGORSKI**

255

SEYMOUR CHWAST is cofounder of Push Pin Studios, renamed the Pushpin Group. His designs and illustrations have been used in advertising, animated films, and editorial, corporate, and environmental graphics. He has created more than one hundred posters and has designed and illustrated more than thirty children's books. His work is the subject of a monograph, *Seymour Chwast: The Left Handed Designer,* and is collected in numerous museums, including the Museum of Modern Art in New York, the Library of Congress in Washington, D.C., and the Israel Museum in Jerusalem. Chwast is a 1983 inductee in the Art Directors Hall of Fame and the recipient of the 1985 Medal for Lifetime Achievement from the American Institute of Graphic Arts.

MILTON GLASER is cofounder of Push Pin Studios. In 1968, he and Clay Felker founded *New York Magazine.* In 1974, he left Push Pin to establish Milton Glaser, Inc. In 1983, he teamed with Walter Bernard to form WBMG, a publication design firm located in New York. His graphic and architectural commissions include the I ♥ NY logo; the complete graphic and decorative programs for the restaurants in the World Trade Center, New York, and the design of the observation deck and permanent exhibition for the Twin Towers of the World Trade Center in 1975; the redesign of the Grand Union supermarket chain—including architectural, interior, packaging, and advertising design; the redevelopment of the Rainbow Room complexes for the Rockefeller Center Management Corporation, New York; the design of an International AIDS symbol for the World Health Organization; and the logo for Tony Kushner's Pulitzer Prize–winning play, *Angels in America.* Glaser has also designed and/or illustrated more than three hundred posters. For forty years he has taught master classes at the School of Visual Arts, New York.

STEVEN HELLER is art director of the *New York Times Book Review* and cochair of the MFA/Design program at the School of Visual Arts. He is contributing editor to *Print, Eye, I.D.,* and *Baseline* magazines. He is the author of more than ninety books on graphic design, popular art, and satiric art, including *Paul Rand; The Swastika: Symbol Beyond Redemption?; Design Literacy; Design Literacy Continued; Graphic Style: From Victorian to Digital* (with Seymour Chwast); *The Graphic Design Timeline; Design Dialogues; Typology* (with Louise Fili); *The Graphic Design Reader; Citizen Designer;* and *Merz to Emigre and Beyond: Avant Garde Magazine Design of the Twentieth Century.* Heller is the recipient of the Art Directors Hall of Fame's Special Educators Award, the Pratt Institute's 1999

Herschel Levit Award, and the 1999 American Institute of Graphic Arts' Medal for Lifetime Achievement. He is currently writing a biography of Alvin Lustig.

MARTIN VENEZKY is director of Appetite Engineers. He has produced work for the Sundance Film Festival, the San Francisco Museum of Modern Art, and Blue Note Records, among others. He was also art director of *Speak,* a magazine of popular culture, literature, music, and art. Through Appetite Engineers, Venezky has also provided his services for nonprofit groups including Frameline, Q-Action/Stop AIDS, the San Francisco AIDS Foundation, and the American Center for Design. He received his BFA in Visual Studies from Dartmouth College and an MFA in Design from Cranbrook Academy of Art in Bloomfield Hills, Michigan. Venezky was listed among *I.D.* magazine's "I.D. 40" list of influential designers, and the San Francisco Museum of Modern Art honored him with a 2001 exhibition of his collected design work: "Martin Venezky: Selections from the Permanent Collection of Architecture and Design." 🎎

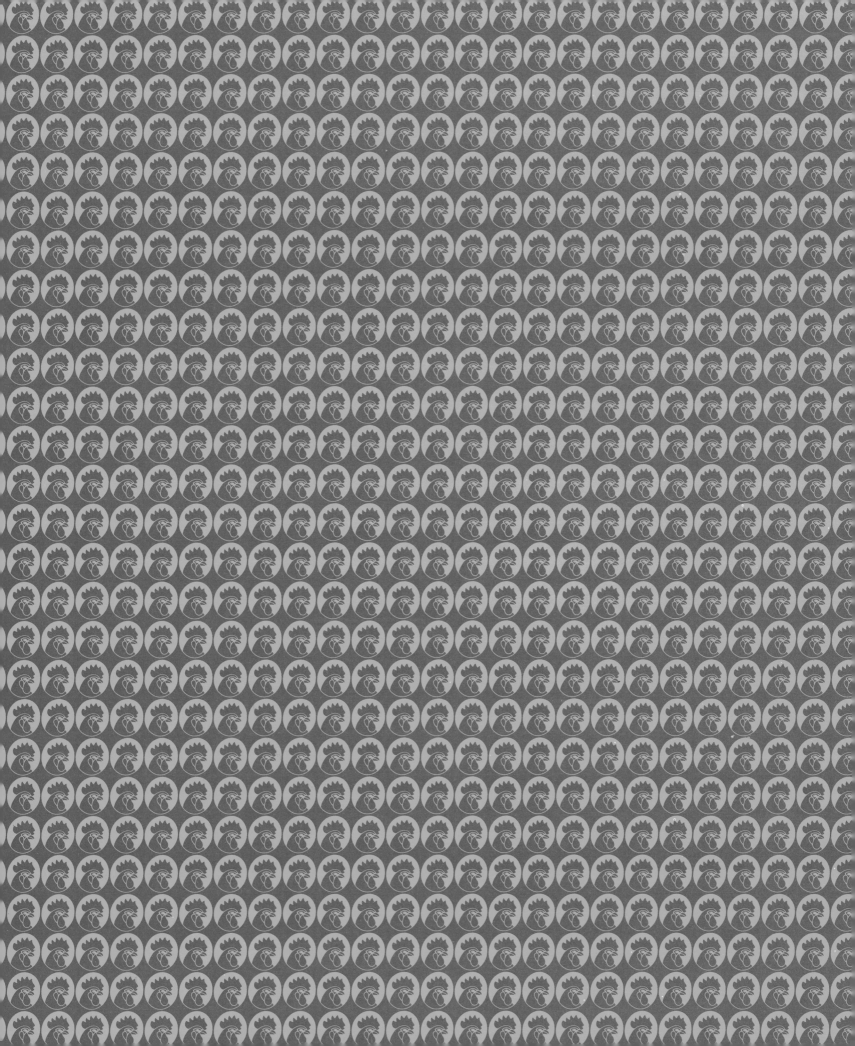

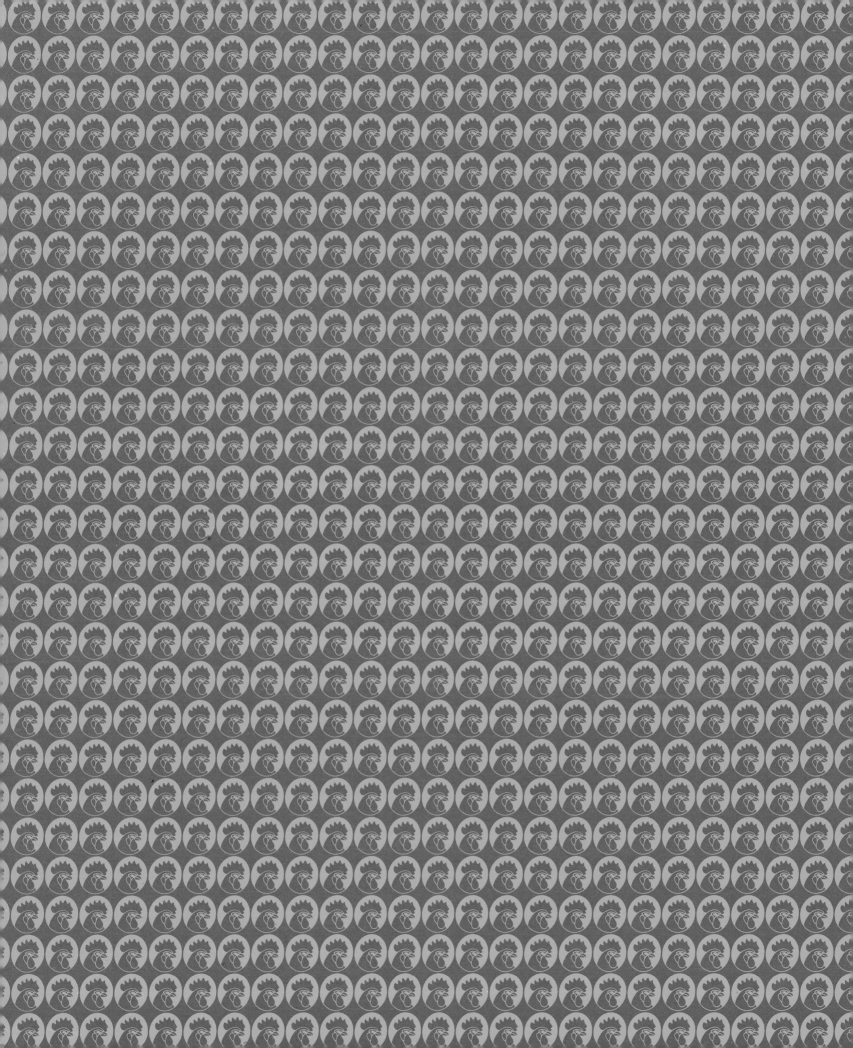